S0-CDQ-345

STUDIES IN MODERN CAPITALISM –
ETUDES SUR LE CAPITALISME MODERNE

CREATING AND TRANSFORMING
HOUSEHOLDS

THE CONSTRAINTS OF
THE WORLD-ECONOMY

This book seeks an explanation of the oft-observed pattern of sharp discrepancy of wage levels across the world-economy for work of comparable productivity. It explores how far such differences can be explained by the different structures of households as "income-pooling units," examining three key variables: location in the core or periphery of the world-economy; periods of expansion versus periods of contraction in the world-economy; and secular transformation over time.

The authors argue that both the boundaries of households and their sources of income are molded by the changing patterns of the world-economy, but are also modes of defense against its pressures. Drawing empirical data from eight local regions in three different zones – the United States, Mexico, and southern Africa – this book presents a systematic and original approach to the intimate link between the micro-structures of households and the structures of the capitalist world-economy at a global level.

Studies in modern capitalism. Etudes sur le capitalisme moderne

Editorial board. Comité de rédaction
Maurice Aymard, Maison des Sciences de l'Homme, Paris
Jacques Revel, Ecole des Hautes Etudes en Sciences Sociales, Paris
Immanuel Wallerstein, Fernand Braudel Center for the Study of Economies, Historical Systems, and Civilizations, Binghamton, New York

This series is devoted to an attempt to comprehend capitalism as a world-system. It will include monographs, collections of essays, and colloquia around specific themes, written by historians and social scientists united by a common concern for the study of large-scale, long-term social structure and social change.

The series is a joint enterprise of the Maison des Sciences de l'Homme in Paris and the Fernand Braudel Center for the Study of Economies, Historical Systems, and Civilizations at the State University of New York at Binghamton.

This book is published as part of the joint publishing agreement established in 1977 between the Fondation de la Maison des Sciences de l'Homme and the Press Syndicate of the University of Cambridge. Titles published under this arrangement may appear in any European language or, in the case of volumes of collected essays, in several languages.

New books will appear either as individual titles or in one of the series which the Maison des Sciences de l'Homme and the Cambridge University Press have jointly agreed to publish. All books published jointly by the Maison des Sciences de l'Homme and the Cambridge University Press will be distributed by the Press throughout the world.

For other titles in the series please see end of book

CREATING AND TRANSFORMING HOUSEHOLDS

The constraints of the world-economy

Coordinated by
Joan Smith, University of Vermont
Immanuel Wallerstein, State University of New York
at Binghamton

With
Maria del Carmen Baerga
Mark Beittel
Kathie Friedman Kasaba
Randall H. McGuire
William G. Martin
Kathleen Stanley
Lanny Thompson
Cynthia Woodsong

CAMBRIDGE
UNIVERSITY PRESS

EDITIONS DE LA MAISON DES SCIENCES DE L'HOMME
Paris

Published by the Press Syndicate of the University of Cambridge
The Pitt Building, Trumpington Street, Cambridge CB2 1RP
40 West 20th Street, New York, NY 10011–4211, USA
10 Stamford Road, Oakleigh, Victoria 3166, Australia
and Editions de la Maison des Sciences de l'Homme
54 Boulevard Raspail, 75270 Paris Cedex 06

First published 1992

Printed in Great Britain at the University Press, Cambridge

A cataloguing in publication record for this book is available from the British Library

Library of Congress cataloguing in publication data
Creating and transforming households: the constraints of the world-economy / Joan Smith,
Immanuel Wallerstein, coordinators.
p.   cm. – (Studies in modern capitalism)
Includes bibliographical references and index.
ISBN 0 521 41552 7 hb   0 521 42713 4 pb
1. Income distribution. 2. Wages. 3. Households. 4. Capitalism. 5. Economic history.
I. Smith, Joan, 1935–   . II. Wallerstein, Immanuel Maurice, 1930–   . III. Series.
HC79.I5C74 1992
339.2′2 – dc20   91-29344   CIP

ISBN 0 521 41552 7 hardback
ISBN 0 521 42713 4 paperback
ISBN 2 7351 0X76 1 hardback (France only)
ISBN 2 7351 0477 X paperback (France only)

Contents

Preface

This book is the fruition of work conducted over many years by the Research Working Group on Households, Labor-Force Formation, and the World-Economy of the Fernand Braudel Center for the Study of Economies, Historical Systems, and Civilizations. The group's membership has evolved over the years, but the authors of this volume formed its core during the key years of the collective research whose results we now present. This book is a joint product, planned and conducted from beginning to end by the entire group. This is not to be read as a collection of essays but as a single monograph, despite the multiple authorship of the various chapters. The argument of the book is a singular one, and the book should be seen as a continuous exposition from beginning to end.

The earlier work of this group can be found in the proceedings of a conference that we held jointly with the Sociology of Development Research Center of the University of Bielefeld (Federal Republic of Germany) and which was published as Joan Smith, Immanuel Wallerstein, and Hans-Dieter Evers, eds., *Households and the World-Economy* (1984). The very first published statement of the group, by Immanuel Wallerstein, William G. Martin, and Torry Dickinson, appeared in *Review* in 1982. An interim report on our research, by Randall H. McGuire, Joan Smith, and William G. Martin, appeared in *Review* in 1986.

This project received support from the National Endowment for the Humanities, for which we are most grateful (Projects RO-1900-81 and RO-20647-84). We acknowledge with gratitude the repeated secretarial assistance of Rebecca Dunlop.

JOAN SMITH AND IMMANUEL WALLERSTEIN

I

Introduction

Households as an institution of the world-economy

Immanuel Wallerstein and Joan Smith

The idea that there exists an "informal sector" of economic activity
is a relatively new one. In the early 1970s feminist theorists raised the
issue of domestic work as productive labor. At about the same time,
Italian authors began to discuss *l'economia sommersa*, referring to small
entrepreneurial activity in central Italy which evaded various legal
restraints. Authors writing about eastern Europe began to discuss
the phenomenon of artisans utilizing collectivized facilities for after-
hours work that were privately contracted for, the clients wishing to
avoid the long delays of "official" repair channels. Anthropologists
began to reopen the question of the structure of the household in
Third World areas.

The reality of course was not new, but the intellecutal discussion
was, especially in relation to the standard analyses of the post-1945
period. Two things had happened. On the one hand, the world
revolution of 1968, as one of its consequences, posed a challenge to
the standard (and simplified) categories of mainstream social
science, both in its liberal and Marxist variants. Simultaneously, the
stagnation of the world-economy (the Kondratieff B-phase) led, as it
had always done previously, to an expansion of the "informal"
sector. Because of the first change, some social scientists were more
sensitive to observing this phenomenon, especially since it had
become more visible because of the second change.

Our own interest in the structure of households was a product of
this changed intellectual climate. We added, however, an additional
twist. We took up an ancient observation, that wage levels are quite
disparate within the world-economy. We wondered whether the
explanation of this persisting disparity might not have something to
do with the phenomenon of *non-wage* labor, and the ways in which
households were constructed.

For 100 to 150 years now, we have talked less of households than

3

of families. In this discussion, we have had an image of the family and its historical evolution that has permeated our consciousness and served as part of the general conceptual apparatus with which we have viewed the world. This image had three main elements. One, the family was previously large and "extended" but today (or in modern times) it has been getting smaller and more "nuclear." Two, the family was previously engaged primarily in subsistence production but today it draws its income primarily from the wage employment of adult (but non-aged) members. Three, the family was previously a structure virtually indistinguishable from economic activities but today it is a quite segregated or autonomous institutional sphere. This image of the family, as perpetrated by world social science, has been an obstacle to our understanding of how households have in fact been constructed in the capitalist world-economy.

Though still quite pervasive as a basic assumption in the world view of the majority, in the last twenty years or so this image of the family has come under severe scholarly attack. There have been at least four themes in that attack.

First, it is argued that this conventional image of the family involves an evolutionary premise that all families everywhere are moving in a given direction, and that the degree to which they have thus moved is a measure of the degree to which the "society" in which they are located may be thought of as "advanced" or "modern." That is to say, this image of the family is an integral part of a "developmentalist" notion which assumed that there exist multiple "societies" in the world, evolving in parallel directions, albeit at different paces, and that all are evolving furthermore in the direction of "progress" (Goode, 1963).

But developmentalism itself has come under severe challenge in recent years as a framework within which to interpret modern historical change. The logical and historical "autonomy" of the various "societies" presumably evolving in "parallel" fashions has been questioned. Rather, some have argued, all these so-called societies have in fact been or become part of an integrated historical system, that of the capitalist world-economy, which is arranged hierarchically in a self-reproducing system, and in which so-called core and peripheral zones perform very different roles and hence are structured quite differently. It would presumably follow from this that the patterns of the family (its composition, its modalities) might look systematically different in the different zones.

Secondly, the idea of the "nuclear" family as something historically "progressive" has been very much associated with the idea that the adult male was thereby "liberated" from the tutelage of his father and assumed independently his own responsibilities. This same adult male came to be identified as the "breadwinner," since it was he who presumably sought wage work outside the household with which to "support" his family. This notion in turn became a basic element in our concepts of the world of work and the world of politics, peopled presumably ever more by these adult proletarian male individuals who faced employers and (sometimes) banded together politically. Along with this conceptualization of the male "breadwinner" has gone the concept of the (adult) female "housewife" (Parsons, 1955).

These concepts of "normal" family roles have of course also been under severe challenge – first of all by feminist scholarship and women's studies in general, which have contested the degree to which this kind of nuclear family (which of course has in fact existed, at least in some places at some times) can be considered to be "progressive" or "liberatory," in that the "liberation" of the adult male from his father was bought, if you will, at the expense of the increased subordination of the adult female to this same adult male, not to speak of the increased subordination of the aged father to his adult male son (Eisenstein, 1979).

In addition, quite apart from the political and moral conclusions to be drawn about this kind of family structure, women's studies has raised basic questions about the underlying assumptions about how economic value is created. Specifically, we find ourselves in the midst of a long, still ongoing, debate about how best to conceptualize the economic significance of "housework" and where it fits in the macroeconomy as well as in the budgetary realities of the household itself.

Thirdly, since the 1970s there has been the growing literature on the so-called "second economy," variously referred as "informal" or "underground" or "submerged." The image of the nuclear family implied a parallel image of a "nuclear economy," with equally clear boundaries and a specified, specialized role. This "nuclear economy" was in theory composed of legal, autonomous enterprises, each with its employer and employees, producing goods and services for the market within the framework established by state laws. This new literature has called attention to the multitudinous economic activities that occur outside this framework – evading legal restrictions or obligations such as taxation, minimum wage laws, and forbidden production (Redclift and Mingione, 1985).

Once again, the implications were double. It was not only that the model of economic production that underlay analysis was shown to be wrong, or at least inadequate to cover empirical reality, but also that the model of family income sources was correspondingly wrong. The adult male often had two employments, not one, and the second employment was frequently one in which the income was not wage income. Similarly, both the "unemployed" adult male and the adult female "housewife" were frequently quite actively involved in this "informal" economy and therefore the basic description of their occupation – unemployed, housewife – was wrong, or at least incomplete (Smith, 1984b).

A fourth challenge to the traditional image has resulted from the enormous expansion of the so-called welfare state, particularly since the Second World War, and particularly in Western (or core) countries. These states have come to accept a wide series of obligations vis-à-vis citizens and/or national residents in general and additionally vis-à-vis specific categories of persons in particular, obligations which involve the periodical allocation of revenues to individuals on some specified criteria.

As the amounts have grown and the political encrustation has become deeper (despite continuing shrill opposition), it has become impossible to ignore the impact of such so-called "transfer payments" on income, and that in two respects. On the one hand, transfer payments have come to represent an even larger percentage of toal income, indeed for some families the majority. And on the other hand, transfer payments are frequently conditional, and thus it becomes apparent that the "state" has thereby a very potent and quite obvious mechanism of affecting, even directing, the structure of the family (Donzelot, 1979).

And if all this were not enough, the careful reconstruction of family history, which has become a major subfield of social history in the last twenty years, has shown that the widespread image of the rise of the nuclear family does not bear the weight of careful archival inspection. The picture in empirical reality turns out to be extremely complex with no very simple trend-line, and one that varies considerably from region to region.

It seems therefore that there is much demand for a reconceptualization of the ways in which these presumably basic institutional spheres – the family, the workplace, the state – relate to each other in our modern world. We shall start with three rather simple empirical observations and argue that no conceptualization which does not encompass these three observations will be adequate as an explanatory model.

Observation number 1 is that most individuals live on a daily basis within a "household" which is what we term the entity responsible for our basic and continuing reproduction needs (food, shelter, clothing), and that this household puts together a number of different kinds of "income" in order to provide for these reproduction needs. We make a distinction between households and families. The former refers to that grouping that assures some level of pooling income and sharing resources over time so as to reproduce the unit. Often the members of a household are biologically related and/or share a common residence, but sometimes not.

We can classify the multiple forms of income into five major varieties, and observe that most households get some of their income in *each* of the five forms, at least if you measure their income not on a daily basis but on an annual or multi-annual basis. These five forms are wages, market sales (or profit), rent, transfer, and "subsistence" (or direct labor input). None of these five categories is as straightforward and uncomplicated as we sometimes pretend.

Wages means the receipt of income (usually cash, but often partially in kind) from someone or some entity outside the household for work performed. The work is usually performed outside the household, and the hours of work are normally circumscribed and legally constrained. We speak of someone being employed full-time when this person works a prescribed number of hours per week (these days, circa 35–45), 52 weeks a year (but these days, most often with "vacation" weeks, often legally prescribed). In some parts of the world, work days are longer, vacations shorter or non-existent; these norms are thus a minimum for "full-time"-ness. Someone is "unemployed" if, having been employed full-time, this person is no longer so employed but is seeking to resume being so. However, we are also aware that many persons receive wages for work that is part-time – in hours per week, in weeks per year (viz., "seasonal" employment), in years per lifetime (viz., "target" employment). And we know that sometimes this employment can involve work "in the home," especially if the wages are based on piecework rather than on hourly compensation.

Market (or profit) income seems straightforward in the case of commodity sales. If someone in the household makes something and sells it in the local market, then the net income is clearly "profit." This profit is generally used for expenditure on immediate consumption, although some part of the net income may be used for "investment." Petty commerce is only a minor variant on petty manufacture in terms of its significance for providing household income. It is more difficult, however, to decide what is happening when "services" are being offered. If one babysits, or takes in washing, the income is often thought of as market income, similar to petty commodity production or marketing. If however one is a freelance editor or computer programmer, the income is more often thought of as akin to wages. It may not be terribly important to resolve such a classificational problem.

Rental income seems to cover any income deriving from the remunerated use by someone outside the household of some entity to which one has (legal) property rights. We rent space in our own home to "lodgers." We rent tools or facilities to neighbors. We deposit money in banks and draw interest therefrom. These days we also "invest" money in stocks and bonds and receive dividends. In theory, this last is a process of joining others to produce market income (and therefore a form of profit), but in practice it is a form of income much closer to that obtained by renting our property. It requires no work, only the forgoing of use. We can also rent our own persons. If one stands in a line for someone else, that is called selling a service. But suppose we substitute our presence for someone else's obligation (say, military service), as has been legal in many parts of the world, is this not more akin to rental (forgoing "normal" civilian life in return for an income)? And how is one to classify one of the newest of all commodifications, the income of the "substitute" uterine progenitor?

Transfers are receipts of income for which there is no immediate work-input counterpart. But of course the "immediacy" of the counterpart is difficult to circumscribe. If one receives state transfer income (old age insurance, unemployment benefits, work-injury compensation, welfare), it is certainly possible to argue that there have been significant counterparts at some prior point in time. To the extent that such transfers are based on "insurance," there have been cash inputs at previous times which required work-inputs to earn them. And even when the transfer payments require no prior insurance payments, it may be argued in many cases that they represent deferred compensation, collectively distributed, for previous work-inputs.

Private transfers are even more obscure in form. Most households receive irregular but predictable (and anticipated) private transfers of income (frequently designated "gifts"). They receive these transfers from their "extended" families (annually on anniversaries, but often more importantly on the occasion of births, marriages, and deaths). They also receive such transfers from those super-extended families we sometimes call "communities," a category which overlaps with but is not identical to another super-extended group, our circle of "friends." But are such transfers transfers? Are there not obligations of reciprocity, more or less faithfully observed? Perhaps these transfers should be thought of as ways of adjusting lifetime income to uneven curves of expenditure (for example, on the occasion of births, marriages, deaths).

Finally, subsistence income is the most confusing category of all. Our use of the term derives from a model of a virtually non-existent entity, the self-sufficient household which reproduces itself fully from what it produces and is thus truly autarkic. This autarkic model is largely a phantasy. However, it should not therefore be forgotten that virtually every household produces *some* of what it requires to reproduce itself, that is, produces some subsistence income.

The household may do this by hunting, gathering, or agriculture to obtain food for consumption. Obviously, this kind of household subsistence production is of diminishing significance, since the percentage of world labor-time (however remunerated) in such activities is on the decline. Household self-manufacture seems on the other hand as important a source of income as it ever was, even if the items thus produced are less likely to be the presumed basics (preserved foods, clothing, the house itself) and more likely to be the increasing number of "do-it-yourself" manufactures (in whole, or more often in part). And household subsistence services on the other hand seems to be actually increasing overall, rather than decreasing in labor input. Households not only still for the most part prepare their own food, but they continue to "maintain" their shelter and clothing. Indeed, they probably spend far more time maintaining their shelter and clothing as the number of appliances available to be tools in this process increases. The tools do not seem to reduce the labor input in terms of time – probably the reverse – even if they usually make the labor input require less muscle-power (Smith, 1987).

The mere listing of the multiple forms of income makes it very obvious that real income for real households is normally made up of all these components. The proportions vary (and are, as we shall see, difficult to compute), but two things at least seem clear. First, few households in the modern world, anywhere, can afford over a lifetime to ignore any of these sources of income. Secondly, wage income, even for households who are thought of as fully "dependent" on it, remains only *one of five* components, and as a percentage probably rarely approaches, even today, a massive proportion of the total.

Observation number 2 is that there seem to exist rather dramatic differences in the real wage levels of persons doing more or less identical work at similar skill levels across world space and world time. That is to say, to put it in its most concise form, a skilled mason employed in construction activities receives considerably higher wages (however measured) in London than in New Delhi, and in London in the late twentieth century as compared to London in the early nineteenth century. This is such common knowledge that it is often not regarded as something which requires explanation.

Yet, on the face of it, this empirical reality flies in the face of almost all standard economic explanations for wage levels. It should not be so, and if it is so momentarily, normal economic flows should end such anomalies over a relatively short space of time. According to most conventional accounts discrimination is impossible to maintain since "if all firms are profit-maximizers, then all will demand the services of the low-wage individuals, bidding their wages up until the wage differential is eliminated" (Stiglitz, 1973: 287). It is said to be "irrational" in a capitalist world-economy that similar/identical activities should not be similarly compensated. In general, when explanations for such an "anomaly" are offered, they tend to be self-consciously non-"economic" in character. The wage differentials are said to be due to "historic" factors, or to "cultural" differences, or to variations in "political" systems. But of course these are no explanations at all, but simply the listing of possible intermediate processes. One would want to know how these other constraints came into existence and when. This is all the more true when we observe that particular wage differentials can and do change but that the pattern of wage differentials nonetheless persists.

Observation number 3 is that all the members of a household (or virtually all) produce *some* income for the household (on an annual basis probably, on a lifetime basis surely), and that the various sources of income are not to be *exclusively* identified with any particular members of the household. That is not to say, however, that there are not systematic patterns or correlations that vary with gender, age, class, and ethnic group.

Wages are identified with adult males. They are identified to the point that female wage work, child labor, employment of the aged or of retired workers constitute a phenomenon that is noticed and therefore that is studied. Yet we know that wage work has never been exclusively the preserve of adult males. To be sure, the amount of wage work by adult females, children, and the aged has varied considerably (although without as yet long trend lines) in what may be cyclical patterns. Still it is probably true to say that at most times and in most places the majority of wage workers have been adult males, and the majority (or at least a large plurality) of adult males have engaged in at least some wage work during their lifetimes.

The earning of market income on the other hand is so flexible a procedure that it is hard to identify it consistently with gender or age roles. Worldwide and over time, men and women have engaged in it, even if some parts of the world seem to show cultural biases towards the higher participation (as well as the non-participation) of certain groups in market activities. One of the flexible features of market activities is that they are less tied to collective schedule making than wage activities. It is therefore usually quite easy to do them for small amounts of time, facilitating their combination with other income-producing activities, and allowing them to be, so to speak, schedule fillers.

Many rental activities are collective household acts (at least in theory) and in addition require very little time. After all, what we mean by rent is income derived from a legal claim rather than from current activity. Of course, the renter may be simultaneously purchasing services or commodities in addition to paying a rent, as when a "lodger" is served food or has clothes laundered. The rental of persons (which is not the most common of phenomena) may however be gender- and age-specific.

Transfers are also made in a sense to the collective household but, not unlike other forms of income, they are usually made via an individual who is the legal recipient of or the excuse for a transfer.

The forms of transfers are many and the recipients therefore are in fact widely distributed across gender and age.

Finally there is subsistence income. Subsistence income shares with market income a considerable flexibility in the allocation (when and for how long a particular activity occurs) and shares with wage income an *imperfect* correlation with a particular age–gender role. We do identify subsistence income with the adult female, but that is for the same reasons we identify wage labor with the adult male. On the one hand, everyone – men and women, adults, children, and the aged – does some subsistence work, with variations according to time and place, with perhaps cyclical patterns, and with no long-term trend-line. But on the other hand, at most times and places the majority of the subsistence income has been produced by adult females, as this is what is implied by the concept "house-wife," which has been a constant of the organizational pattern of the capitalist world-economy.

What then may we conclude from these observations? One thing surely: that all members of the household (except infants and total invalids) are capable of obtaining income for the household by their labor inputs, and in most cases participate in income-securing activities. One other thing, which must however be stated more hesitantly: there are some patterns of gender–age correlation with income-procuring activities but it is far from perfect, and most persons engage in several different income-procuring activities – in a week, in a year, in a lifetime.

One last point should be made about income-pooling. What we are describing is how income comes *into* the household. This says nothing necessarily about how it is spent. Households may be structured in more or less authoritarian fashions. The income may be allocated unequally. Furthermore, the in-coming of the income may be hypothetical. A particular member of the household, earning somehow cash income, may skip a step in the redistributive process, by keeping part or all of the cash to spend. This is a "political" act. From the point of view of this analysis, this cash is still "household income," since it in fact forms part of the pool that is redistributed. A member who keeps the income earned and spends it may not, as a result, be allocated other income for the expenditures in question. In any case, the internal structure of the households, and how power and goods are distributed internally, is not treated in this discussion.

How then should we reconceptualize the interrelations between the household, the workplace, and the state? We suggest that we can make most sense of what is going on if we utilize a set of five orienting propositions, alerting us to what seem to be the processes at work.

(1) The appropriate operational unit for analyzing the ways in which people fit into the "labor force" is not the individual but the "household," defined for these purposes as the social unit that effectively over long periods of time enables individuals, of varying ages of of both sexes, to pool income coming from multiple sources in order to ensure their individual and collective reproduction and well-being. We shall call the multiple processes by which they pool income, allocate tasks, and make collective decisions "house-holding."

The composition of the household is thus a central object for empirical research. We do not presume that all members of the household are necessarily kin, much less a nuclear family, although no doubt in most cases most members of a household are kin and probably close kin. Nor do we presume that a household is necessarily a group resident in the same house, or even in the same locality, although once again this is often the case. Households are defined as those who have de facto entered into long-term income-pooling arrangements. This to be sure entails some set of mutual obligations, although no particular set is included in the definition.

This mode of defining the household is beset by all sorts of boundary problems. How long is long-term? How much pooling constitutes pooling? How many obligations constitutes an ongoing set of mutual obligations? Since persons enter and leave households periodically (certainly by birth and death, and quite often for other reasons), over what sequence of time ought one to measure the pooling activities? We deliberately leave these issues without answers at the level of definition, thus both making it an object of study and not presuming that there is only one set of possible boundaries for a household.

(2) There is a further reason for our vagueness about boundaries. The household as an income-pooling unit is not a primordial essence. It is an historically created institution, both as an institution in general and in its particular varieties. Of course it is not the only such historically created institution. Our holistic conception of the capitalist world-economy as an historical system leads us to consider that the institutions of this system – the states and the interstate

system, the enterprises, the classes, the nations and ethnic groups, the social movements, the sciences, the educational and health structures – are all equally historically created in a single, interrelated process which is a continuing one.

It follows that we must ask why any of these institutions has taken the form that it has, generically as a form and specifically in all its variations. None of this history is to be considered theoretically accidental, having no explanation other than it just happened to be that way for "historical" or "cultural" reasons.

In this case, the bounding of households is itself an historical process which not only can but must be analyzed, as it is probably the key process in the functioning of householding and is what integrates this particular structure into the larger network of structures that constitute the capitalist world-economy. If bounding is key, then it behoves us to see what are the kinds of pressures to which the households are subject which lead them (or even force them) to modify their boundaries. We see three major kinds of pressures which thus constitute our third, fourth, and fifth orienting propositions.

(3) The capitalist world-economy operates through an axial division of labor which is hierarchical and involves commodity chains of production processes, some of which are more core-like and some of which are more peripheral. Any particular unit of production participates in one or multiple commodity chains. Furthermore, any particular unit of production competes with other units of production for its percentage of the total production for a specific point in the one or multiple commodity chains.

The number of competing units of production at particular nexuses of the commodity chain(s) is continually varying, and can vary hypothetically from one to a very, very large number. This is the continuum of monopoly/competition. As the number of competing units in the world-economy as a whole goes down at any nexus toward one, the ability of the units of production located at this nexus to increase their net profit goes up, and as the number goes up toward some very large number, the ability to obtain net profit goes down. This is essentially the difference between being "core-like" and being "peripheral."

Furthermore, the total net profit extracted at any nexus of a chain is related to the total net profit (or extracted surplus-value) in the sum of all the nexuses. Thus, as one nexus becomes more or less profitable, it affects the level of profitability of other nexuses in the commodity chain or chains of which it is a part. That is to say, coreness or peripherality is a relation of one nexus to other nexuses. The nature of the actual economic activity is irrelevant, what matters is the degree to which, at any given point in time, participants ("owners") at this nexus are in a more or a less favorable position to obtain a larger or less large proportion of the total surplus-value created in the commodity chain.

Commodity chains typically are very long with many nexuses. Typically, too, the production units of a given nexus are located in a large number of political units, although the more core-like the nexus, the fewer the number of countries containing production units belonging to that nexus. And typically, it is difficult to go from one end of a commodity chain to the other without crossing frontiers (often many frontiers).

The modes of remunerating labor at different nexuses of the commodity chain are multiple. Two things are true: Most commodity chains will have various modes at different nexuses. Many nexuses will have more than one mode; that is, different production units at the same nexus may use different modes of remuneration.

Finally, as the world-economy goes through its cyclical patterns of global expansion and global contraction, which reflect global ability to extract surplus-value and therefore to accumulate capital, there will be pressures of varying intensities on the units of production to reduce costs. Global contraction will lead to squeezes which force units of production to find ways of reducing costs. One such way of course is to reduce the cost of labor. This may in turn lead to changes in the mode of remunerating labor.

Now what has all this to do with the structure of households? A very great deal. A household is a unit that pools income for purposes of reproduction. If the income it receives is reduced, it must either live on less income or find substitute income. Of course, there comes a point where it cannot survive on less income (or survive very long) and therefore the only alternative is to find substitute income.

The household with the least flexibility, as total income goes down, is the household most dependent on wage income, since the ability to obtain wage income (or a certain level of wage income) is a function of the offer by someone outside the household of that wage employment. A household can most readily affect its total income by investing its labor power in activities it can autonomously launch. It can do this most obviously in terms of subsistence income, and it can also try to do this in the securing of market and rent income. It can even try to invest its time in the securing of additional transfer-income, though this may be more difficult.

But the ability to secure non-wage forms of income is itself a function of the boundaries of the household. One that is too small (say, a truly nuclear family) may simply not have the hours available to generate the necessary income. On the other hand, a very extended household may have too much of a gap in income realistically to hope to overcome it. Such very extended households have however become relatively rare in the poorer strata of the world's households, which tend to vary from very small to medium in size. Ergo, typically, stagnations in the world-economy create pressures on small household structures to enlarge boundaries and to self-exploit more.

Seen from the perspective of the employer of wage labor, it is preferable, other things being equal, to employ persons who are less rather than more dependent on wage income (let us call such households semi-proletarian). For a wage worker in a semi-proletarian household is more able to accept a low real wage since this worker may be able to assume that, via self-exploitation, other compensating forms of income will be available to him or her. The more "proletarian" (that is, wage-dependent) the *household*, the more the individual wage worker is compelled to demand higher real wages (a so-called "living wage"). This is for example why we see, in times of stagnation in the world-economy, relocation of industries from one zone to another. They are moving primarily to reduce wage costs, and they can do this because of the household structures prevalent in the zone into which they are relocating.

If this is so, then both the cyclical rhythms and the secular trends of the capitalist world-economy should affect the modal boundaries of household structures. The cyclical rhythms – the expansions and contractions of the world-economy – should lead to a shifting rhythm of modal household composition. Periods of expansion should see a shift in the direction of relatively greater wage-dependence and relatively narrower boundaries of inclusion, while periods of stagnation should see a shift in the reverse direction. Obviously, we are talking only of shifts and not sudden and complete transformation. And obviously too this will vary according to the degree to which particular sub-areas benefit from or are hurt by the global rhythms.

In addition, however, the world-economy has secular trends. The stagnation phases of the world-economy's rhythms are not symmetrical to its expansion phases. There results a certain "ratchet" effect, which leads to some long-term *slow* upward curves. The one that is most relevant here is the slow upward curve of worldwide proletarianization, which should find some reflection in a *slow* upward curve of the type of household structures most consonant with wage-dependence.

(4) Thus far, the pressures on household boundaries of which we have been speaking seem to be non-tangible, proceeding from obscure market forces to whose abstract consequences households feel it necessary to respond by altering their composition and perhaps their mode of functioning and internal decision making. No doubt these obscure market forces are real and no doubt too households can perceive their effects and respond to them.

There are other forces which are more direct, more immediate, and more imperious. We tend to call such forces "political" and to locate them primarily in the state machinery – or rather in the multiple levels and forms of state machinery: laws and policies which direct households about a large number of possibilities and issues which determine their composition; possibilities and requirements of coresidence; financial and legal responsibilities, fiscal obligations; right to physical movement; constraints on the physical location of economic activities; rules concerning hours and remuneration of work; rules about market behavior; eligibility for transfer income.

Indeed the list of matters about which the state legislates is extremely long, even in the more "laissez-faire"-oriented political regimes. Not only does the state legislate on a vast gamut of matters affecting the structure and composition of households, but it legislates constantly. That is, the rules are never set once and for all. They are regularly being revised.

The bases on which particular states decide to revise their rules are to be sure multiple. One major factor is the attempt of the state to maintain its own budgetary balance and the collectivity's economic survival (as reflected say in a "balance of payments"), as this state faces the changing realities of the world-economy within which it operates. A state may decide it wishes to be the locale to which a large industry in another state may consider relocating because of world economic stagnation. It may then take concrete steps to ensure that the household structures of at least a portion of its citizenry are such, or become such, that the owners of the large industry will find a local market for wage labor at wage levels they find attractive.

Or a state may need to restore its budgetary balance which has been upset by some changes in the realities of the world-economy. It may then decide on major fiscal or social welfare reforms, which will affect the inflows to and outflows from the state's treasury. Such changes may have a significant impact on budgetary calculations for particular groups of household structures, forcing them, in order to survive, to recompose the household.

Of course, the state may even be more direct. It may actually ordain household structures, by controlling the right to migrate (across frontiers, or from rural to urban areas), or by decreeing certain legal obligations of kin to each other, or by making its own obligations to provide household income contingent on households being structured in specific ways, or by forbidding urban land to be used for "agricultural" purposes.

Thus, our fourth orienting proposition is that states always have policies about household composition and boundaries and that furthermore such policies are not simply givens, but change. States therefore constrain households. But conversely the state itself is the vector of political forces, and households participate in these political forces which put pressure upon the state to move in specific directions.

(5) Both the obscure market forces and the more visible state-machineries appear to the household as something external to it, to which it has to "respond" in some way. But the realities of the world-system of which we are a part enter into the "internal" mental frameworks which we utilize to respond to these other apparently "external" forces.

Households think of themselves as belonging to "communities," multiple communities. If the boundaries of the community are derived from the obscure market forces, we call it a "class." If the boundaries are derived from or related to existing or potential state structures, we call it a "nation." In some sense, both class-consciousness and nationalism are conceived of as simultaneously subjective and objective realities. That is, we "feel" ourselves to be of a given class, of a given nation, but we also know that, since they are defined in terms of "external" phenomena, membership is alterable. We can theoretically change our class affiliation, our national allegiance. Some people do (even if most do not). The possibility is nonetheless felt to be there, and by and large it is considered "legitimate" for a household to make a change should it wish to and/or should it be possible to do so. The "legitimacy" of such change is subject to certain constraints relating to the moment of change – it is frowned upon to shift membership at moments when the community is in crisis.

There is a third type of community affiliation which, in common conception, is thought simply to be there and which people claim is not somehow determined by "external" structures. We call this "ethnicity" and by that we mean a collection of cultural norms, perhaps a common language, sometimes a religious affiliation, which marks us off from others *of the same class and nation.* It is furthermore believed that this community membership is not subject to change. That this is not in fact true does not diminish the importance of the widespread belief that it is true.

Our "ethnicity," our "culture" (or "subculture") is a crucial defining category for household structures – in two ways. Households are the prime socializing agency into the norms of ethnicity. We learn these norms as children within a household, and we are most immediately constrained to observe them – as adults or children – by others in the same household.

But what norms is it that we learn in a household and consider to be our "culture" or a good part of it? The norms relate to all areas of activity, but first of all and most importantly to the operation of the household itself. We are taught rules of legitimacy concerning sexual behavior. We are taught obligations (and their limits) of observing *non*-market criteria in internal household transactions. We are taught norms about our sharing obligations, that is, with whom we ought to pool income despite the fact that the income is often juridically defined as owned by an individual.

We are also taught norms about how to relate to the work world and to the state. We are taught to be more (or less) "industrious." We are taught to be oriented to "upward mobility" or to accept our "place." We are taught to be more submissive to the state ("law-abiding") or more intransigent (individual "independence" or collective "rebelliousness"). We are taught to be more or less self-denying, more or less self-indulgent. We are taught to define inter-community obligations narrowly or broadly.

As one draws up the list of all the things that are involved in one's ethnicity, two things become obvious. It is a very broad list, impinging not merely upon the household structure but quite explicitly on how these structures should relate to economic and political institutions. Secondly, the list itself is constantly evolving. That is, the "norms" of a given "ethnic group" are themselves changing; indeed the very boundaries (and names) of the groups evolve. We see then that, far from being somehow just there, somehow more "internal," ethnicity is simply a third modality by which the forces in the total historical system mold each other.

It consequently should come as no surprise to find a triple correlation which, while not total, is strong: ethnicity, type of household structure, ways in which household members relate to the overall economy. We are very aware of this phenomenon in its most unpalatable form: discrimination in the work (or political) arena. But it operates as well, and more frequently, in subtler guises: by orienting households to greater or lesser wage-dependence, by legitimating (or not) certain kinds of market or subsistence involvement, by pressing toward or away from certain kinds of transfer payments.

A household normally has a single "ethnicity." If, by marriage, there is a "mixture," the "intrusive" element tends to "convert," if not formally, at least de facto. If this does not happen, the household has survival problems. The household's ethnicity constitutes a set of rules which very largely ensure that it will operate in specific ways. If, because of changes in the world-economy, such modalities of action are no longer useful, ethnic groups find themselves under "external" pressure to evolve, that is, to change their "norms," even to change their ethnic boundaries.

There is at this point one bugaboo to set aside. It may be said that our concept seems to diminish, underplay, or even eliminate the autonomous role of the household – the household as actor, and not as dependent variable. Not at all! The household is as "autonomous" as the "state," the "firm," the "class," or indeed as any other "actor." As autonomous or as little autonomous. All these so-called actors are part of one historical system; they compose it. They are "determined by" it, but they also "determine" it, in a process of constant interaction that is so imbricated that there is no prime mover. Had we set out to reconceptualize and analyze the "state" or the "firm" or the "class" it might have equally seemed, once the matter were laid out, that its "autonomy" as an actor had been denied. What is inherent in a holistic view of an historical system is that the actors are simultaneously produced by the system and produce (that is, constitute) the system. The whole issue of who is autonomous is a non-issue.

These then are our five orienting processes: the household as an income-pooling unit as our basic unit of analysis; the household as an entity whose boundaries and composition are subject to continuing change; the impact of the cycles and trends of the world-economy upon household structures; the role of the state-machinery in molding and remolding household structures; the role of ethnicity as a modality of socializing household members into particular economic roles, and the changeability of these norms. They add up to a concept of "household" and therefore of "householding" that serves as a basis of our analysis of empirical reality.

We decided to look at eight "regions" in three parts of the world at five points in time. Our three parts of the world are the United States, Mexico and southern Africa. We hoped thereby to catch differences between "core" zones and more "peripheral" zones.

But since each of these zones was itself economically complex and composite we decided to look at smaller entities within the zones that we called "regions" – units that we thought were identifiable as playing some primary economic role (but different ones) and within which households in some sense really "lived." Thus, within the US we looked at the New York City area, the Detroit area, and the Binghamton area. We also looked at Puerto Rico. Within Mexico we looked at the Mexico City area and rural central Mexico. Within southern Africa, we looked at the Witwatersrand and Lesotho. While Lesotho is a separate political jurisdiction from South Africa, it is physically surrounded by South Africa, it has served as part of its hinterland, and its economic history has been very much intertwined with that of South Africa.

In terms of movements of time, we took as our base the presumption of the existence of Kondratieff-length cycles and decided to study each region at the approximate mid-point of each of the presumed A- and B-phases of the last 100 years or so. This gave us the following set of dates: 1885, 1910, 1935, 1955, 1975.

Whatever might be argued about the heuristic value of the time–

space choices we made, we faced an even harder issue in deciding what kinds of data to collect. For one thing, since we began by reconceptualizing categories, it followed that much of the data available did not fit our categories or fitted them only imperfectly. Furthermore, as everyone knows, as one goes back in time and outward from core to peripheral zones, the "hardness" of the data declines, sometimes precipitously.

We decided that our only hope was to be catholic in taste. We would use, with due precautions, whatever data existed. We would use quantitative material where it could be found (government data, including of course census materials, time and budget studies, survey data). We would use archival data that was relevant. We would search for "ethnographic" data – field notes, oral history, syntheses of scholars. We would concentrate on data relating to "working-class" households (defined broadly). And we would be sensitive to ethnic variations that seemed important in any given space–time unit.

What we would try to obtain was a picture of the boundaries of households, the principal sources of their "income" and some approximation of the proportions of each kind of income, and some sense as to who in the household "earned" what sorts of income. We would try to put this into relation both with a picture of the labor force (and therefore labor "needs") in each space–time unit and with a picture of state policy concerning households.

We hoped thereby to make a triple comparison: between different kinds of regimes (and of course first of all between more core-like and more peripheral ones); between A- and B-phases of the world-economy; over time, in terms of secular trends. From this triple comparison, we would derive some preliminary conclusions about the patterns of householding in the capitalist world-economy.

We shall therefore present our empirical findings in the following manner. We shall devote Parts II, III, and IV to the historical transformations of household structures in three zones of the world: the United States, Mexico, and southern Africa. In each part, we shall sketch the evolving relationship of the zone as a whole to the world-economy, and look at the changes over time in state policies that related to household structures. We shall also present a dia-chronic picture of the sub-regions we have selected in terms of a number of specific phenomena. The first will be the transformations in the "income package" of income-pooling households, that is, the relative role of the various forms of income we have outlined. We shall also look at the ways in which the nature of these components may have changed, particularly subsistence income and transfer payments.

Secondly, we shall give what evidence we have on changes in household size and whether it can be seen to relate to the issue of the economic viability of differently bounded households.

Thirdly, we shall try to spell out, to the extent that data is available, the fluctuating role of others than adult males in wage employment: that is, the three categories of adult females, children, and the elderly. Of course, we realize that the boundary line between the three age categories – children, adults, elderly – is socially defined and is itself something that changes. We not only want to look at adult males versus all others, but we are interested in whether the increase in the role of "all others" involves a concomitant rise in the wage employment ratios of adult females, children, and the elderly, or not.

Finally, we shall try to sort out, to the degree we can, how much cyclical fluctuation there is in these patterns according to Kondratieff A/B-phases and how much secular evolution.

These presentations are by country and by region within the country. We shall then try to draw some conclusions from this exploratory study in the form of propositions about which new lines of research may be constructed.

II

The United States

Introduction

Kathie Friedman Kasaba

For the United States, the period after the Civil War witnessed a spectacular and steady rise in economic wealth. These were also the years during which the US solidified its central role in the world-system, strengthened its military power, and improved its political standing.

At the point where the hegemonic role of Great Britain in the capitalist world-economy began to wane, the United States entered into a long multifaceted competition with Germany to be the successor hegemonic power, a competition that was finally resolved in 1945. From 1945 to circa 1970 the US stood as the unquestioned hegemonic power. After 1967/73, with the onset of another long Kondratieff B-phase of stagnation in the world-economy, the relative position of the US began to be eroded. This has had some relatively immediate and negative effects on the level of economic well-being in the US.

The rise to hegemony of the US, in the period 1945–70, was based in large part on its "efficiency" in all spheres of production. In terms of the workforce this meant a steady and significant expansion both of the waged labor force and of the level of real wages. In terms of household structures, this meant, as we shall see, considerable transformations.

The biggest single change in the structure of the workforce over this period was the virtual disappearance of the agricultural sector as a significant user of labor. This went along with a spectacular expansion of the percentage of labor employed in the service sector. The percentage change in the manufacturing sector was comparatively small.

This hundred-year period also saw some very significant political transformations in the United States. The United States moved steadily in the direction of an increasing role of the state (both at the

federal and the individual state levels) in assuring the well-being of
its citizenry in various ways – what we have come to call generically
"welfare state" reforms. This increasing role of the state meant of
course an increasing attempt to control specific aspects of household
structures. At the same time, the increasing role of the state
internally (the welfare state) and externally (the US role in the
world-system) meant that the budgetary requirements of the state
also expanded spectacularly. This led to a great quantitative leap in
taxation as well as changes in the tax structure and this too had a
direct impact on household structures.

The story of the US state's increasing role internally can be told
most succinctly via the three primary moments of its expansion: the
Progressive era reforms from circa 1890 to the First World War; the
New Deal reforms of the 1930s; and the Great Society reforms of the
1960s.

Throughout much of the nineteenth century the United States
maintained a policy of relatively unrestricted immigration. Most
migrants originated in northern and western Europe. One of the
main attractive features for these early immigrants was the availability of land. Later as the frontier began to close, the railroad,
manufacturing, and mining sectors expanded significantly in demand for low-wage labor. From the late nineteenth century and up
to the First World War these sectors attracted large numbers of
migrants from China, Japan, and eastern and southern Europe.
During the First World War, when this immigration was inter-
rupted, and after 1924 when it was largely curtailed, the manufacturing sectors in the northern US attracted Black migrants from
agricultural areas in the southern US as a substitute. During this
same period, Chicanos and Mexican migrants were increasingly
drawn into the workforce in the western and southwestern states.
After the Second World War, legal and illegal immigration from
Latin America, the Caribbean, and some Pacific areas played a
similar role. The policies governing movement of labor – liberal de
jure at first, liberal de facto later – have been a crucial state
contribution to the expansion of US industrial strength.

Legal and administrative restrictions on the rights and freedoms
of migrants, which began at the time of their incorporation into
the US, fundamentally shaped the nature of their wage work,
other income-producing options, and household and community
structures. Although increased migration created the possibility of

low-wage labor, the absence of well-established community or ethnic networks made it more difficult for some migrants to supplement their wages with other sources of household income. This threatened to create a strong upward pressure on wage demands, in order for households to reach a minimum level of collective reproduction.

The intent of "Progressive era" reformers and the consequences of the reforms should be set against this backdrop. Included among these reforms by municipal and local state governments were protective labor legislation for women, abolition of child labor, and more stringent enforcement of compulsory schooling, sanitation and safety rules for factories, working men's compensation, and more restrictive building and real estate codes, which included the regulation of industrial home work in tenements (Dubofsky 1975: 77).

Overall, the reforms can be viewed as part of the effort to ameliorate some of the worst "excesses" of the wage system, particularly those that threatened to disrupt or destroy the daily and generational reproduction of the industrial labor force. In order to maintain a culturally acceptable standard of living in the context of extremely low and irregular wages, workers and their families required far more than merely wages.

Progressive era reforms, by regulating to a large degree who (in terms of age, gender, and marital status) would be entitled or available to be wage workers, tended to push women and children in the direction of creating sources of income other than wages. That women and children, on the one hand, were comparatively better "protected" from the harshness of formal wage earning made them all the more available for ther pooling of non-waged income from domestic labor, petty commodity production, petty commerce, inter-household exchanges – not to mention unregulated wage earning. On the other hand, the reforms can be seen as well as part of organized labor's attempt to control the supply of labor as fully as possible in order to protect the market value of their skills from erosion. In this light, the gradual closing of the Asian and European immigration door between 1917 and 1924 should be viewed as part of organized labor's struggle for a "family wage."

The labor and relief policies of the New Deal can be viewed as furthering similar tendencies with regard to households. But unlike the reforms of the Progressive era, state policies of the 1930s responded to the enormous social dislocations of a workforce previously having been made much more dependent for their livelihood on waged income. Prompted by massive unemployment together with public insurgency, the government took steps to stabilize the wage system.

Three dimensions of the New Deal are of particular relevance to the tendencies previously mentioned. Agricultural subsidies (e.g., Agricultural Adjustment Act, 1933) disrupted sharecropper household arrangements in the South, encouraged increased mechanization, and consequently resulted in the displacement and urban migration of great numbers of tenant farmers and sharecroppers. In other words, one important effect of New Deal agricultural policies was to transform peasant-workers and semi-proletarians into a class of low-wage earners, thus augmenting the absolute size of the wage labor force.

Another effect of the New Deal recovery policies was the massive input of state transfer payments to households in the form of direct relief (e.g., Federal Emergency Relief Administration, 1933–36) and the expansion of state employment in the form of work relief (e.g., Civilian Conservation Corps, and Public Works Administration, both in 1933; Works Progress Administration, 1935). With FERA the federal government, for the first time, assumed responsibility for relief giving, and not only to the traditional categories of "unemployables," but to all persons, unemployed or not, whose resources were inadequate to provide them the necessities of life (Piven and Cloward, 1971: 74). Although such direct relief giving was eventually narrowed to widows, orphans, the blind, and disabled, and subsumed under the 1935 Social Security Act, the long-term consequences were such as permanently to involve the federal government in providing non-waged income to households, who would then be obligated to restructure their family lives in order to obtain it.

The final consequence of the New Deal considered here was the creation of a "dual welfare system" (Boris and Bardaglio, 1987: 144). Under the arrangements for federal relief giving described previously, it was generally White adult male citizens who were eligible for public work jobs and unemployment compensation, having once been connected to the formal wage labor force. Women with children were generally categorized as unemployable, and thus received direct relief (or Aid to Dependent Children) if no man were present. Similarly, the minimum wage mandated by the Fair Labor

Standards Act (1938), because it did not cover domestic service or agricultural labor, had the effect of institutionalizing inequality with regard to wages and access to benefits according to race and citizenship, in addition to gender. On the one hand, this "dual welfare system" maintained women in households as providers of domestic labor and as potential low-wage workers. On the other hand, non-citizens were subjected to forced repatriation when laid off from their low-waged jobs, becoming with their families a potential reserve of low-wage labor to be drawn upon from the other side of the border.

The "Great Society" legislation of the post-1945 period (peaking in the 1960s) enlarged the flow of transfer payments from the social welfare programs of the 1930s, in addition to creating new types of non-waged benefits to households. Social Security benefit levels rose, as Aid to Families with Dependent Children expanded, in terms both of expenditures and of eligibility. Though ADC was designed during the 1930s depression, in part to keep single mothers (typically widows) out of the wage labor force, recipients of AFDC in the mid-1960s (primarily single and divorced mothers) were encouraged to join the low-waged workforce. By 1971, federal AFDC policy required women whose children were under 6 to enter the labor force. The Medicare, Medicaid, and food stamp programs added new state transfer income to households. Overall, benefits – cash, in-kind, and service – rose at a rate of about 8 per cent each year between 1965 and 1972 (Piven and Cloward, 1982: 118).

At the same time the Equal Pay Act (1963), Civil Rights Act (1964), and the Affirmative Action Executive Order (1967) expanded the relative size of the wage labor force. To the extent to which these policies reduced wage discrimination, formally employed members of households were able to increase the waged portion of their contribution to the total household income mix. Partly as a result of the relative increase in the waged part of household income, and partly as a result of households responding to eligibility requirements for state transfer payments, the size of households diminished during this period (Hacker, 1983: 89). Furthering this trend, the Federal Housing Authority and the Veteran's Administration typically subsidized housing that was appropriate only for small nuclear family households. The tendency for household income-pooling boundaries to contract was strengthened by the urban renewal programs of the Great Society era which cut apart ethnic communities across the US. This made the inter-household exchange of non-wage labor and income more difficult, just as it was becoming more necessary.

CHAPTER I

The Detroit story: the crucible of Fordism

Kathleen Stanley and Joan Smith

Detroit is perhaps the quintessential American city. In many ways its history mirrors that of the nation as a whole. In the 1890s, Detroit was already a diversified manufacturing center with a fairly large immigrant population. This was the period in which the automobile industry came to dominate Detroit, and Detroit's contribution to the growing production of consumer durables that was coming to dominate the American economy. In the 1930s, Detroit was the locale of fierce class struggle. By the 1950s, the city came to epitomize the American Dream – highly paid, unionized workers whose wives stayed at home in lower-middle-class suburbia and whose children went to college. This was to last but a moment. By the mid-1960s, poverty and unemployment were becoming increasingly visible; Whites were fleeing to the suburbs and Blacks were left to deal with a city in decay. In recent years, the "flight of capital" has worsened an already bad situation for Detroit's working class as unemployment in manufacturing has increased dramatically, and unions have lost much of their bargaining power.

Detroit, of course, is the birthplace of Fordism, of that particular combination of production and consumption practices which became the hallmark of American capitalism. In Aglietta's classic account,

Fordism is a stage that supersedes Taylorism. It denotes a series of major transformations in the labour process closely linked to those changes in the conditions of existence of the wage-earning class that give rise to the formation of a social consumption norm and tend to institutionalize the economic class struggle in the form of collective bargaining ... It marks a new stage in the regulation of capitalism, the regime of intensive accumulation in which the capitalist class seeks overall management of the production of wage-labour by the close articulation of relations of production with the commodity relations in which the wage-earners purchase their means of consumption. Fordism is thus the principle of *an articulation between process of production and mode of consumption.* (Aglietta, 1979: 116–17)

This articulation of the processes of production and consumption was accomplished via the wage. The crucial element of Fordism was the presumption of the so-called family wage – a male-earned wage sufficient for the support of a dependent wife and children. However, in fact, even in Detroit, this presumed bastion of Fordism, the family wage was never a reality for the majority of wage earners. Before the Second World War, the male wage was always supplemented by the wages of children and sometimes of wives, as well as by considerable amounts of subsistence labor. In the postwar period, with the commodification of many household tasks, women were "freed up" to enter the labor force. It has in fact been their wages in conjunction with their unwaged labor that has allowed this most American of cities to maintain its population at some minimal standard. In what follows we will review the shifts in the livelihood and income-pooling patterns of working-class families in Detroit.

By 1890, Detroit was already an industrial center *par excellence*. Well over half of all employment was in manufacturing and a full 32 percent of the manufacturing labor force was employed in just five industries: foundry products, railroad cars, cigars and cigarettes, boots and shoes, and men's clothing (USBC, 1890d). These leading local industries were among the leading industries nationally as well. Nevertheless, wages were quite low and Detroit's average industrial wage was less than 60 percent of the national average for industrial employment.

Largely because of these low wages, Detroit's leading industries outproduced their national counterparts (with productivity measured here as a ratio of value produced to average wages in that sector). Furthermore, in those sectors which were *not* competitive with their national counterparts, there was a strong inducement to lower wages either because wages in those sectors were, relative to the national sectors, too high; or, since they already paid high wages relative to local standards, they could afford to reduce wages as a way of improving their standing vis-à-vis their national counterparts. During the 1890s, then, Detroit's labor force experienced continued downward pressure on wages.

The structure of Detroit's labor force facilitated the low wages

Table 1. *Composition of the Detroit labor force*

	1890	1910	1940	1950	1970
Population in the labor force (%)	38.7	46.2	36.8	47.8	39.9
Women as percentage of labor force	21.5	22.4	23.3	26.2	35.6
Blacks as percentage of labor force	2.1	1.5	7.4	11.6	17.0
Foreign-born as percentage of labor force	51.9	42.8	23.5	n/a	n/a
White women as percentage of White labor force	21.4	22.3	24.0	26.1	34.4
Black women as percentage of Black labor force	26.9	29.0	26.2	26.8	41.3
Foreign-born women as percentage of foreign-born labor force	19.0	15.8	15.2	n/a	n/a

Source: Calculated from USBC (1890a, 1910c, 1940c, 1950c, 1970b).

paid to its workers. There is no question that immigrant labor was the key to building Detroit's labor force (see Table 1). Well over 70 percent of the city's 206,000 residents were either foreign-born themselves or had at least one foreign-born parent (USBC, 1890a). Of these, over 15 percent had come from Poland, making Detroit's Polish population one of the largest ethnic groups in the city.

In spite of the proportion of immigrants, the sex ratio favored women. The proportion of the Detroit labor force made up of women during the early periods was considerably greater than the US as a whole. Moreover, between 1890 and 1910, that proportion grew in Detroit while it was actually diminishing at the national level.

A third important feature of the Detroit labor force was its overwhelming proportion of youth. In 1890, the proportion of the city's population composed of young adults (20–29) was 17 percent greater than the national average (USBC, 1890a). One effect of Detroit's age structure was an increase in the number of potential wage earners relative to the total population. There was an abundance of labor and this had the predictable effect of pulling down wage levels.

Wages could not, however, be reduced to the point where the survival of the working class was compromised. While there are no available data on household or family income in Detroit for this period, there are indirect ways of measuring the capacity of individual industrial wages to guarantee the generational replenishment of the labor force. By comparing the wage levels of adult males to some standard estimates of cost of living, we can assess the adequacy of wages to meet the needs of working-class families.

On average, Detroit's workers during this period earned a yearly wage of $448.55. In the early 1890s, the Michigan Bureau of Labor prepared a report on the monthly budgets for a carpenter's and a laborer's household (Michigan Bureau of Labor and Industrial Statistics, 1892). From this we have calculated an average worker's budget of $473.40 which comes near to but is still more than the average annual wage (Oestreicher, 1979; Glazer, 1965).

While on the surface the average wage seems to have been almost adequate to cover the cost of basic necessities, this average conceals considerable variation in incomes. Semiskilled, unskilled, and service workers (39 percent of Detroit's labor force) made a great deal less than the average. The laborer whose budget was reported by the Michigan Bureau of Labor, for example, faced an annual shortfall of $86, or 27 percent of his total income. Women, who on average earned less than half the wages of men, fared far worse and would have found being the principal support of a household extremely difficult.

Furthermore, by the 1890s, Detroit was in the middle of a severe depression which was considerably worse, judging by unemployment levels, than in the nation as a whole. In 1890, overall unemployment in Detroit was close to 17 percent (reaching as high as 30 percent during the decade) and, in 1896, 81 percent of those who were working reported lost time, averaging 58 days per year (USBC, 1890d).

Clearly, households had to employ a variety of strategies in order to piece together a "living." The different basic patterns of household formation and income-pooling will be examined for native-born Whites, Polish immigrants, and Blacks. Although Blacks constituted only 2 percent of the population in 1890, they began immigrating to Detroit in large numbers with the closing down of European immigration and the onset of the First World War (Mandle, 1978). These three groups have been chosen for study in an attempt to represent the ethnic diversity of Detroit and to understand its consequences for household patterns.

The structure of Detroit households varied among the ethnic groups making up the city's population. In 1890, the average size of coresidential households was 4.88 persons – a figure which masks considerable variation among groups. Polish households were considerably larger than the average, while Black households were considerably smaller. Blacks, in fact, had the smallest households of any group – only 3.6 persons on average. Native-born White Americans had the smallest families and households of all White groups, largely because of relatively low fertility rates. Polish women, on the other hand, had extraordinarily high fertility rates (along with high rates of childhood mortality) (Zunz, 1982).

Coresidential households were organized primarily around nuclear families (parents and dependent children) with some variation among groups. In 1880, most families were nuclear in structure: 74 percent of native Whites, 93 percent of Polish, 86 percent of Blacks (Zunz, 1982). The composition of these nuclear families was not always the same, however. Unlike the nuclear families of native Whites and Polish immigrants, 60 percent of the Black nuclear families were "either childless couples or single parents rather than complete families with both parents and children present" (Zunz, 1982: 257). Extended families were frequent only among native Whites.

Detroit households responded to the depression years by reducing their size – a strategy, as we will see, which was also employed in the 1930s. During these years native White families reduced their coresidential household size by 17 percent and Black families by 7 percent. Residential membership also became more complex, especially for Blacks, who decreased their proportion of nuclear families by 25 percent and dramatically increased both the number of extended families (10.5 to 17.5 percent) and the number of solitaries (3.5 to 16.3 percent) (Zunz, 1982: 70, 250).

There were, however, exceptions. Polish households continued to have a high degree of nuclearity and increased the average size of coresidential units by 4 percent. This then raises an important question. It is generally taken to be axiomatic that households reduce their dependency ratios during hard times. But as we see with Polish households in Detroit, this is not always the case. Obviously then such reductions are not automatic but contingent. In what follows we will show that household patterns for Poles differed markedly from those of other groups because their patterns of subsistence differed. Further, as we shall see, it was these patterns of subsistence that allowed Polish households to thrive in good times as well as to survive in bad.

Polish families obviously were more able to utilize a larger household size for survival than the two other groups. From the available descriptive data (Napolska, 1946; Orton, 1981), it would appear that Polish families brought with them skills associated with their recent past as peasants, which could be put to use outside the wage nexus and which were enhanced by the cooperation of larger numbers of individuals within the household unit. Polish women, for example, were apparently one of the few groups to keep extensive vegetable gardens and livestock in Detroit during this period; it is possible that as much as 50–60 percent of food costs were covered by this subsistence production. In addition to this subsistence work, Polish women were also responsible for managing the money income (usually wages) contributed by other family members. Virtually no married Polish women worked outside the home for wages (Zunz, 1982: 233).

In Polish households, when a family needed additional cash, the usual solution was to put children to work, even at the expense of their schooling. Most Polish sons began contributing regular wages (80c a week) between the ages of 10 and 14 (Orton, 1981). Many young women joined their brothers in the workforce earning 50c a week for factory work and 25c a week for housework (Orton, 1981). Wages earned by the children of immigrant families seem to have been turned over entirely to their mothers to be used in meeting household expenses.

Native White families, on the other hand, were the most likely to keep their children in school. This was possible in part because of the higher wages received by native White men, 72 percent of whom were either professional or skilled workers (USBC, 1980a). As in other ethnic groups, the lower the father's income, the more likely teenaged children were to leave school and earn wages. While native-born White women were more likely to work for wages than other White women, the actual proportion remained quite low. The predominant strategy for increasing cash income in these households was to take in boarders and lodgers. By 1900, approximately 20 percent of native White households had boarders.

Black households were both the most complex and the most fragile in times of crisis. The very low fertility of Black women meant that fewer children were available to contribute income while it also reduced the number of dependents in most households. Black men were almost always unskilled laborers (73 percent) who earned very low wages and were most likely to face unemployment. This may account for the high number of solitaries – usually men – which increased by 365 percent during the crisis of the 1890s. This increase in the number of solitaries had a direct impact on the practice of boarding in the Black community. In just twenty years, between 1880 and 1900, Blacks went from having very few boarders to having the largest percentage in the city. This was obviously an important strategy for increasing income during the depression.

Married Black women were twice as likely to work for wages as other women (5.4 percent versus 2.3 percent) during the 1890s (Zunz, 1982: 23), and, by 1900, over 34 percent of all Black women in Detroit earned wages (Hill, 1929). The employment of Black women was also necessitated by the rise in the number of female-headed households during the economic downturn. By 1900, 27 percent of all Black households in Detroit were headed by women (Zunz, 1982).

Many households, from all ethnic groups, were simply unable to cope with the severity of the crisis and the number of public relief cases shot up dramatically. Detroit's solution was, in many respects, innovative. "As the depression of 1893 dragged on over the next three years, more than fifteen hundred families, mostly Polish, received a half-acre plot of undeveloped public or, in a few cases, private land on the city's outskirts, where they raised vegetables for their own use or to sell" (Orton, 1981: 184). The first year of the plan, 945 families raised between $12,000 and $14,000 of vegetables, an average of about $14 worth of produce per household. The second year, 1,546 families raised $27,792 worth of produce, an average of nearly $18 per household (Michigan Bureau of Labor and Industrial Statistics, 1896). For these families, then, about 9 percent of their food expenses were met through these purely subsistence activities for the years mentioned in the report. Since food expenses made up 41 percent of the typical household budget (Michigan Bureau of Labor and Industrial Statistics, 1892), these families were able to reduce their total budgets by at least 4 percent through gardening according to the official figures. In reality, given the subsistence practices of immigrant families, the proportion was in all likelihood considerably larger.

In summary, approximately 40 percent of male workers were earning substandard wages in 1890 (see Table 2). While average wages were generally adequate, there was a great deal of unemployment

Table 2. *Household income in Detroit*

	1890	1910	1935	1955	1977
Percentage of adult males earning substandard wages[a]	40	32	50	20	30
Percentage of waged income from wives and children[b]	Native Whites: 15 Poles: 19 Blacks: 22	Native Whites: 18 Poles: 26 Blacks: 27	Women's wages increasing in importance	Whites: 20 Blacks: 28	*City* Whites: 49 Blacks: 53 *SMSA* Whites: 15 Blacks: 27
Average wages as percentage of cost of living[c]	94	66	60 (income)	80	84 (income)
Extent of market activities and rental income[d]	*Rental:* Moderate for native Whites, low for others *Market:* ?	*Rental:* Up slightly for Poles, very high for Blacks *Market:* ?	*Rental:* Overall – 20% Blacks – 42% *Market:* ++	*Rental:* Whites – ? Blacks – 17% *Market:* ?	*Rental:* ? *Market:* ++
Extent of subsistence activities	High for Poles, low for others	?	++	Declining	—
Extent of transfer payments[e]	Native Whites: Low Poles: Moderate Blacks: Moderate	?	++	Whites – ? Blacks – 40	Whites – 44 Blacks – 53

Notes: [a] These are rough guesses based on a combination of wage data, cost of living data, and unemployment rates.
1890: Unemployment was at least 20%; probably 50% of men were unskilled laborers or irregularly employed skilled workers, although some did support families but at lower standard of living. Therefore, we estimate that roughly 40% of men were earning substandard wages.

1910: No data on unemployment; we do know that only workers in auto and auto-related industries (35% of male workers) could comfortably support households at average standard of living. We assume that one-half of the remaining 65% earned seriously low wages – 32%.

1935: 50% of the labor force was without regular, full-time employment.

1955: Unemployment was 8%; 23.2% of workers were low-waged and we assume that half of them were men. Therefore, we estimate that around 20% of male workers were low-waged or unemployed.

1977: 18% unemployment; 20.7% of White men had some unemployment, 39.0% of Black men had some unemployment. Therefore, we estimate that at least 30% of male workers were receiving substandard wages.

b1890: *Native Whites:* Around 29% of women (mostly single) worked at an average wage of $245 (.29 × $245 = $71 average contribution). Men earned around $500. So women contributed about 12% of waged income. This was rounded up to 15% to account for contributions by unmarried sons.

Poles: Most men were laborers earning $387. By 1900, 20% of Polish women were earning wages (.20 × $245 = $49). We assume that one son was also earning wages at .80 per week ($42 annually). Thus, the total contribution from women and children was $91 or 19% of total waged income.

Blacks: Men earned at most $387 as laborers. 36% of Black women worked (.36 × $245 = $88.2 or 19% of waged income). This was rounded up to 22% to account for contribution by unmarried sons. (Note: This is probably an underestimation since we know that, by 1900, 27% of Black households were female-headed, where women contributed nearly all waged income.)

1910: *Native Whites:* About 33% of women were working at an average annual wage of $424 (.33 × $424 = $140). Men earned $780 (in auto plants). So women contributed 15% of waged income. This was rounded up to 18% to account for sons.

Poles: Men earned around $673 (between laborer's and autoworker's wages). 22% of women were working (.22 × $424 = $93 average contribution). Single sons likely to contribute wages (maybe 25%) from work as laborers (.25 × $565 = $141). The contribution of women and children was $234, or 25% of waged income.

Blacks: Men made at most $565. 42.6% of women worked (.426 × $424 = $181 or 24% of waged income. This was rounded up to 27% to account for contributions made by unmarried sons.

1935: Insufficient data to calculate, but we do know that women's wages were of increased importance during the depression.

Notes to Table 2 (*cont.*)

1955: 35% of all households had 1 + wage earners (36% of White and 38% of Black households). Most of these additional wage earners were women who made, on average, $2,692 (men made $5,604) (.36 × $2692 = $969 for Whites or 15% of waged income; .38 × $2692 = $1,023 for Blacks or 15% of waged income in two-earner households). However, 15.4% of Black households and 6.1% of White households were female-headed where women contributed 100%. So:

Whites: 0.939 × 0.15 = 0.141
0.062 × 1.00 = 0.061
 ————
20.2% of waged income

Blacks: 0.846 × 0.15 = 0.127
0.154 × 1.00 = 0.154
 ————
28.1% of waged income

1977: *City* –
Whites: 48.9% of women in labor force; 33% of households female-headed. No wage data but we can assume that women made 60% of male wage (.484 × $60 = $29) or 23% of waged income when both husband and wife present. So:
Whites:

0.67 × 0.23 = 0.154
0.33 × 1.00 = 0.330
 ————
48.4% of waged income from women

Blacks: 49.6% of women in labor force; 44.0% of households female-headed (.496 × $60 = $29.8 or 23% of waged income when both husband and wife present). So:

0.56 × 0.23 = 0.129
0.44 × 1.00 = 0.44
 ————
56.9% of waged income from women

SMSA: Data is from USBC (1980a) and is for married couple families.

1890: Average wages ($445) calculated from USBC (1890a). Adequate income = $473; calculated from data in Michigan Bureau of Labor and Industrial Statistics, 1892.

1910: Average wages for manufacturing workers were $530.88 (USBC, 1910b). Cost of living is estimated to be 4,800 (calculated from Nearing, 1921).

1935: Average income calculated from data in Mayor's Unemployment Committee (1932). Adequate income = $944 from Stecker (1971).

1955: Average wages ($4,841) calculated from data in USBC (1960a). Data is for Detroit SMSA. Adequate income = $6,072 (Monthly Labor Review, 1959).

1977: Median income ($13,980) is from City of Detroit, Planning Department (1980) and is for the city of Detroit. Adequate income = $16,560 (Monthly Labor Review, 1977).

1935: Percentage of families with rental income; data from Mayor's Unemployment Committee (1932) and USBC (1930a).

1955: Percentage of Black households receiving rental income (Wolf and Lebeaux, 1969).

1955: Percentage of households receiving transfers is extrapolated (Wolf and Lebeaux, 1969).

1977: Percentage of households receiving transfers is extrapolated from City of Detroit, Planning Department (1980).

and many households experienced serious budget shortfalls. The ways households responded to these shortfalls varied by ethnicity. Native Whites sent young women into the labor force and took in boarders. Poles sent sons and daughters into wage labor and engaged in fairly extensive subsistence activities. Blacks responded by sending a high proportion of women into the labor force. The severity of the depression, though, forced a significant number of households (especially those of immigrants and Blacks) to rely on charity.

In 1910, 38 percent of the Detroit labor force was in manufacturing. More than 45 percent of all manufacturing workers were employed in the five top industries – motor vehicles, foundry products, tobacco, brass and bronze castings, and men's clothing. Three of these sectors were directly related to the newly emergent automobile industry and accounted for 35 percent of all industrial employment in Detroit.

Though officially in a period of economic expansion, Detroit workers were under severe economic pressure. The downturn of the 1890s and early 1900s, coupled with the increased efforts of the city's manufacturers to enter the national market, left the workforce of Detroit substantially worse off in 1910 than in the previous period of economic contraction. Wages in Detroit during the period of industrial expansion were about 25 percent lower than national average in all but three sectors. Furthermore, as compared to Detroit's wage structure in 1890, many of the city's industrial employers had reduced wage scales considerably (USBC, 1910b).

What had emerged by 1910 with the advent of the automobile industry was a strongly bifurcated industrial structure and labor force. In 1910, the automobile industry proper accounted for 20 percent of all industrial employment with another 15 percent in auto-related industries. Workers in these industries received wages higher than the Detroit average while a little lower than the average for the national sector. This situation gave Detroit auto manufacturers a decided advantage relative to producers in the rest of the country, while still giving Detroit auto workers an advantage relative to the rest of the city's labor force. Workers in other major industries in Detroit received extremely low wages relative to both Detroit and national sectoral averages. In automobile plants in 1909, the average daily wage was $2.70, while for common laborers in other industries it was just $1.81.

What emerged during this period was a set of conflicting pressures on the area's wage structure. Low wages continued to be the fuel of the local economy while, at the same time, the local economy was becoming increasingly geared to an automobile industry whose workers were relatively well paid. The Detroit labor force expanded along with the automobile industry. The first few decades of the twentieth century were ones of massive population increase in Detroit. Between 1900 and 1910, the population grew by 63 percent (USBC, 1910c). Immigrants from abroad poured into Detroit – more than 90,000 in the century's first decade alone. The increase in Detroit's Black population was particularly dramatic, thanks largely to the closing of European immigration and the wartime expansion of industry. In 1900, only 4,111 Blacks lived in the city. Twenty years later, the figure was 40,838 – an increase of almost 9 times. A major proportion of this new immigration consisted of working age people who, having been raised and educated elsewhere, helped to subsidize the expansion of Detroit's industrial economy. During the 1920s, for example, 45 percent of Black males in Georgia aged 15–34 left the state; a significant proportion of them came to Detroit (Mandle, 1978: 74).

Most of these migrants, unlike in earlier periods, were single males. This created a massive shift in the sex ratios of the city. This trend continued throughout the expansionary phase. By 1920, there were 144 foreign-born men, 137 Black men, and 110 native-born White men for every 100 women in their category.

The average Detroit manufacturing worker received a yearly income of $530.88 in 1910 (USBC, 1910b). Though slightly higher than the US average ($518.07), the Detroit wage scale was increasingly polarized between high-wage skilled workers and low-wage semiskilled and unskilled workers. From budget studies for the period, we have extrapolated $800 as the minimum cost of living for a family of five in Detroit (NICB, 1921). This annual income was attained by few in the Detroit working class. In the relatively highly paid automobile industry, only skilled workers could hope to earn this much, and only by working six days a week fifty-two weeks a year. Common laborers who worked the same could expect to earn only $565 – approximately 30 percent below minimum requirements. Women could expect to earn only $424 – approximately 47 percent below the official minimum cost of living.

Clearly, very few households could rely on the earnings of a single wage earner. Between 1900 and 1920, women of all three groups increased their labor force participation rates slightly (Table 1). Overall, women's rates of labor force participation increased during the expansionary period of the 1910s, then fell back during the 1920s as male wages increased and employment stabilized. Women in Detroit were a bit more likely to earn wages than women in the nation as a whole – just under one in three as opposed to one in four nationally.

Black women in Detroit remained much more likely than any other group of women to work for wages. In 1920, one of four married Black women worked for wages compared to only one of twenty married immigrant women. In New York, however, almost half of married Black women earned wages. These variations between cities can be explained by the local job situation for Black men. In cities such as Detroit, where men had access to industrial employment, fewer wives worked than in cities where Black men were in domestic service (Jones, 1985: 162).

Black households in Detroit could earn extra income (and utilize women's labor) by keeping boarders. Many Black migrants, induced to come to Detroit by labor recruiters sent to the South, arrived without family or friends. The arrival of so many Blacks so fast, at one point a quadrupling in eighteen months, was a strong encouragement to the phenomenon of boarding, which helped both the new migrants and old residents to hold down housing costs (Haynes, 1969).

While the few Polish families who kept boarders used the money to help purchase homes, Blacks lived almost entirely in rented quarters, and used the money from boarders simply to cover the increase in living costs.

[A]t least one-third of ghetto households between 1915 and 1930 contained lodgers at any one time ... Maturing Black families relied increasingly on income from lodgers because they could not count on their own sons and daughters for financial support. Polish households, on the other hand, became more nuclear over the years; gradually children started to work and turn over their wages to their parents, thereby lessening the need for boarders. (Jones, 1985: 189)

The few children Blacks did have tended to establish independent households or at least retain their wages for their own use to a much greater extent than did Polish children.

The amount of work necessary to maintain households increased dramatically with the flood of Black immigrant lodgers. Female lodgers helped with housework and child care and, in larger households, the addition of at least one woman boarder became necessary at certain points simply to share in the additional housework. It is interesting to note that the proportion of wage-earning young Black women declined by over 10 percent during the decade, which reflects, at least in part, the increase in unwaged housework as a means to insure family survival.

Polish household patterns remained fairly stable over this period and, for the most part, represent continuations of earlier trends. Boarding did increase as young immigrant men poured into a city already facing a housing shortage, but this phenomenon was relatively short-lived. Further, and more important, the character of such "doubling up" was different in Polish neighborhoods from what it was among Blacks. The additional income from boarders was not used to supplement extraordinarily low wages, but to add to wages so that living standards could be improved. Black households used income from boarders barely to stay alive, Polish households to buy new homes.

By 1910, Polish families were probably experiencing some shortfalls in their waged income, but they had already put into practice subsistence activities that could more than make up the difference. For that reason, they could use subsistence production (which now included some keeping of boarders) not only to meet current needs but to build up a surplus for investing in housing. The important point is this. While all households depended on income other than that generated by the male head of household, that income functioned very differently depending upon how various groups had weathered prior economic storms.

In spite of Detroit's industrial expansion, very few households could survive on the wages of a male breadwinner (see Table 2). One fairly predictable effect was a sharp increase in the proportion of the city's population in the labor force (see Table 1) which reduced the dependency ratio. All households sent more women into waged labor, the most dramatic increase being among immigrant families. Black women would have certainly increased their rates of labor force participation even more had it not been for the unparalleled opportunities to earn money in the Black community by taking in boarders.

Detroit was the big city hardest hit by the depression of the 1930s.

By January of 1931, 32.4 percent of Detroit's labor force was unemployed. A large number of those still working were reduced to part-time employment. Altogether, more than half of the labor force was without regular, full-time employment (Fine, 1975).

Even those still working saw their incomes shrink drastically. In 1929, median family earnings were $35.05 per week. By 1932, median family earnings had dropped to $10.82 per week – a decrease of two-thirds in just three years (Mayor's Unemployment Committee, 1932: 7). Wages in the auto industry were slashed from $6 and $7 a day for some auto workers in the 1920s to $3 and $4 a day in some plants and still less in others. "Michigan's autoworkers averaged only $700 to $1,000 a year by 1932, a 50 percent cut from their 1929 average of $1,600. Prices meanwhile had dropped only 20 percent" (Babson, 1984: 53). Since skilled workers generally faced the steepest wage cuts, the depression tended to equalize the incomes of various groups of workers.

Women workers faced fewer layoffs and consequently their wage earning assumed increasing importance.

The steep layoffs in Detroit's heavy industries idled many men whose wives and daughters still worked in service or retail trades. Unemployment among Michigan's wage-earning women was 30 percent lower in 1935 than among men, and in Detroit the number of working women actually rose by 10,000 during the 1930's – even as the number of employed men fell by 74,000 ... Three out of four wage earners were still men but women's wages, before and after marriage, had taken on an added importance within blue-collar households. (Babson, 1984: 71)

In short, household incomes in Detroit during the depression were totally inadequate. Average weekly income from all sources (earnings, boarders, etc.) was $12.25 (Mayor's Unemployment Committee, 1932: 10). Yet food costs alone for "minimum adequate sustenance" of a family of five were estimated to be $7.65–$10.25 by the United States Children's Bureau. The typical family then was just barely able to meet their basic nutritional requirements with little or nothing left over for rent, clothing, and other necessary items.

A minimum working-class budget was prepared by the Detroit United Community Services in 1921. During that year, it cost $1056.36 annually to reproduce a family of five. By March 1935, the cost of living in Detroit had declined to $944 (Stecker, 1971), but average incomes amounted to only 60 percent of that figure. Auto workers, at least those who were still working, were faring considerably better than other workers. Their average earnings covered about 90 percent of the cost of living.

Under these extreme circumstances, many households could no longer survive in Detroit. In 1932 alone, 150,000 Detroiters (mostly men) fled the city in search of jobs elsewhere. This completely reversed earlier sex ratio patterns, and women now outnumbered men. The sole exception was foreign-born men, who were far less likely to leave the city than men of other groups.

From the available evidence it seems clear that working-class households employed every possible strategy in order to survive.

Without unemployment insurance or federally funded welfare to cushion the blow of economic catastrophe, tens of thousands of unemployed workers exhausted their savings just to keep food on the table and shelter overhead. As the crisis deepened families sold their furniture and dishes, pawned their jewelry and other valuables, and turned to neighbors and relatives for support. But individual measures proved increasingly futile. Hundreds, then thousands, of Detroiters were evicted from their homes for non-payment of rent or mortgage, forcing entire families to live in tents, shacks, lean-tos, and garages. Public begging, burglaries, and Prohibition violations grew dramatically; at night, lines of hungry men began to form behind Detroit's big hotels, waiting for garbage cans to be brought out. (Babson, 1984: 54)

The basic pattern seems to have been one of attempting to maintain and stabilize, when possible, existing households. In the early years of the depression, both the number of new marriages and the number of divorces decreased. From 1929 to 1932, the city's birthrate per 1,000 fell from 23.5 to 15.7 (Fine, 1975: 248). By the decade's end, one-quarter of all White couples and 40 percent of Black couples were childless (Daines, 1940).

Not surprisingly the depression meant for most Detroit households a "stripping down" period. As the depression wore on, the number of people who lived together and could count on mutual daily support declined. In 1920, the average household size in Detroit had been 4.5 persons; by 1940, it had dropped to 3.4. Paradoxically, Black households, the hardest hit during the depression, sustained a proportionately smaller decrease. In consequence, although Blacks had in 1920 the smallest coresidential household size (4.0), by 1940 they had the largest (3.76). Apparently, Blacks having sustained a considerable degree of poverty prior to the depression years, had already declined to the "survival" size. White households were being forced into this strategy only in the course of the 1930s downturn. Prior to that period, White households, even in the face of inadequate wages, could sustain themselves with a combination of several wage-earning members plus informal labor.

As the depression deepened, households were forced to do without basic necessities, and the number of cases of starvation rose (Babson, 1984: 57). Evictions for non-payment of rent rose dramatically, reaching 150 a day during some months. As many as 50,000 home owners lost the equity in their property during a sixty-day period in 1931 (Fine, 1975: 247). Many families took refuge in the tents and shanties mentioned earlier. Other families doubled up, thereby creating larger, more complex households in which the sharing of resources was more widely distributed. Still other families were forced to separate and to take residence with different family and friends.

Some 15–20 percent of all households received money from boarders, an average of $7.42 per week in 1932 (Mayor's Unemployment Committee, 1932: 10). However, many households undoubtedly took in friends and relatives who were not able to contribute financially. As in previous years, Blacks were the most likely to receive additions to their households. In 1930, 42.5 percent of Black families were keeping lodgers (USBC, 1930a).

Market-oriented activities, many of them illegal, became increasingly important sources of income for some households as the formal economy declined. Gambling and bootlegging, which had both become important in the 1920s, provided entrepreneurial opportunities and employment for both Blacks and Whites within the "informal economy" (Widick, 1972: 32–33).

Mutual assistance, which effectively widened the networks of income-pooling, was extremely important during these years. In their survey of over 1,200 households, the Mayor's Unemployment Committee found that

Seven percent of the families received an income from the disposal of property since January 1930, 25 percent received financial aid during the past year, 15 percent received contributions of food during the past year, 11 percent received contributions of clothing during the last year ... 42 percent of the families had aided others since January 1930 ... the aid given running as high as $300, there being forty-five families that gave that much financial aid, the median being $61.00. (Mayor's Unemployment Committee, 1932: 11)

These figures would seem to suggest that as many as 80–85 percent of all households were either giving or receiving financial assistance, a form of non-governmental transfer payments.

Among Whites, these networks of mutual exchange were both kin-based and reciprocal. In contrast, the pattern of Blacks was considerably different. Because of recent migratory patterns, Blacks had few kin in Detroit. Without biological kin groups, Black households created substitute "families."

During the Depression, Black housewives often found themselves to be part of a cohesive community despite high rates of residential turnover. This was due in part to patterns of racial segregation which severely restricted the geographical size and location of Black neighborhoods; families might move, but if they stayed in the same city they were bound to remain near their old friends ... The collective ethos among neighbors sprung from necessity as much as physical proximity. Residents of a Chicago tenement had to share facilities like bathrooms, hotplates, stoves and sinks because of the inadequacy of their individual apartments. They also exchanged goods and services among themselves; a girl might "do the hair" of a neighbor in return for permission to use her pots and pans. Another woman might trade some bread for a glass of milk. (Jones, 1985: 229)

Public relief assumed increasing importance for many households. In 1931, the "thrift-garden" plan of the 1890s was revived. The gardeners were either welfare clients or the unemployed who were not yet on the welfare rolls. Three hundred acres of land were set aside and divided into individual garden plots of 100 × 40 feet. In addition to the 2,785 field gardeners, the Detroit Thrift Gardens Committee furnished seeds and instructions for 1,604 home gardens. The first year of operation the 4,369 field and home gardens produced a crop valued at $218,450 ($50 per gardener, about 46 percent of their annual food budget, or 12 percent of their total budget), and produced food for an estimated 20,000 people. The second year, 6,200 gardeners produced $310,000 in crops (again $50 per gardener), and benefited 31,000 persons (Fine, 1975). The project was discontinued after 1936, although it is certain that many households continued their home gardens on their own. It is equally certain that Polish households, who seem to have had more subsistence skills and practices already in place, would have been keeping extensive gardens, even if they were not formally enrolled in the program.

Other public relief was hardly adequate. At most, families received basic groceries. Many were denied even this limited assistance. By 1931, households whose average weekly income was $2.05 per person were cut from the relief rolls. Only later did Works Project Administration (WPA) jobs provide thousands of Detroit households with enough income to pay rent and buy food. By 1940, 38 percent of all employed persons in one Black area of Detroit were employed by the WPA, from which they received $52 per month (Daines, 1940).

Blacks were disproportionately represented on the relief rolls. Although they constituted only 7.6 percent of the population, they made up 30–35 percent of relief cases. By the mid-1930s, at least 40 percent of all Black families in which the adult male (husband) was absent were receiving assistance. Some Black men apparently deserted their families specifically in order to allow them to qualify for assistance (Jones, 1985: 225). By 1940, 40 percent of all Black households in one area of the city were receiving WPA or some other type of assistance (Daines, 1940).

Probably the most dramatic alternative to traditional household patterns in Detroit in the 1930s was the spread of working-class militancy and the growth of unionism. Early in the depression, Unemployed Workers' Councils were formed as "collective forms of protest and self-help" (Babson, 1984: 57). These Councils were organized primarily on a neighborhood basis and worked to block evictions, establish soup kitchens, and pressure the Welfare Department to provide more adequate relief.

After the initial years of the depression, workplace agitation also rose. The first sitdown strikes in 1933 to protest wage cuts and deteriorating working conditions collapsed, as hunger drove the strikers back to work. These work actions were, however, the precursor to the militant industrial unionism of the mid-1930s. In 1936–37, wave after wave of sitdown strikes rocked the city. While these strikes were initiated by auto and auto-related workers, they soon spread to virtually every workplace, including the cigar factories, small shops, hotels, and even the Woolworth's lunch counter.

These activities and organizations reflected, in very fundamental ways, emerging working-class alternatives to previous household arrangements. The degree of cooperation and resource sharing necessary to make the sitdown strikes successful, for example, virtually turned Detroit's working class into one large income-pooling unit. Moreover, these strikes were part of a process which would eventually change the kinds of resources households would have at their disposal or could demand albeit with varying rates of success – not only higher wages but also unemployment and health insurance, disability pay, and less tangible resources, such as better working conditions, sick leave, and shorter work days.

It was only during the postwar economic expansion that Detroit began to resemble the model of a modern Fordist city in which presumably everyone works for wages, and wages are adequate to sustain a nuclear family independent from a wider household arrangement. But as we shall see, this description fails to fit a substantial proportion of Detroit's labor force even in the halcyon days of the postwar period.

As in the previous upswing of 1910, the 1950s saw an expansion of Detroit's labor force participation rates. In 1940, only 36.8 percent of Detroit's total population was in the labor force. By 1950, this figure had climbed to 47.8 percent in Detroit, while in the US as a whole it was only 39.6 percent (see Table 1). In 1950, Blacks had, for the first time, a higher representation in the Detroit labor force (11.6 percent) than in the US labor force as a whole (10.3 percent). Also for the first time, Blacks in Detroit had a lower rate of labor force participation (40.6 percent) than Whites (48.9 percent) (USBC, 1950a). This represents a reversal of the situation in earlier periods when a much larger proportion of Blacks had been drawn into the labor force.

Women in Detroit increased their representation in the labor force by 12.4 percent between 1940 and 1950; a bit slower than in the US as a whole (14.4 percent). In 1950, women made up 26.2 percent of the Detroit labor force, and 28.9 percent of all women in Detroit worked (USBC, 1950a). Black and White women increased their rates of labor force participation equally (about half a percentage point each) and, for the first time, were almost equally likely to work. By 1960, 32.9 percent of women in the Detroit SMSA were in the labor force (USBC, 1960a).

In the 1950s, three sectors (motor vehicles, metal-working machines, and foundry products) accounted for half of all industrial employment in Detroit (USBC, 1950a). But relative to the previous period, the economy had diversified. In 1939, 61.5 percent of the industrial labor force was employed in the motor vehicles sector; by 1958, this had dropped to one-third.

By the 1950s, Detroit had solidified its position as a high-wage area. Only 3 of Detroit's 17 leading industries paid less than the average national sectoral wage (USBC, 1959). But this higher than average wage was an effect of the continued dominance of the high-wage automobile industry. Workers in Detroit's other leading sectors generally earned less. Nevertheless, there was a general smoothing out of local wage disparities. And, in fact, the proportion of low-wage workers in Detroit had declined by one-quarter. In this case the rising tide had lifted all ships or at least a portion of them.

There were, however, clouds on the horizon. In spite of Detroit's relative prosperity in the 1950s, stable employment was still fairly uncertain. The city's unemployment rate of 7.8 percent in 1950 was 15 percent higher than the national rate (USBC, 1950a). Moreover, the city's economy went through a series of very rapid ups and downs which sometimes pushed the employment rate considerably higher.

No other American city in the 1950's suffered the severe dislocations which were the lot of Detroit – changes which were often underestimated, since most government and private reports or analyses were based on the statistical concept of metropolitan Detroit, not the city itself. The image of Detroit as the "automotive center of the world" was also misleading because it created the impression that whatever happened in the auto industry was automatically reflected in the city. Actually, while the auto industry survived its "feast or famine" production schedules and sales to reach new and unpredicted success in the 1950's, the city of Detroit steadily deteriorated. Chronic unemployment plagued many auto workers, particularly in Detroit due to: (1) the effects of the four postwar recessions, (2) the elimination of small manufacturers and the loss of defense jobs, (3) the impact of automation and technological changes, (4) the decentralization of the auto industry, and (5) the disastrous years at Chrysler, whose plants were concentrated mainly in the city . . . The recession of 1953–1954 hit the auto industry very hard ... Under pressure from the UAW [United Automobile Workers], the Department of Labor did a resurvey of unemployment and reported 121,000 out of work in the Detroit area . . . 1955 was a boom year for the auto industry, and the UAW won a modified form of a guaranteed annual wage, suggesting that prosperity had returned to the city. However, Chrysler had not yet recovered, nor were the unemployed rehired elsewhere, with auto production gradually shifting out of the city. (Widick, 1972: 137–38)

As industry moved from Detroit to the outlying communities (a trend which began with the construction of defense plants shortly before the Second World War), the gap between the living standards of city and suburbs widened. In 1959, the median income for the city of Detroit was $6,069; for the suburbs it was $7,472, a difference of 23 percent. Similarly, in the city itself, 19 percent of all households had a total income of less than $3,000, while for the urban fringe this figure was only 8.6 percent (USBC, 1960a).

Not surprisingly, these differences reflected the racial composition of the city and its surrounding metropolitan area. In 1960, the Detroit SMSA had a non-White population of 15.1 percent. The city of Detroit, on the other hand, had a non-White population of 29.2 percent (USBC, 1960a). As industry moved to suburban industrial zones, it generally brought with it the younger, more affluent segments of the White working class, leaving behind the older White population and a fairly young Black population.

The central city of Detroit had a higher rate of unemployment (9.9 percent as compared to 5.9 percent for the urban fringe), a higher rate of labor force participation for married women (28.9 percent versus 25.7 percent), and a lower rate of labor force participation for men (80.6 percent as opposed to 85.9 percent). This shift in the gender composition of the labor force was related to the movement of industry to the suburbs where 43.9 percent of the labor force was in manufacturing compared to only 37.4 percent in the central city (USBC, 1960a).

Data collected by the Bureau of Labor Statistics in 1959 indicate that a "modest but adequate" level of living for a family of four cost $6,072 annually. Individual wages were often insufficient to attain this standard of living. Men in the metropolitan area earned $5,604 on average, and many – a slight majority of 55 percent – were able to rely on these wages for the support of their families (USBC, 1960a). However, men in the city of Detroit earned only $4,091, which resulted in budget shortfalls of over 30 percent. And of course, women would have found the support of a family extremely difficult on their wages alone. Women in the Detroit area earned, on average, only $2,692 in 1960 (USBC, 1960a). Predictably, the ability to achieve this standard of living also varied by race. The median total income of all families in the Detroit area was $6,825, while for Blacks it was only $4,385 (USBC, 1960a).

As in other periods, coresidential household size was one way of adjusting resources to needs. In general, there was a convergence of household size among the various groups. Average household size was only slightly smaller in the central city (3.20 persons) than in the SMSA as a whole (3.44 persons). Non-White households were only slightly larger than average (3.78 persons in the SMSA and 3.90 persons in the city). Larger households were becoming common only among better-off families in the suburbs or among the poor for whom a wider sharing of resources was indispensable. The more "typical" wage-earning household attempted to achieve a "modest but adequate" standard of living by reducing the number of persons dependent on a single wage.

The most common way of making up for insufficient (or just barely sufficient) male wages was to send additional household members into the labor force. 36.6 percent of all households and 37.9 percent of non-White households had more than one wage earner. More often than not, this extra wage earner was the adult woman/wife. In the 22.5 percent of all households in which both husband and wife worked, median household income was raised to $8,318. In the 23.8 percent of Black households in which both husband and wife worked, median household income rose to $6,446. This was clearly a major strategy for achieving or improving upon the "modest but adequate" standard of living. By 1960, 27.0 percent of married women in the Detroit metropolitan area and 28.9 percent of married women in the city proper were employed (USBC, 1960a).

Black households were less likely to rely on a single wage earner. They experienced higher rates of separation and divorce, and they were more likely to have either no children or more than four. The average number of children in Black families with children was 3.6, whereas for White families it was 3.2 (USBC, 1960a). In 1960, 15.4 percent of all Black households in Detroit were headed by women (compared to 6.1 percent among Whites). In one predominantly Black neighborhood of Detroit, Wolf and Lebeaux (1969) found that 45 percent of the households lived on earnings alone, 32 percent acquired their income from a combination of earnings and transfer payments, and 20 percent lived on transfers only. Most transfer payments were either social security, some form of disability payment, or pensions. Only 8 percent of households received Aid to Dependent Children. Seventeen percent of the households received income from roomers. Wolf and Lebeaux also found evidence of informal exchange networks in Detroit such as those described by Stack (1970). Such networks, usually organized through women, created fairly large income-pooling units in which various types of resources were shared.

Assistance between households was still fairly common among all households in Detroit during the 1950s. Approximately 70 percent of the households surveyed by the Detroit Area Study reported giving or receiving assistance in 1956. Most of this assistance was in the form of services rather than money although financial help between households was not uncommon.

Polish households which remained in the traditional Polish neighborhoods maintained relatively stable household patterns over time. As in earlier periods, Polish families were resoundingly nuclear. Male wages were generally sufficient for family needs and wives rarely worked. But there was a major change over earlier periods. Children remained in school rather than going to work at early ages. Polish-American households turned to two other strategies to supplement earnings. Men worked overtime. Polish-American men and women both tended to evaluate men according to their ability and willingness to earn extra money through overtime (Wrobel, 1979). It was a point of both pride and privilege. More importantly, it was a major resource for Polish-American households. A second strategy was to maintain some level of home production. Approximately one-third of all households surveyed by the Detroit Area Study reported some subsistence work (growing and canning vegetables, or making clothing).

However, though still practiced by a few families, home production was declining in importance. By the 1950s, households in Detroit were largely commodity dependent which greatly affected the kinds of strategies they could utilize to improve their lives. As can be expected, when resources proved inadequate, it was becoming increasingly common to send married women into the labor force, a trend which continued through the 1970s.

Though eventually wages were the central ingredient to survive, as we have seen, Fordism in Detroit was a more complex historical phenomenon than is generally supposed. Only a slight majority of families were able to rely exclusively on the wages of a male breadwinner. At least two wage earners were required for many households to achieve "standard" consumption patterns and some, even with two wage earners, were forced to accept a considerably lower standard of living. Clearly Fordism did not guarantee higher consumption incomes to all workers and may even have required a polarization of the labor force into high-waged and low-waged in order to combine high profits and high levels of working-class consumption of commodities (for part of the working class). Moreover, Fordism in Detroit was a relatively brief phenomenon of the 1950s. By the late 1960s, Detroit's economy was already beginning to decline in ways that fundamentally altered household patterns.

During the 1970s, Detroit continued to be a relatively high-wage area. Eighteen of Detroit's twenty-one leading industries paid wages higher than the national average for that sector. The auto industry continued to dominate the local economy. The same three sectors (motor vehicles, metal-working machines, and foundry products) still accounted for 45.2 percent of all industrial employment, and all three still paid wages which were higher than both national and local averages (USBC, 1970a). But behind these rosy statistics lay real problems. Between 1950 and 1970, the proportion of Detroit's labor force which could not find employment lasting longer than twenty-seven weeks increased by 76 percent and, by 1970, totaled nearly 18 percent of the labor force. Coupled with this was a 91 percent increase in the number of low-wage workers in spite of Detroit's relatively high average wages.

Unemployment was becoming a serious and long-term problem in Detroit. By 1970, Detroit's unemployment rate of 15 percent was more than double the national average of 6.5 percent. By 1980, Detroit's unemployment rate stood at 18 percent (USBC, 1970a; USBC, 1980a).

By the 1970s, Detroit's labor force had become increasingly polarized between high-waged auto and auto-related workers on the one hand, and on the other, low-waged, unemployed, and underemployed workers, many of whom were to be found in the burgeoning service sector. Two features of Detroit's population and labor force sustained this polarization.

One was the area's growing Black population. By 1970, over three-quarters of a million Blacks lived in the Detroit area. In 1970, Blacks made up 18 percent of the population. By 1980, this had increased to 20.5 percent in the Detroit SMSA and 63 percent in the city of Detroit (USBC, 1980a; City of Detroit, Planning Department, 1983). Throughout this period, large segments of the Black population, especially in the inner city, became increasingly marginalized economically.

A second important feature of Detroit's labor force in the 1970s was the very rapid increase in the numbers of female wage earners. In 1970, 35.6 percent of Detroit's labor force was made up of women. This represents an increase of 36 percent between 1950 and 1970. From 1970 on, women's wage-earning activities increased even more rapidly. By 1980, 46 percent of all women and 52 percent of women with children in the city of Detroit were in the labor force (City of Detroit, Planning Department, 1983). Black women, both with and without children, were more likely to work than their White counterparts, and to work longer hours – 35.3 hours per week versus 33.6 hours per week. In one Black neighborhood with relatively high incomes, 72 percent of the women with children were in the labor force (City of Detroit, Planning Department, 1983).

Women's increased wage earning was necessitated, in part, by the increase in female-headed households. By 1980, 40 percent of all households in Detroit (44 percent of Black and 33 percent of White households) were headed by women. Overall, this represented an increase of 48 percent in just ten years.

Male employment patterns also influenced women's wage-earning activities. Black men had much lower rates of labor force participation than White men (65.3 percent versus 79.4 percent), and when employed they usually worked fewer hours per week (38.4 hours versus 41.4 hours) (USBC, 1980a). Unemployment also affected the races differently. In 1979, 20.7 percent of White men reported some unemployment (an average of 14.5 weeks), while 39 percent of Black men reported some unemployment (an average of 19.8 weeks) (USBC, 1980a).

Given these figures, it is hardly surprising that so many women were earning wages. What is surprising, given the extremely bleak employment picture for Black men and high incidence of Black female-headed households, is the relatively small difference between the labor force participation rates of Black and White women (49.6 percent versus 48.4 percent). This might indicate a slightly different character to the wage-earning activities of Black and White women. Black women were nearly always working in order to provide basic necessities for their households. While this was also true for many, if not most, White women, the latter's earnings could at least in some cases be used to raise, rather than simply maintain, the household's standard of living.

In 1980, median household income in the city of Detroit was $13,980 (City of Detroit, Planning Department, 1983). While this was well above the poverty level for a family of four ($7,412), it amounts to only 84 percent of the income estimated to be required to reproduce such a family at an intermediate standard of living ($16,560) (City of Detroit, Planning Department, 1983).

The composition of this income varied by ethnic group. Approximately 74 percent of White households had income from earnings, 32 percent had income from social security, and 12 percent had income from public assistance. Black households were a little less likely to have income from earnings (still 70 percent) or social security (26 percent) but were more than twice as likely to acquire income through public assistance (27 percent) (City of Detroit, Planning Department, 1983).

Household size continued to decrease and this seems to have been a major method of adjusting consumption needs to available resources and incomes. Average household size was around three persons per household (2.81 for Whites, 3.00 for Blacks).

It is probable that at least three major types of market-oriented activities increased during this period. Given the large number of working mothers in the Detroit labor force and the general lack of child care facilities nationwide, many other women were able to increase their household's income by providing child care in their homes. A second major category of market activity which seemed to be on the rise nationwide was the circulation of already used household goods (Herrmann and Soiffer, 1984). A third category of possible market activity existed in Detroit and other urban areas. This set of activities revolved around the operation of illegal drinking establishments and the drug and weapons trade, which were often, but by no means exclusively, found in urban ghettos. According to one inhabitant of Detroit's inner city, "There's a lot of money around here. If you go into the right thing, like you're selling dope . . . It's just a hell of a thing. That's the only way to make any money now . . ." (Ezekiel, 1984: 106).

In general, the economic downturn of the 1970s appears to have intensified household patterns and trends which had begun in the postwar period (increases in women's employment and the proportion of female-headed households, decreases in household size). By the 1970s, households in Detroit were almost completely dependent on money income. As inflation and unemployment eroded this income, there were a limited number of options. Subsistence production was no longer a viable alternative to wages. Consequently three major trends emerged: a dramatic increase in women's contribution to households' waged income; an increasing reliance on public assistance by those who had become most marginalized (Black and/or female-headed households); and the growth of a substantial underground economy.

Let us conclude by commenting on the household patterns observed in Detroit and the larger economic processes in which they are embedded and to which they must necessarily respond. Several long-term secular trends may be observed in Detroit, as well as more cyclical fluctuations in waged and unwaged activities. Perhaps most important is the expected increase in dependence on waged income as consumption became commodified. While in the 1890s, unwaged labor of various kinds could be used as a substantial (if still partial) substitute for wages, by 1980 this was no longer true. None of this is surprising. What is surprising is the degree to which Detroit households depended on unwaged activities. The particular mix of waged and unwaged activities varied over time but dependence on income from "informal" sources remained a constant. Gardening provided households with a significant portion of their food until after the depression of the 1930s, when it declined in importance and eventually became a recreational activity. The keeping of boarders and lodgers was also important until after the depression when it too disappeared. In the 1970s and 1980s, market activities remained important but they were of a different nature (child care, garage sales, illegal drug trade). Public assistance assumed increasing importance over the years as a source of income, particularly for female-headed households.

Increasing wage dependency also led to a long-term decline in household size as households sought to coordinate their consumption requirements and resources. As the costs of their reproduction increased, families generally had fewer children. With fewer children the structure of the households subsistence economy was altered.

A third major trend was the increasing participation of women in the wage labor force. In Detroit, women's employment increased at a fairly steady rate until the 1970s, when it increased dramatically. There is only one exception to this general trend, which occurred in the late 1910s and early 1920s when some women dropped out of the labor force as men's wages increased. Before the Second World War, women's rates of labor force participation were higher in Detroit than in the nation as a whole, but in the postwar era of high wages they have been slightly lower.

It is clear that the family wage system was a reality for only a minority of Detroit's working-class families. The home of "Fordism" had created an orphan.

CHAPTER 2

New York City: the underside of the world's capital

Kathie Friedman Kasaba

A century ago New York City, the "economic capital" of a new core area in the world-economy, candidate for future "world capital," still attracted low-wage laborers and petty entrepreneurs from all over Europe, many of them from peasant backgrounds. After the Second World War, the region became one of the highest-wage areas in the world-economy, its steady rise marking the hegemonic position of the United States in the world-system. Yet, by the close of the 1970s, New York City had once again become dependent upon low-wage immigrant populations for its prosperity. The "new" immigrants from Asia, the Caribbean, and Latin America, who labored in sweatshops and small family businesses, now complemented the high-salaried professionals found in global corporate and finance centers headquartered in the city (Portes and Sassen-Koob, 1987). Economic life in New York City seems to have come full circle over the past hundred years.

By 1890, more than half of New York City's population (age 10 and older) had been incorporated into the labor force, most on an irregular or seasonal basis, or for only parts of their lifetime. Men comprised nearly 74 percent of the wage earners. Nearly 40 percent of these were employed in manufacture, mostly of consumer goods; 29 percent were engaged in trade and transportation; and 26 percent in domestic and personal service (USBC, 1890a, III: 570–71). The expansion of the manufacturing labor force was not the result of the emergence of a group of industrial giants, as in Detroit. The pattern in New York was rather that of an expanding number of firms in given industries with fewer workers in each. It might be called deconcentration or increased competition. This was especially true of the clothing industry, the city's largest employer. Though the clothing industry went from 30 percent of industrial wage earners in 1880 to 40 percent by 1910, the average clothing manufacturer in

1910 employed roughly one-third fewer workers than thirty years earlier (Hammack, 1982: 41).

Who was it that composed New York City's labor force during these years? European immigration was critical to labor supply. The appearance of a massive foreign and largely impoverished laboring population markedly influenced the structure of the city's labor force and household income-pooling structures. The foreign-born comprised in 1870 over 44 percent of the population; in 1890, about 42 percent. Although Ireland and Germany led in providing low-wage immigrants to New York employers before this period, by the last decade of the nineteenth century they were eclipsed by Russia and Italy as the new leading areas of origin of the city's working poor. By 1890, Russian Jews comprised over 3 percent of the city's population, Italians (from southern Italy) over 2 percent (Claghorn, 1901: 465–68; Rosenwaike, 1972: 42). More important than their share in the general population, however, was the dominance of these two groups in the city's largest employment sector. Fully 75 percent of the clothing workers in the city by 1897 were Jewish men. Italian women, however, comprised 7 out of every 8 home finishers of garments in 1902 (Pope, 1905: 52; Kessner and Caroli, 1978: 22).

Clothing production brought workers higher annual average wages in New York City in 1890 than in the nation as a whole, $565 compared to $427. The same could be said for industrial wages generally, $649 for city workers, and only $484 for their national counterparts (USBC, 1890d, I: 23–115; II: 390–409). The limited impact of these comparatively higher wages on workers' standards of living is brought into focus by considering that, by 1903, a family of five required at least $850 to maintain itself in the city (More, 1907: 92). What kind of household structures permitted the payment of such low wages to immigrants with such high expectations of life in America?

Although comprehensive surveys of household income and expenditures were rare in this period, in 1893–94 a young social settlement worker, Isabel Eaton, interviewed numerous New York City clothing workers, from the better-paid capmakers to the poorly paid shirtmakers. Her meticulous investigation of garment households provides us with a lens to focus on the impact of the Great Depression on income-pooling structures and practices.

The entire period 1873–96 was characterized by economic depression, but the last four years were particularly severe. Although money wages fell, real wages remained relatively constant as a consequence of the rapid decline in the prices of workers' food and clothing. But the fact that money wages decreased less and at a slower rate than most prices did not remove the burden of the unemployed, who had to be supported by the remaining irregularly employed wage earners. At the depression's worst, between 1893 and 1897, more than one-third of the city's population was unemployed (Kessler-Harris, 1968: 13, 74–75). In that year, garment workers saw their customary wages reduced by half (Eaton, 1895: 4).

The average family size of garment workers ranged from four to five, mirroring that of the city as a whole. The relatively better-paid capmakers tended to have smaller families (4 members) than the poorly paid shirtmakers (5 members) (Eaton, 1895: 4–5; USBC, 1890a, 1: 941). It is quite possible that shirtmakers, of necessity, relied on more family income contributors than capmakers, since they worked more months per year than the latter, and still earned smaller annual incomes from the trade (Eaton, 1895: 6; see Table 3 below). Clearly most families could not and did not get by on the income provided by the principal wage earner, the adult male garment worker. Yet, only 2 out of the 81 families surveyed by Eaton reported more than one gainfully employed wage earner, regardless of family size or particular branch of the trade (1895: 9–10).

How did these families make ends meet? In order to remain viable economically and as a family, members "stretched" income by stretching the rather elastic tenets of a domestic ideology which mandated a household founded on the partnership of a full-time adult male breadwinner with a full-time wife and mother remaining at home. Family members formally employed in the clothing trades, usually adult men, widows, and single daughters, became the conduit through which industrial home work was channeled to wives, mothers, and young children. During the busy season, tailors commonly ran their machines fifteen to sixteen hours a day in the shop, and then took home large bundles of unfinished garments for their wives and children to work on at piece rates, in order to augment the wages of the adult male breadwinner (Eaton, 1895: 19–22). Thus, in the "pauses" of their cooking, child minding, or other unremunerated domestic labor, full-time mothers were frequently unreported wage-earning "home-finishers," sewing underwear or children's kneepants. The children, if they were at least 14, could be legally withdrawn from school to earn wages for the family. It was quite common for younger children to vend newspapers before schools opened in the mornings and to pull bastings after school in the evenings (Eaton, 1895: 6; Claghorn, 1901; Kessner and Caroli, 1978; CSA, 1894: 20–22).

Taking in boarders and lodgers was another income-generating strategy. Often it occurred as a stage in a family's life-cycle when children were still too young to contribute to family income (More, 1907: 58). Generally however, in cities like New York, where many opportunities for industrial homework and employment in light industry outside the home existed, fewer women worked at provisioning boarders (Kessler-Harris, 1982: 124–25). The depression, however, temporarily increased the prevalence of this mode of earning money income. The *Forward* in 1903 noted that "during the 1890s desperate families had put three boarders in the front room and two borderkes (female boarders) in the kitchen, but today the rooms are too small" (cited in Howe, 1976: 171).

Given their lower wage rates and larger families, more than 40 percent of the shirtmakers surveyed by Eaton utilized the strategy of making all available family members work for money income. Among the better-paid capmakers, with slightly larger families, only 25 percent reported additional money income to their own wage earnings (Eaton, 1895).

During the depression years, measures taken by households to "stretch income" and/or reduce money expenditures required the application of considerably more subsistence labor, primarily by women. Included among women's non-wage work activities during the depression were the organization of the frequent moves to smaller and less costly apartments, and aggressive shopping for bargains. The availability of cheap second-hand goods and ever-cheaper new goods wholesale (clothing, shoes, furniture) in the neighborhood shops and pushcarts assisted families' efforts to maintain their standards of living (Rischin, 1962: 55–56). Since the first Tenement House Law in 1867 had prohibited the keeping of horses, cows, sheep, goats, or swine in tenements, the importance of "agricultural" subsistence income had declined substantially, but it had not yet vanished entirely.

It is clear from most sources on the depression era in the city that many households expanded their income-pooling boundaries beyond the coresidential family unit in order to be able both to give and receive limited amounts and types of assistance from friends, kin, and neighbors. Some even received money from the "old country." Neighbors reportedly often sent up left-over food to a family in need or at least fed the children of such families, and contributed clothing to them their own children had outgrown. If a family were dispossessed, or a mother and child were deserted, neighbors often seemed to provide extra room. Among the German and Irish on the West Side, one social settlement worker observed:

> The readiness to give and share seems to me to be one of the chief traits in the relation of neighbor to neighbor . . . The neighbors lend everything they have from the kettle or coffee pot to their best black shirt for a funeral. One woman lent her christening robe nineteen times. Your neighbor is even willing to lend money "unless you are false to her," but in that case there would "be an end of it even if you went down on your knees." You are thought "stingy" if you won't give as much as you can. (Herzfeld, 1905: 33–34)

According to Herzfeld, families were reluctant to accept aid from charitable institutions, preferring to pawn special pieces of clothing and furniture, to rely on the labor of wives, mothers, and children, and to accept gifts and services from kin and neighbors. The price of accepting charity was often social ostracism, which seemed too costly for these families to bear (Herzfeld, 1905: 39).

Despite the multiple and numerous strategies available for maintaining and reproducing their households during the depression era, the squeeze on money income was a heavy burden. Among the group of clothing workers surveyed by Eaton, only 4 percent were able to get by on their money income; fully 70 percent of the capmakers and more than 60 percent of the shirtmakers were in debt to grocers, butchers, and landlords (Eaton, 1895: 34–37).

Table 3 summarizes the composition of the household income package for the city's garment workers during the 1890s. At best, an adult male's wage earnings comprised only one-half of his family's maintenance needs; at worst, one-third. Households, therefore, put all available family members to work, at both money-producing and subsistence activities. Particularly for the larger families of the poorly paid shirtmakers, the money income contributions of wives and children were more important than subsistence income. Households expanded their boundaries in order to share and draw upon non-wage, subsistence, and transfer income, but they narrowed their membership boundaries to blood kin for purposes of pooling wage income.

Table 3. *Family size and average annual real household income of garment workers, 1893–94*

Average family size:	Capmakers 4 persons	Shirtmakers 5 persons
Income		
Adult male wages	$198 (51%)	$140 (33%)
Rent and other cash income, including women's and children's wage earnings	103 (26%)	203 (48%)
Subsistence income	86 (22%)	76 (18%)
Total income	387	419

Source: Eaton (1895: 4, 6–7, 34–35).

It is quite plausible that the global economic stagnation of the period accounts for the clear indication of increased workload by household members. Generating subsistence income was no doubt important, but garment workers' families found it very difficult to obtain the money to pay for rent and groceries, as well as to remit to the poorer and aging members of their extended family households on the other side of the Atlantic.

By 1910, New York City had emerged as the preeminent center for light manufacturing in the United States (USBC, 1910b: 703–04). The occupational distribution of the labor force remained similar to what it had been in 1890. Trade and transportation accounted for 25 percent of the gainfully employed, domestic and personal service for nearly 16 percent, and clerical for 11 percent. The manufacturing labor force increased in proportion only slightly from the previous period, to 41 percent. Furthermore, the percentage of the population gainfully occupied remained identical to 1890 at 56 percent (USBC, 1910c, IV: 180–92).

In order to arrive at a clearer understanding of the increase in manufacturing productivity during this period, it is useful to examine both the organization of production and reproduction of the city's labor force. New York continued to be characterized by a diversity of manufacturing industries, including clothing, printing and publishing, foundry products, and tobacco manufacturers. Unlike other industrializing cities in the US at the time, small firms with minimal capital investments, carrying on limited production, dominated the economic terrain. From the 1870s through the 1920s, the same general trend connected otherwise diverse enterprises – an increasing number of business units and continuously smaller units of production, each employing fewer and fewer workers. Employers experienced this fiercely competitive industrial structure as a series of unceasing pressures to reduce production costs, particularly wages, in order to stay in business. The experience of industrial wage earners, on the other hand, was characterized by intense job insecurity, wage cuts, and regular bouts of seasonal unemployment.

What was the composition of this enormously productive labor force? Between 1900 and 1920, the city's "working population" (those with access to at least irregular wages) grew in absolute numbers by more than 72 percent (Conk 1978: 89). Much of this increase can be traced to the rise in the migration of adults of working age. Reared and trained outside the United States, their low-wage labor constituted a subsidy to New York City employers. The percentage of foreign-born Whites rose to 45 percent of the population. Native-born Blacks, although increasing, were still only 2 percent of the population in 1910 (USBC, 1910c, III: 232–33). Women increased their share in specifically industrial employment to 33 percent, while the share of children (under 16) fell to less than 1 percent. The most noteworthy change over the period was in married women's labor force participation – from 4.9 percent of the labor force in 1900 to 9.4 percent in 1910, and 9.6 percent in 1920 (Hill, 1929: 269).

The formal wage employment of children under 16, on the other hand, continued to decline. This was aided, after 1910, by the legal requirement that children between the ages of 7 and 14 attend school. Additional restrictions on children's income-generating activities, such as the 1912 Street Trades Law, made it more difficult, though by no means impossible, for children to contribute small amounts of wage and market income to their households. Understaffed municipal agencies were not in a position to enforce these restrictions strictly, particularly not the prohibitions against employment of children in tenement manufacturing (Cohen, 1982: 448–49; Daniel, 1905: 624–29).

The average annual wage in manufacturing jobs in New York City was $584 in 1910. Clothing workers, who constituted nearly 30 percent of this workforce, earned on average only $567. But in comparison to the national average of $518, or $477 for the garment trades, the city was becoming a high-wage area, at least in terms of money wages (USBC, 1910b: 514–24, 703–04, 746–51). By 1914 however, the minimum cost of living for a family of five was estimated to be $876; by 1917 it had risen to between $980 and $1,018 (Kyrk, 1953: 206–07). Thus, although New York was becoming a higher-wage area, and its workforce more dependent upon wages than any other source of income, one adult male full-time wage was not at all enough to maintain an average size family. Although 86 percent of all families surveyed by the 1911 Immigration Commission derived part of their income from husbands/fathers, in only one-third could the household survive on his wages alone. On the average, only 65 percent of a household's total money income was provided by an adult male (USIC, 1911, XXVI, 1: 232).

The income strategies household members created to make ends meet varied significantly by ethnicity and race. This is to say, they were in large measure the consequence of both different migration patterns and labor market discrimination. Jews migrated in whole families, while the seasonal migration of adult males, single and married, characterized the Italian movement into the city. Relatively few single adult women in either ethnic group migrated alone. An important component of the Black population in New York by 1905 was comprised of single adult migrants, both men and women (Gutman, 1976: 522).

Most Jewish (73 percent), Italian (86 percent), and Black (95 percent) men earned wages in blue-collar jobs. But there the similarity ended. Fully 86 percent of Black men were in the most unskilled and irregularly paid segment of the labor market at the time, compared to less than 50 percent of Italian men, and only about 30 percent of Jewish men (Gutman, 1976: 523). As a consequence, fewer Black households (19 percent) were able to depend for money income solely on the wages of their adult male members, than were southern Italian (38 percent), Russian Jewish (20 percent), or US-born White (64 percent) households (USIC, 1911, XXVI, 1: 232).

Wives and mothers contributed money income to their households, in about one-third of the cases studied by the Immigration Commission, but this amounted to little more than 10 percent of the money pooled by family members. Although the Commission reported that 23 percent of Black married women and 22 percent of Italian married women were employed at home, a significant

amount of income-producing work by married women went unrecorded. Taking in laundry, for example, was an important home
industry for Black mothers with young children, although it brought
in a smaller income than going out to work. Italian mothers engaged
in home work for the garment industry in disproportionately large
numbers. Working behind the counters of family shops and small
enterprises, Russian Jewish wives and mothers contributed significant amounts of market income to their households (USIC, 1911,
XXVI, 1: 226, 232; Ovington, 1911: 141, 62; Pleck, 1979: 376).

A common source of money income for some households, and one
which was dependent largely on unrecorded women's and children's
labor, was rent from boarders and lodgers. Before the war and
restrictive legislation put a virtual end to new European arrivals,
more than a quarter of the city's households reported this type of
income (USIC, 1911, XXVI, 1: 198–99). But the incidence of boarding varied significantly by nationality and race. If overcrowded
households can be used as a measure of the presence of boarders,
then this practice was the rule among wage earners' families in the
city. Given the standard of one-and-a-half persons per room, fully 65
percent of Italian households, 61 percent of Russian Jewish, 57
percent of Black, and 50 percent of Irish-American households were
overcrowded, compared to only 30 percent of US-born White
households (Chapin, 1909: 81). According to the Immigration
Commission, Russian Jewish (48 percent) and southern Italian (22
percent) transformed friends and neighbors from the "old country,"
as well as some kin, into rent-paying boarders. In addition, southern
Italian families (31 percent) preferred to reduce their rent costs by
occupying an apartment jointly with one or more families. About
one-third of the Black households surveyed by the Commission
contained boarders and lodgers (USIC, 1911, XXVI, 1: 198–99).

The 1911 Immigration Commission made it a point to survey
households in heavily immigrant districts of the city to assess the
incidence of child labor. Accordingly, children's money income was
reported in over one-quarter of all households surveyed, and averaged a critical 20 percent of household money income. The households most likely to have money income from children were Russian
Jewish households, while US-born Black households were the least
likely (see Table 4 below). The difference again resides in migration
patterns and labor market discrimination. While Jewish migration
from Europe was comprised largely of the permanent transfer of

families, Black migration was generally a movement of young single adults, two-thirds of whom were between the ages of 15 and 39. Black parents in the city often relied for child care on grandparents or other kin in extended family households in the South. Moreover, Black children, especially boys, were reported to be attending school (rather than at home or at work) in much higher numbers (92 percent) than any other US- or foreign-born population in the city (USIC, 1911, xxvi, 1: 220). On the one hand, it seems as if the disproportionately high labor force participation rates of Black mothers may have compensated for the virtual absence of child employment in Black households. On the other hand, it is more than likely that Black children were combining school work with a variety of unrecorded income-generating activities, contributing labor, money, and subsistence goods to their households.

Although New York City households had become more wage-dependent during this period of economic expansion, income derived from market activities continued to be important for recent European immigrants. Fully 18 percent of all male migrant household heads surveyed by the Immigration Commission were "in business for profits," compared to 9 percent of female heads of households. This type of income-producing work was especially noted for Russian Jewish men (26 percent) and women (15 percent), and southern Italian men (18 percent). Less than 2 percent of Black men in New York City in 1905 reported income derived from "enterprise" (USIC, 1911, xxvi, 1: 217–18, 232).

Low wages in the expanding garment industry and other immigrant-dominated trades were increasingly subsidized by non-wage domestic labor, both of employed and non-employed household members. Even in 1902–03, inspectors of the Tenement House Department were still reporting, albeit infrequently, the keeping of goats, pigs, or poultry in dark cellars (NYC, THD, 1, 1902–03: 110–15). Social investigators also noted the time-consuming searches for free fuel on city streets, especially near warehouses and construction sites. This was typically the work of mothers and young boys (Chapin, 1909: 117). Estimates of minimal household budgets for this period always "presuppose[d], on the part of the mother, a high grade of efficiency in mending and remaking" clothing for the family. In garment workers' families, when materials could be taken out of the shops, men often sewed new clothing for family members (Chapin, 1909: 163–65, 167). A somewhat flexible pricing system and access to easy credit facilitated immigrant women's practice of stretching low wages by bargaining for the household necessities that had to be purchased. One method of making do with very low wages, especially popular among young wage-earning women not residing with their families, as well as with Italian and Black family units, was to do all of their laundry at home, despite the expansion of inexpensive commercial laundries (Chapin, 1909: 170–71; Clark and Wyatt, 1911: *passim*).

Table 4 summarizes the average composition of household income in New York City for a diversity of racial, ethnic, and immigrant groups. At most, wages comprised 69 percent of the income pooled, but this was true only for US-born White households, where an adult male's earnings averaged half of all income, from any source. Subsistence production and other non-wage domestic labor, correspondingly, averaged less than one-third of household income. Among all other racial and immigrant groups adult male wage contributions were far less, and income from non-wage labor was far greater. Income derived from work outside market relations was an important component of households' standards of living, and an important subsidy to the industrial expansion of the period.

Mayor LaGuardia's Committee on Unemployment Relief in 1935 spelled out the dimensions of the joblessness crisis to New Yorkers in stark terms: "One out of every three men and women gainfully employed in 1930 is now unemployed due to lack of work, and in the city's population of seven million over two and a half million are intimately affected by the resultant loss of family incomes" (NYC, RM, 1935: 9).

The burden of joblessness was, however, not distributed evenly among employment sectors. Of all occupational divisions, manufacturing had the highest rates of unemployment in 1930 – nearly 16 percent of men and 10 percent of women. Public service occupations had the smallest number of unemployed, while professional and trade-related jobs also remained fairly stable. In the clerical fields, only 6 percent of men and nearly 5 percent of women were unemployed (Bayor, 1978: 10; Cohen, 1977: 133–34). The selective distribution of unemployment in the 1930s marked the accumulated impact of years of ongoing transformation of the city from an expanding center of consumer goods manufacturing to a metropolis dominated by commerce and the service sector.

Although the manufacturing workforce was clearly declining over

Table 4. *Composition of household income, New York City, c. 1910*

Ethnicity	Real income, all sources $	Husband's earnings (1)	Wife's earnings (2)	Children (3)	Total wages (1 + 2 + 3)	Rent from boarders/lodgers (4)	"Other sources"[a] (5)	Subsistence production (6)
Native-born White	$1,176	$679 58%	$34 3%	$92 8%	69%	$25 2%	$2 0.2%	$344 29%
Black	$1,029	$344 33%	$161 16%	$29 3%	52%	$17 2%	$23 2%	$455 44%
Irish-American	$1,255	$636 51%	$53 4%	$141 11%	66%	$35 3%	$18 1%	$372 30%
Russian-Jewish	$1,207	$480 40%	$8 1%	$252 21%	62%	$73 6%	$1 0.1%	$393 33%
Southern Italian	$1,129	$468 41%	$55 5%	$131 12%	58%	$21 2%	$8 1%	$446 40%

Note: [a] Receipts from investments, usually rent and/or contributions from friends and kin.
Sources: Chapin (1909: 70–72); USIC (1911, xxvi, 1: 226, 232).

the long run as a proportion of the total labor force, industrial employees nevertheless continued to dominate the city's wage labor market. Between 1920 and 1930, manufacturing wage earners decreased their share of the gainfully occupied from 38 to 32 percent. Trade, transportation, and communication workers increased from 25 to 27 percent; clerical employees from 16 to 17 percent. Public service jobs accounted for 8 percent of the labor force in 1930, compared to less than 7 percent a decade earlier. The numbers employed in domestic and personal service occupations rose from 12 to 14 percent, reversing a trend from the late nineteenth century (USBC, 1920a, IV: 130–31; USBC, 1930b, IV: 1086). A national study conducted during the depression on "families that were above the average in education and income" reported, against that author's expectations, that the number of families hiring "full-time help" had nearly doubled from 1927 to 1933 (Morgan, 1939: 33). This most probably reflected the increasing polarization between income, gender, and racial-ethnic groups during this period of economic stagnation. Falling wages for full-time household help made it possible for some families previously not able to hire domestic workers before the depression to do so in 1933. On the other hand, intensifying privation drove more persons into domestic employment.

War slowed the migration both of temporary and permanent low-wage workers from Europe. After 1924, such migration was nearly completely curtailed through restrictive legislation. However, between 1900 and 1920 Blacks doubled their share of the population in the city, and redoubled it in the single decade of the 1920s. The bulk of this growth originated in migration of rural Blacks from the southern Atlantic coastal states and the West Indies. Restrictive legislation also had the impact of widening the stream of Puerto Rican labor flows to the city increasing especially during the 1920s. Economic stagnation in the 1930s reduced the rate of this migration considerably. Between 1930 and 1934 return migration rates rose to include nearly 20 percent of all Puerto Ricans then resident on the mainland. But, in total for the twenty years between 1920 and 1940, the Puerto Rican presence in the city increased more than eightfold, from 7,000 to 61,000, and the city's share of all Puerto Ricans living on the mainland grew from 62 to nearly 88 percent (Rosenwaike, 1972: 117–19; Calzada, 1979: 223–27).

Child and young adult employment declined dramatically

between 1920 and 1940. Nearly 6 percent of children (aged 10–15) were employed in New York City in 1920; this was down to less than 2 percent by 1930 (USBC, 1930b, IV: 95). In 1920, almost 44 percent of youth (aged 14–17) were gainfully employed, compared to only 24 percent in 1930, and 9 percent by 1940 (USBC, 1940b, III: 356). On the other hand, women maintained their share in wage employment. Thirty-four percent of women (aged 15 and older) were in the labor force in 1920, compared to 33.7 percent (of those aged 14 and older) in 1940 (USBC, 1920a, IV: 800; USBC, 1940b, III: 347). Married women, in particular, were slightly more frequently drawn into gainful employment outside the home, from less than 10 percent in 1920 to nearly 12 percent in 1930 (USBC, 1930b, IV: 80; USBC, 1940b, III: 347).

The overall trend, apparent from 1890, for New York City wage earners to receive wages equal to or higher than the national average for their respective employment sectors continued well into the midst of the depression. The average city manufacturing worker earned $1,234 in 1939. Clothing workers, who comprised about 22 percent of this labor force, earned, on average, somewhat more, $1,310. The national average manufacturing wage was then $1,153; in clothing it was only $1,088 (USBC, 1940b). New York had become, relatively, an even higher-wage zone during the depression for those able to maintain full employment.

Cost of living estimates over the period caution against undue optimism, however. At the beginning of the period, in 1921, an average family of five was said to require $2,264 annually in order to "live comfortably" (*New York Tribune*, May 23, 1921). By 1935, a "maintenance level of living" for a manual laborer's family of four was estimated at $1,375 (Stecker, 1971: 5). Few fully employed manufacturing workers, not to mention the fully or partially unemployed, were able to provide for a family solely on the basis of their wage earnings. The tension between family reproduction costs and wages was reflected in the composition of households and their income-pooling practices.

Economic depression seems to have had the effect of diminishing family size. The 1930 census for the city reported a median family size of only 3.36 persons. As in the past, Black families were the smallest (2.61 persons), and foreign-born White families, the largest (3.76). For all New York City families, regardless of race, income, or occupation, the dominant family type in 1930 was husband and wife only. This was the case for nearly 50 percent of the Black and 25 percent of the White families studied (USBC, 1930b, VI: 56, 66).

Although families were shrinking, households were growing in size and complexity. As an alternative to return migration to areas where subsistence and market income were more readily available, some low-wage laborers and/or recent arrivals to New York City expanded the boundaries of income-pooling households. While the 1930 census reported that nearly 90 percent of all New York City families contained no lodgers, detailed surveys of particular neighborhoods reveal considerable "doubling up," and movement of the unemployed to kin and friends (USBC, 1930b, VI: 67; Simkhovitch, 1938: 13).

The median household size for Puerto Rican families in 1925 was 4.8 persons, a number strongly affected by the presence of boarders and lodgers, particularly during the depression. In some cases, multi-family, or extended family dwellings were reclassified as households with lodgers, since census-takers would list only one household head. In actuality, however, several married couples or family units often shared living space and expenses equally (Korrol, 1983: 103). The practices of ritual kinship, e.g., godparents, and informal adoptions also extended the income-pooling unit beyond the coresidential nuclear family (Korrol, 1983: 100–02).

Among Black residents, the percentage of kin-related households containing a nuclear family rose from 80 percent in 1905 to 83 percent in 1925 (Gutman, 1976: 514, 529–30). However, households containing simply a nuclear family declined. About 50 percent of all Black households contained one or more lodgers; about 20 percent had one or more relatives other than members of the immediate family (Gutman, 1976: 443, 454). Practically every St. Helena's Islander (South Carolina) resident in Harlem had close relatives nearby willing to help them out, or take them into their homes as their wages diminished, or as they became unemployed. As a result of this practice, very few returned to St. Helena's Island during the depression, although the rate of migration to New York City declined (Kiser, 1969: 33–34, 199).

Not all the unemployed were able to rely on kin and friends to share living space or other necessities. Social settlement workers noted the increasing numbers of homeless men concentrated within particular neighborhoods. Mary Simkhovitch, Greenwich House worker, detailed the shanty town constructed by the homeless at the

corner of West and Charlton streets (Simkhovitch, 1938: 217–22).
Henry Street Settlement workers on the Lower East Side surveyed
the many homeless men who frequented soup kitchens in the winter
of 1933–34 (Henry St. 9).

What were the other means by which family members made ends
meet during the depression? Well over one-third of all New York
City families pursued a multiple wage earner strategy in 1930. For
the city's Black and foreign-born White families the figure rose to
nearly 50 percent (USBC, 1930b, VI: 66). As previously noted,
formal wage employment for children and youth declined, but
married women from both lower- and middle-income families were
increasingly drawn into wage employment outside the home (Wandersee, 1983: 47).

Children below the age of legal full-time wage employment
probably continued to contribute non-remunerated subsistence
labor to their households, much as they had done during the pre-
depression years of 1926–27. They assisted mothers in industrial
homework, ran errands, worked in the shops of their parents or other
kin, or at pushcarts, and above all continued to collect scrap wood
from city streets for fuel. Children's wage jobs, as newspaper
vendors, or bootblacks, were increasingly taken, however, by adults
(Shulman, 1938: 13).

In 1935–36 the Bureau of Labor Statistics, in cooperation with the
Works Progress Administration, did a national study on family
incomes and expenditures that included a detailed sample of New
York City families. Because only families not on relief were included
in the report, the results are biased in a wage and salary direction
(USBLS, 1935–36, 643: 2–4, 7). In light of this, it is interesting that
wages comprised only 65–80 percent of real household income. In
fact, the group categorized as "wage-earning families" depended less
on wages than did "clerical worker families" (see Table 5 below).
The difference between them is due probably not only to higher
wages, but to steadier wages. Black families, both wage-earning and
clerical, drew a great deal more income, relative to White families,
from rent and "casual work" (market activities, sewing, laundry).
White families, particularly clerical workers, in contrast relied to a
far greater extent on transfer income (money gifts, pensions, and
benefits). These differences are probably the legacy of long-run
labor market discrimination and segregation. Black family members
met the depression with continued work overload; White family

Table 5. *Family size and average real household income, by race and occupation, New York City, 1935–36*

	White wage earner	White clerical worker	Black wage earner	Black clerical worker
Family size	3.7 persons	3.4	3.3	3.3
Real household income, total	$2,684	$3,037	$1,930	$2,338
Wages	68%	75%	65%	80%
Subsistence	28%	20%	30%	14%
Rent plus "casual work" done in home (sewing, laundry)	0.6%	0.5%	3.1%	2.6%
Transfers (money, gifts, pensions, benefits)	1.6%	2.2%	1.1%	0.6%
Other non-money income (includes value of owned home and/or value of rent as pay)	2.1%	2.0%	1.0%	2.2%

Source: USBLS (1935–36: I, 94, 101, 107, 157, 164, 171; II, 114–15, 156–57).

members were positioned to reap the benefits of past formal labor force participation.

Table 5 summarizes the real household income mix for non-relief families in New York City in 1935–36. Compared to the 1890s depression, households in the mid-1930s were more wage-dependent, and dependent on more wage earners. The proportionate contribution of subsistence income, including the domestic labor of women and children, changed little from the previous depression, but decreased noticeably from the preceding period of economic expansion. This contrasted with expectations. It is likely that the increased time spent in formal wage employment by wives and mothers, in combination with state transfer payments to households, set some limits and compensated somewhat for the greater amount of subsistence income pooled in previous years.

The global economic and technological arrangements which emerged from the 1930s depression and the war had the effect of restoring a degree of profitability and growth to New York City. The rise of the United States to hegemony in the world-economy after 1945 was the occasion for the consolidation of the role of New York

City as a center for global finance. The city had increasingly captured the headquarters of highly mobile transnational corporations, international banking establishments, trading companies, and a number of auxiliary services in transportation, accounting, advertising, law, municipal services, and high-rise construction.

The expansion of business service employment was matched by and somewhat obscured the accelerated outmigration of industrial firms from the central city. Between 1947 and 1967 the city lost over 200,000 manufacturing jobs. The loss was especially sharp in the labor-intensive clothing and food-processing industries. As a consequence, overall employment levels showed virtually no growth from the mid-1950s, and declined considerably more by the late 1960s (Vietorisz and Harrison, 1970: 178–81, 184). As of 1958, employment in manufacturing had declined to 24 percent of the labor force; trade, transport, communication, and utilities to 11 percent. Government employment had risen to 11 percent (Vietorisz and Harrison, 1970: 284).

When New York City's runaway manufacturing base is disaggregated, a more complex picture of the period emerges. In the case of the garment industry, it was the larger shops with standardized production and high-wage unionized workforces which left the city. The less mechanized, lower-wage apparel branches, as well as the industry's highest-paid marketing and design operations, remained (Roniger, 1974: 20). In fact, apparel-related manufacturing continued its historical dominance throughout this period, representing the trades of nearly one-third of the manufacturing labor force in 1958 (USBC, 1958, III: 6–23, (31) 16–20).

Patterns of population movement and labor force composition complemented these changes in the city's occupational structure, and help to explain them. By mid-century, although the city's population growth stabilized, there were some important changes in its social composition. The trickle of immediate postwar suburbanization turned into a flood during the 1950s and 1960s. Higher-wage skilled workers, white-collar workers, professionals, managers, and business proprietors migrated to outlying areas. Paradoxically, for a period of declining opportunities in industrial employment, the migration of largely unskilled Black and Puerto Rican wage earners and their families to the city accelerated. Between 1950 and 1960, Blacks increased their numbers in New York City by almost half (to 14 percent of the population), and Puerto Ricans one-and-a-half (to

8 percent of the population) (Rosenwaike, 1972: 131–40; NYC, CEE, 1973: 23–24, 38). The paradox was only apparent.

A Harvard University study on the New York Metropolitan Region in the late 1940s signaled the future and underscored the then critical role of Puerto Rican labor flows in "protecting" industrial sectors that might otherwise have been "endangered":

> The rate of Puerto Rican migration to New York is one of the factors that determines how long and how successfully the New York Metropolitan Region will retain industries which are under competitive pressure from other areas. To the extent that some of these industries have hung on in the area, they have depended on recently arrived Puerto Rican workers who have entered the job market of the New York area at the rate of about 13,000 a year. (Cited in Rodríguez, 1979: 213)

Connections between Puerto Ricans in the city with kin and friends on the island kept potential migrants informed about the mainland job market. As a consequence, during the recurrent recessions of the mid-1950s and 1960s, the rate of migration slowed and the number returning to Puerto Rico rose (Lopez, 1974: 319–20, 376).

One of the more impressive changes in the composition of the city's labor force, and one which surely was related to the processes of selective suburbanization, had to do with the age of the population. Increasingly, the city became home both to those too young for full-time wage employment (age 15–24) and to those too old (over age 65). This may account, in part, for the increase in public welfare spending from about 12 percent of the city's budget in the 1950s to 25 percent by 1970 (NYC, CEE, 1973: 23–24, 38).

By 1950, the labor force was nearly one-third female (USBC, 1950b, II: 100). Sixty percent of all single women were formally employed. But the largest increase was among married women; 22 percent had entered the labor market (USBC, 1950b, II: 253). Among non-White women, labor force participation was considerably higher. Forty-eight percent of non-White women were engaged in formal wage earning, 55 percent of single women and 39 percent of married women (USBC, 1950b, II: 113).

The increasing number of women wage earners, especially married women, was one of the chief means by which households not only made ends meet, but improved their standard of living. Average annual wages in the city were $3,943 for manufacturing in 1958, and $3,003 for garment workers. This put New York City workers behind the national average, at $4,434, for the first time. New York City garment workers, however, still tended to be rather high-waged, when compared to their national counterparts, at $2,610 annually (USBC, 1958, III: 6–23, (31) 16–20).

If the cost of living for nuclear family households remained close to its 1950 average, at $3,649, a true "family wage" would have been possible for a minority of such family types (Knapp, 1951: 153). The Bureau of Labor Statistics, in its report on consumer expenditures and incomes in New York City for 1950, observed that relatively few families relied on more than one wage earner (see Table 6 below). Interestingly, it was the families of skilled wage earners, with relatively high wages and steady work, that were most often comprised of more than a single wage worker. Unfortunately, the report is no more specific than this (USBLS, 1950). The slight decrease in both average household and family size to 3.2 persons in 1950 may be an indication of what made a family wage possible for some households (USBC, 1950b, II: 90).

Of what was the household consumption fund composed during these years of relative economic expansion? "Money income," a BLS category representing an aggregate of wages, profit, rent, and transfer income from unemployment insurance, social security, pensions, public assistance, and gifts, comprised on average little more than half of the total real household income. This aggregate probably marks a fair degree of economic polarization between those most dependent on transfer income and those dependent on wages, salaries, and profit. If the technique described in the Postscript for approximating the proportion of household income derived from subsistence activities is applied here, subsistence income comprised 36 percent for high-wage clerical households and 53 percent for the households of the unemployed (see Table 6 below). However, in a context of increased commodification of household goods, increased government regulation of subsistence-generating activities, and increased female labor market participation, it is unlikely that poor urban families would be able actually to produce through subsistence activities half of their household's income, and moreover, to survive on it.

One of the means by which this group of households was able to get by, and (for some) experience a higher standard of living, was by drawing on past savings and buying on credit or installment plans.

On the average, households surveyed in 1950 had a deficit of nearly $200 (Williams, 1956: 1017, 1021).

If, however, the household consumption funds of the unemployed and poor are disaggregated, as they were in the 1966 Urban Employment Survey for Central Harlem, a more complex and sharper picture of income pooling emerges (Vietorisz and Harrison, 1970: 225–36). More than one-third of low-income families contained two or more wage earners. This represents a greater incidence of multiple wage earning than was observed in the 1950 study. This may have been an indicator of the approaching economic downturn. But coping with the consequences of low-wage work in this way was probably more deeply embedded over the long term in this region.

It seems to have mattered little, however, whether households contained one, two, or more wage earners in terms of their receiving state transfer income. Wages were so low and so infrequent that roughly equal numbers of households containing one wage earner and those containing two or more received some form of state transfer income – about 10 percent in each case. Overall, nearly 20 percent of all families surveyed depended upon public assistance, usually as a supplement, rather than as a replacement, for wages. This was the case for twice as many female-headed (26 percent) as male-headed households.

In addition to reliance on state transfer income, about 20 percent of the poor households reported other income, presumably from some type of market or entrepreneurial activities. While this is not surprising information about those households which lacked wage earners, or even about those which supplemented inadequate state transfer payments, it is noteworthy that nearly half of the households which pooled wages also pooled market income – and still remained poor. The survey clearly demonstrated the necessity for multiple income contributors pooling many types of income in a very poor area, even during a period of economic expansion in a core region of the world-economy.

Table 6 summarizes the results of the 1950 Bureau of Labor Statistics study regarding income-pooling patterns in New York City. As previously mentioned, the table reveals the increased possibility and actual incidence of true "family-wage" households. But, at the same time, the table masks the increased polarization between households. The members of poor households, dependent on

Table 6. *Family size and annual real household income, by occupation and race, New York City, 1950*

Occupation	Average family size	Number full-time wage earners	Total real household income	Percentage money income	Percentage subsistence income	Percentage Black[a]
Clerical and sales workers	2.7	1.0	$8.121	52	36	13
Skilled wage earners	3.3	1.1	$7,479	61	35	17
Semiskilled wage earners	3.0	0.7	$7,321	56	36	12
Unskilled wage earners	2.8	0.9	$7,077	51	43	21
Not gainfully employed	2.4	0.3	$6,699	39	53	11

Note: [a] Spanish-speaking families were classified as White in the data.
Source: USBLS (1950: I, 49).

combining income from transfer payments, market activities, wages, domestic labor, and other subsistence production, in order to make ends meet were one important element in the restoration of profitability and growth in New York.

The accelerated relocation of manufacturing jobs to the Sunbelt and overseas during this period disproportionately affected the New York City labor force. In 1960, the number of employed were 3.3 million; in 1970, 3.1 million; but by 1975, only 2.7 million. Unemployment in 1970 was 3.8 percent, but reached 11.2 percent by 1976 (USBC, 1970b, I: 283). By 1976, manufacturing employment accounted for only 16 percent of the city's wage earners or, in more graphic terms, half of what it had been in the immediate postwar boom. In the garment trade alone, the New York region lost 158,000 jobs between 1950 and 1970 (Sassen-Koob, 1983: 188).

Until 1970, it appeared as if employment growth in the finance, real estate, and government sectors would somewhat compensate for the loss of manufacturing jobs. But as Hughes and Sternlieb commented, "the conventional wisdom of the 1960s – of white-collar office jobs effectively supplanting their manufacturing counterparts – had been rendered obsolete" (Hughes and Sternlieb, 1978:

16). Between 1968 and 1977, the process of job loss accelerated, affecting new sectors; 334,000 goods-handling jobs and 99,000 retail and consumer service jobs were lost between 1968 and 1972. Between 1969 and 1977, Manhattan's central business district suffered a 15 percent decline in office employment and a 30 percent decline in factory employment, much of which was in white-collar administrative and managerial-level jobs (Sassen-Koob, 1983: 188).

In the midst of overall economic stagnation in this period, we nonetheless find sharp employment increases in particular sectors. The New York City Department of Labor, for example, continually reported on labor shortages in domestic service, the taxi industry, and the garment trade (Roniger, 1974: 59). In the 1970s, in scenes reminiscent of the turn of the century, Chinatown's garment industry expanded; excluding sweatshops and home work, the number of factories located there rose from approximately 180 in 1970 to 400 by 1979. Sassen-Koob notes "a growing awareness in the industry that wages in New York City are increasingly competitive with those in the garment industry in Southeast Asia" (Sassen-Koob, 1983: 194). Expansion of employment in jobs less easily recorded, such as in the garment sweatshops and industrial home work for the electronics industry, have also been noted by investigators (Sassen-Koob, 1985: 239). More recently, between 1977 and 1980, there have been employment increases in some of the higher salaried service sector positions; up by 7.7 percent in finance, insurance, and real estate; by 9.4 percent in communications and media; and by 24.7 percent in business services (Sassen-Koob, 1983: 193).

The trends of simultaneous employment growth and decline during this period are descriptive both of New York City's changing position in the global division of labor and of a recomposition in the structure of the city's labor force. More precisely, global migration flows and increased female labor force participation complemented, if not facilitated, the presence of economic expansion in the midst of stagnation.

During the years under examination the city experienced migration of largely unskilled workers from the Caribbean Basin and Southeast Asia. One-quarter of all new arrivals to the US between 1966 and 1979 located in New York City. By 1970, the percentage of foreign-born or mixed-parentage reached 42 percent of the city's total population, a figure comparable to that of 1890. Similar also to the immigration flood of the turn of the century was the fact that most new arrivals were from low-wage areas of origin.

At the same time, women increased their labor force participation. By 1970–71, 42 percent of all women in the New York SMSA (age 16 and older) were counted in the labor force. Among Black women the figure rose to 47 percent, and among Puerto Rican women it fell to 28 percent (USBC, 1970b, 1: 283, 407, 441). Particularly noteworthy was the fact that nearly 37 percent of married women, with husbands present, were in the labor force; among them 19 percent had children under age 6 (USBC, 1970b, 1: 283).

Overall teenage labor force participation was low in 1970. Only 7 percent of males and 5 percent of females (age 14–15) were reported in the New York SMSA labor market (USBC, 1970b, 1: 361). But the picture is substantially changed when slightly older teenagers from specifically low-income households in predominantly Black neighborhoods were examined. In 1971, Wallace found, for ages 16– 19, that 49 percent of Black males and 42 percent of Black females were in the labor force. In the same low-income areas, only 36 percent of White males and 39 percent of White females were reported to be at work. Although school attendance was usually cited as the reason for non-employment, it was nevertheless widely acknowledged that many young people in school also had part-time jobs, or were searching for them as a means of supplementing household income or personal spending money (Wallace, 1974: 29–32).

Part of the increased wage labor force participation is probably a response to the intense rise in prices of household necessities after 1969 when wages ceased to provide added purchasing power (Roniger, 1974: 41). Moreover, as in the earlier period, the average city wage in 1977 for manufacturing, at $9,242, was significantly less than the national average at $11,479. Garment workers, in particular, earned low wages at $6,250, although they continued to seem high when compared to the national average for the trade at $5,845 (USBC, 1977: 6–21, (33) 28–34). With the lower level minimum cost of living for a metropolitan family of four estimated at $7,061 in 1970, it is of course possible that a minority of families may have been able to survive on the wages of one breadwinner, although increasingly unlikely (Ruiz, 1971: 59). The median family income in

1970 was \$9,682, but only \$7,150 for Black families, and \$5,666 for Puerto Rican families (USBC, 1970b, 1: 387, 417, 451).

How did families and households make ends meet under these reduced economic circumstances? Three general patterns into which households recomposed during this period may be deduced (The Conference Board, 1975: 7; USBC, 1970b, 1: (34) 111, 391). One type was a smaller coresidential household. In 1970 household size averaged 2.93 persons (2.88 for Whites, 3.18 for Blacks). By 1973, it had been reduced to 2.6 persons. Moreover, by 1973, households composed of one individual constituted 28 percent of all households in the city. Increasingly commodified consumption in the context of inflationary pressures may have had the effect here of adjusting daily and generational reproduction needs to available income. These may have been among the 47 percent of households surveyed in 1973 which contained only one wage earner.

A second type of household was based on multiple income earners. By 1973, about 30 percent of households contained two or more wage earners. This pattern was related to the expansion of unskilled service sector, informal sector, and manufacturing jobs, many of which had been generated by the growth of the high-salaried service and business sectors, and the life-styles of those employed in them. This type most clearly resembles New York City households of the 1890s garment workers, although by this later date the possibilities for producing subsistence income had declined significantly.

The third type of household contained no wage earners, and comprised nearly 24 percent of those surveyed in 1973. Presumably, these households comprised the nearly 10 percent of all families who received income from "self-employment," the 20 percent that received social security, and the 8 percent on public assistance (USBC, 1970b, 1: 389). They may also have received unreported wage income, from the expanding "downgraded" manufacturing sector, i.e., sweatshops, industrial home work, in addition to the informal service sector. Of necessity, these poor households probably had fluid income-pooling boundaries, in order to increase the opportunity to piece together many income sources. Consequently, they may have included large numbers of new immigrants, as well as single parents who relied on income contributions from outside the coresidential unit. A 1977 Community Service Society inquiry into the backgrounds of applicants for aid at an East Harlem Income

Maintenance Center revealed the variety of income types and pooling patterns of poor families. During the 1970s economic downturn, families resorted to welfare primarily to replace or augment another type of income that had recently become unavailable. Before applying for public assistance, nearly 40 percent of poor families had supported themselves with wages; another 40 percent had depended upon kin and friends. Only 13 percent had been previously supported by state transfer payments (NYC, CSS, 1977: 48–51).

In the midst of a cycle of economic contraction, New York City experienced a fair measure of expansion and increased profitability. The flight of high-wage industrial jobs combined with the arrival of unskilled workers, immigrants, and women on the labor market produced growth in the low-wage manufacturing and service sectors. Household structures were not neutral to these pressures. Their membership boundaries became more rigid for the high-salaried, and more malleable for the low-waged. The burden of work increased for all members of poor households, since the wages of a traditional male breadwinner were rarely sufficient.

Several long-term trends and cyclical fluctuations may be identified in the historical development of the New York City labor force and its income-pooling practices. First, over the entire period, 1875–1975, increasing numbers have been drawn into the ranks of wage labor in the city, and wage earnings have grown to dominate the household income package relative to other income sources. This may be seen as one consequence of the increased commodification of household consumption goods. A second trend may be observed in the relation between wage and non-wage work. Non-wage labor and non-wage income have gradually become a necessary supplement to wage work, rather than a replacement for/or alternative to it. In part, this is evidenced by the transformation of "housework" from the production of domestic goods to the servicing of purchased household commodities. Thirdly, the more households have become dependent on the money wages paid to members on an individual basis for work done in the marketplace, the more the income-pooling boundaries have contracted. Even the coresidential household ceased gradually to be a resource pooled or shared by more than a nuclear family in an increasing number of cases.

A final secular trend that should be noted involves the changing composition of the labor force. Over the hundred-year period the members added to the city's wage labor force have increasingly been female. As children and teenagers have gradually been eliminated from formal wage labor, women, at all stages of their personal and family life-cycle, have added wage employment to non-wage domestic labor. This may be read as one indication of a trend toward more time spent in income-producing work by all household members.

In addition to these long-term secular trends, there have been observable cyclical shifts in labor force composition and household income mix. Most important among these cyclical fluctuations between periods of economic expansion and contraction is what occurs within the broad category of "non-wage income." Non-wage income-producing work became more important to New York City households during periods of relative economic stagnation – 1890s, 1930s, 1970s – but the specific character of the work varied from one period to another. In the 1890s, at the height of the "immigration fever," provisioning boarders was a popular method of augmenting household income. Boarding and "doubling up" continued to be an important element of household survival for recent arrivals on the urban labor market and the poor during the 1930s. As opportunities to earn the increasingly important money income narrowed, however, individual household members often struck out on their own. They increasingly relied on their own subsistence income-producing work, as evidenced by the urban shanty towns constructed by "homeless" males, both adults and youth. State transfer income and charity also became more important during this depression era, as in the next.

The economic contraction of the 1970s was characterized by the growing importance of state transfer payments to New York City households, but also by the increase in "casual" and unregulated work. Some of the growth has been in low-wage commodity producing work in sweatshops. Much of it was service-producing work for market income on city streets. And all of it was reminiscent of the patterns of the 1890s depression. The similarity is not only in the nature of the work itself, but in the immigrant character of the labor force. There is, however, at least one important difference between income-producing patterns in the 1890s and the 1970s. A defining feature of the most recent economic downturn has been the household's greater dependence on the combined wage and non-wage contribution of adult women, and increasingly, of mothers with non-adult children.

CHAPTER 3

Binghamton: the secrets of a backwater

Randall H. McGuire and Cynthia Woodsong

The great economic engines that powered the growth of the United States as a core zone lay in the major metropolitan centers, such as Detroit and New York. But the process involved in this growth also worked themselves out in hundreds of smaller manufacturing cities around the nation. Broome County, New York, had established itself as such a secondary center by 1880.

Broome County is located in southern New York along its border with Pennsylvania and is the smallest urban county in the state. The major city in the county, Binghamton, grew as a manufacturing center in the late nineteenth century. Around the turn of the century two new towns, Johnson City and Endicott, were founded around shoe factories. These three communities have formed a single urban area, which in 1940 had a population of about 150,000, and in 1980 of approximately a quarter of a million people.

Through most of the period from 1890 to 1960, Broome County was a one-industry center. The organization and concentration of labor first in the cigar industry and then in shoe manufacturing dominated capital–labor relations in the area. It is therefore useful to divide the labor force history of the area into three periods: (1) cigars, 1880–1910, (2) shoe manufacturing, 1910–60, and (3) diversified manufacturing, 1960–80. In all periods, the overall average wage for Broome County was less than the overall average wage for the US as a whole. Throughout the period from 1890 to 1980, Broome County remained a small- to medium-sized manufacturing center. At all times, average wage rates in Broome County lagged behind those in other upstate New York industrial areas, as did the cost of living. Female employment has remained consistently higher than the national average.

In 1890, cigar manufacturing was the dominant industry in Binghamton, employing slightly over 26 percent of the labor force.

Table 7. Composite US census data

	1890 City of Binghamton[a]	1910 City of Binghamton[b]	1935 Broome County[c]	1955 Binghamton SMSA[d]	1977 Binghamton SMSA[e]
Population	35,005	48,443	145,159 (BMD)	212,661	301,336
Broome County population	62,973	78,809	165,749	212,661	213,648
Number in labor force	12,865	n/a	71,704	87,141	139,651
Number of women in labor force	4,049	n/a	21,943	30,348	59,354
Percentage of women in labor force	30%	n/a	45% (BMD)	38%	50%
Percentage of labor force who are women	32%	n/a	31%	35%	43%
Youth in labor force	n/a	n/a		20% of age 14–17	40% of age 16–19
Married women in labor	n/a	n/a	n/a	17,143	34,158
Median schooling	n/a	n/a	8.5	10.9	12.5
Manufacturing wage Adjusted to 1967	$427	$452	$1,100 (1939)	$4,000 (1958)	$10,596 (1977)
Consumer Price Index	$1,581.48	$1,674.07	$2,644.23	$4,578.94	$5,838.02
Median family income	n/a	n/a	n/a	$6,251	$19,707
Percentage below poverty level	n/a	n/a	46.5% (BMD)	12%	6.7%
Percentage dwelling units owner occupied	n/a	n/a		65%	68%
Persons per household	6.26	5.71	3.81 (per occupied unit BMD)	3.26	2.74

Notes:

n/a = not available

[a] City of Binghamton (USBC, 1890b, 1890d).
[b] City of Binghamton (USBC, 1910b, 1910d).
[c] Broome County, unless marked BMD (Binghamton Metropolitan District) (USBC, 1940b).
[d] Binghamton Standard Metropolitan Statistical Area (SMSA) which included all of Broome County (USBC, 1960a).
[e] Binghamton Standard Metropolitan Statistical Area (SMSA) which included all of Broome County (USBC, 1980a).

Sources: USBC (1890b, 1890c, 1890d, 1910a, 1910b, 1910d, 1940a, 1940b, 1940e, 1958, 1960a, 1977, 1980a).

The remainder of the labor force was employed in a scattering of industries, none of which employed over 10 percent of the labor force. The major definable ethnic group in the region in 1890 were the Irish, some of whom had been in the community for as much as forty years. Eastern Europeans and Italians together accounted for less than 200 people. The few such individuals in the community were predominantly male and involved in the lowest-paying work. For example, the vast majority of workers in the paving industry were Italians, and they earned an average annual wage of $157.90. Labor recruitment in this period appears to have been from the children of the working class and from rural areas, with some foreign migrants. During one major 1890 strike, when the cigar factory owners brought in strikebreakers from the adjacent areas, they recruited not foreign immigrants, but persons from rural areas of Pennsylvania.

Overall, the population was not particularly young, with a median age of 27 compared to the national median of 22. The population distribution does, however, exhibit a disproportionate number of individuals aged 20–29, 22 percent as compared to a national figure of 18 percent. Fifty-four percent of the individuals in this range were females. The average annual manufacturing wage in Binghamton at this time was $426.76. Wages were depressed in 1890 following major reductions by most employers in 1888. Worker unrest was at its highest in the history of the area in this year, with major strikes in the glass bottle plants and in the cigar factories. The cigar strike involved over 2,000 workers and closed all of the plants in the community. In their official declaration of the strike, the cigar workers said that "wages have been gradually decreasing – until the cigarmakers have been forced to send their wives and children into the shops" (McGuire and Osterud, 1980: 34).

The majority of working-class households were unable to subsist on the wage of a single male wage earner. With the exception of a minority of skilled workmen, all working-class households appear to have had multiple individuals in the labor force.

Women made up 32 percent of the labor force. In 1890, they accounted for 40 percent of the workers in the cigar factories, from 50 to 80 percent of the employees in the clothing and whip factories. It appears that most of these working women were unmarried, as the working class exhibited considerable opposition to married women working. Many of the women came from the rural areas around Binghamton.

Interestingly, women could do the same work as men and received the same wage in some components of the cigar production; this was touted in the local newspaper as one of the industry's good points. Overall, however, women in all industries, including cigars, consistently earned less than men, on average 60 percent of men's wages.

Employment of children was widespread but very poorly reported. The 1890 census reported boys under the age of 17 and girls under the age of 16 as children. These children earned on average 40 percent of men's wages in the cigar and wagon industries, the only two industries for which children's wages are available. Children as young as 10 years old were employed in the cigar plants to strip the vein of the tobacco leaves from the leaf. Other sources report that many worked as assistants in the glass works (McGuire and Osterud, 1980).

Binghamton industries, particularly the cigar factories, depended on a young, primarily female, and highly mobile labor force. Less than half of the people residing in Binghamton for the 1880 census were still there in 1890, despite an overall population increase in the area.

Given this situation, households appear to have adopted one of two strategies vis-à-vis waged labor. The working-class households in the city desired large families so that additional children could be sent into the factories. Rural households in the surrounding area received income from older children, primarily daughters, who had been sent into the city for work. The provisioning of daughters to the city left sons on the farms to perform the heavy tasks of farming identified as men's work. The working-class households in the city derived essential income from the boarding of these rural immigrants, which allowed married and widowed women to remain at home. These practices are reflected in the statistics for household and family size in Binghamton. The average family size (i.e., the number of related individuals) was 4.51, but the average number of people in a dwelling was 6.26. This suggests that the average family took in about two boarders. In one working-class ward, No. 12, these numbers are considerably higher, the average family size being 9.22 and the average number of persons in a dwelling 11.76.

A farmer's market (which continues to the present time in the same location) allowed residents to purchase locally grown foods. People maintained small gardens and raised small stock in town as well. Those persons who owned cows and goats would make cheese and butter, which they would sell to families in town. Wild berries were picked and preserved, and produce was sometimes purchased in bulk for home preserving. Maple syrup was also produced and sold by local residents. Women's diaries from the period 1890–1910 provide insights into the range of women's activities. This work included sewing, cleaning, laundry, and remaking clothes. Boys were hired to shovel snow and young girls were occasionally hired to do extra housework.

In 1910, the cigar industry was on the decline, and the Endicott-Johnson (E-J) shoe company on the rise. This shift in the source of employment and an accompanying shift in the source of labor had a profound effect on Binghamton working-class households. E-J differed from the cigar plants in the type of labor force it desired and in how that labor force was treated. E-J sought to obtain a stable, dependable labor force and attempted to forestall labor unrest and unionization through company welfare plans and a sense of worker loyalty, as opposed to the older strategy of depending on a high turnover rate of unskilled employees. E-J had existed in 1890, under a different name, but by 1910 George Johnson had taken control of the company and it was in the midst of a massive expansion which would culminate in the establishment of twenty-eight factories in the Binghamton area by the late 1920s.

The workers needed for this expansion were recruited from two primary sources, migrants from the depressed regions of rural Pennsylvania, and eastern European and Italian immigrants. In 1910, the population of the area was 28 percent higher than in 1890. The Irish population already in the community entered the shoe plants in small numbers, principally as supervisors and foremen, or in the contracting and retail trade sector. They also dominated government service jobs, especially the police and fire departments.

E-J promoted a company ideology based on an analogy to the family. All workers were considered members of "the E-J family." The company based their welfare programs on the care of the family and encouraged the employment of multiple individuals from the same family. Company officials, especially in this period of expansion, encouraged workers to bring relatives, whether from Europe or from Pennsylvania, to work at the factories. Up to one-third of the employees were women, many of them married. Women received wages one-half to two-thirds of those received by men.

In 1910, the average manufacturing wage in Binghamton was $452 a year. Interviews suggest that working-class families were not relying on only one wage. In 1910, we see the establishment of the pattern of non-wage activities described in detail below in our discussion of 1935. The major difference in the households of 1935 is in their composition.

Most of the immigrant workers coming to Binghamton were young adults who established families soon after their arrival in this country. As they began having children, they sent for relatives in their home country to come and help in the household. In this period, households were formed by the addition of relatives brought in from the place of origin to constitute households of a size large enough to put several persons into the labor force and to cover the essential non-waged activities. These individuals appear to have been incorporated either as boarders or as household members. Boarding was very characteristic of these households. As one individual put it, "they were all family 'cause they all knew each other from coming across." The care of boarders was a woman's responsibility. She might cook for up to twenty boarders daily and take in their laundry and mending (BCOHP, n.d.).

There were numerous farms in the area at this time. Twenty percent of Broome County households were rural, with most of the farms between 50 and 175 acres (USBC, 1910b). Farmers sold produce on the streets to the working-class households of the city. Several large farms which bordered the town kept stands open regularly. Baked goods, produce, and milk were brought in from surrounding farms to be peddled on the streets and in the public market downtown.

We suspect a shift in household organization from households supported through the employment of working-class teenagers (especially girls) and young adults to ones supported by the employment of married women. By 1900, two-thirds of the workers in the cigar plants were women. According to interview data, many of the immigrant wives who came to Binghamton in the first decade of this century worked in these plants because their husbands' jobs did not supply sufficient income to support the family. This precipitated a shift from the employment of daughters to the employment of wives.

E-J with its family-oriented employment policies encouraged and capitalized on this trend. Rural households which previously would have sent only their daughters to Binghamton moved the entire household to Binghamton, leaving only one or two individuals on the farm. The marginal added income that a wife could earn made such a move more profitable than sending a single individual. It is also likely that children and teenagers could find sources of informal employment in town. Diaries from this period, now housed in the Broome County Historical Society, mention house cleaning and yard work as sporadic sources of work.

Somewhere in the 1920s and continuing through the 1930s the pattern changed again, it seems, with increasing employment of teenaged children and women remaining at home. This seems to be explained by increased size of families. During the late 1930s the Endicott-Johnson shoe company dominated the Broome County economy and employed more than 65 percent of the labor force. Over 50 percent of the individuals in this labor force were immigrants or the children of immigrants. Our research initially distinguished between Slovak, Italian, and rural migrant housholds. It soon became clear that, although ethnicity played a major role in structuring interactions and the social lives of the Broome County working class, it had little impact on the composition of households, the division of labor in the households, and the nature of household consumption funds.

In Broome County of the late 1930s ethnicity primarily provided variations on a basic theme. Mutual support for Italian households came from the cortile, a system of fictive kin relations, while the Slovaks depended on institutions such as churches, clubs, and gymnasiums. Slovak women raised geese and used their feathers in the production of pillows and comforters. Italian women produced and sold homemade pasta, while Slovak women sold pastries. We do not, however, have evidence of significant structural differences in the households of these people.

The households of non-immigrant Whites who had migrated from rural Pennsylvania differed from immigrant households primarily in their retention of family farms in Pennsylvania. These farms were clearly not commercially viable entities in their own right. The shoe plants at E-J were essentially providing an alternative to the coal mines of Pennsylvania as a source of off-farm income. Some family members stayed on the farm, providing not only for their own

subsistence but also for provisioning of the Broome County household members with dairy and meat products as well as fruits and
vegetables. Regular car pools were established to facilitate the
movement between city and farm.

The family farm figured prominently in the lives of the children.
During the summer, children too young for full-time employment in
Broome County often stayed on the farm while their parents worked
in the factories. This provided the farm operation with much-needed
labor at peak times, provided gainful activity for out-of-school
children, and kept steady the flow of foodstuffs into the factory
households. As the family grew older, a teenage son might be sent to
work full-time on the farm. These households showed a far higher
portion of subsistence income than the immigrants and a higher level
of income from petty market production.

E-J workers earned an average wage of $936.00 a year in 1938,
which was only 85 percent of the average Broome County manufacturing wage of $1,099.26. E-J company benefits, however, probably
made up for much if not all of the 15 percent difference in pay so that
the living standards of most non-E-J employees did not differ
significantly from that of E-J workers, with the notable exception of
workers in skilled trades such as machinists who earned considerably
more than the county mean.

The adequacy of this wage can be assessed against several
standards. Stecker's 1935 study (1971) of the cost of living in
Binghamton, based on a four-person household, indicates that this
wage would exceed the "emergency level" of $878.10 a year but not
the "maintenance level" of $1,243 a year. E-J claimed that company
benefits increased their wage by 25 percent (Inglis, 1935), and if that
was true the average E-J worker was paid at the "maintenance"
level. Both of these standards fall considerably below what at the
time was considered a "satisfactory American standard of living" –
an income of $1,600 to $2,000 a year (Andrews, 1935: 119). We are
certain that these households were seeking to obtain this higher level.
Automobiles, radios, savings, home ownership, insurance, and the
other material indicators of an "American standard" were considered necessary, and most households had these things. It is worth
noting that households routinely sacrificed one of the characteristics
of an "American standard" – high school education for children – in
order to obtain these other characteristic factors. This will have

consequences for these households in our next time period, the late 1950s.

As was recognized by researchers at the time, these cost of living estimates were lower than the actual social costs of reproduction. These figures underestimate the size of the household and, as importantly, set a base line of consumption at a survival level, and not the socially sanctioned level which workers strove to achieve. Adjustments for E-J benefits are probably generous, as we feel certain that the company would have erred on the high side in estimating the value of their benefits. Wage labor in Broome County during the late 1930s did not provide the opportunity for a family wage for the majority of the working class, requiring that multiple individuals from the same household enter the factories and engage in a host of other non-wage activities. Households routinely incorporated non-nuclear family relatives to increase the size of the income-sharing pool.

In all cases adult males entered the labor force if possible, because their potential wages exceeded that of teenagers and women. A typical adult male's yearly salary was $1,200 and women's jobs paid one-half to two-thirds the rate of men's jobs (McGuire and Osterud, 1980: 69). Teenagers could enter the factory at age 14, and informants indicate that they routinely lied about their age in order to start work earlier. They usually did women's jobs and were paid at the same lower rate. Older teenagers, 16–20, kept from one-half to two-thirds of their wages while younger teenagers remitted the total wage to their parents (BCOHP, n.d.). Most E-J workers were paid piece rates and our wage calculations assume full production in the plants. During most of the 1930s this was not the case, and work slowdowns were the rule. Rather than dismissing workers, the company routinely cut back the number of shoes in production, reducing the possible piecework wage. The annual salary estimates we have used in our tables clearly overrepresent the contribution of waged labor to householding at this time.

Children between the ages of 8 and 14 engaged in a variety of money income activities, including being mother's helpers, market sales, and babysitting. One of our informants indicated that at age 10 she babysat after school for three hours a day, five days a week, and received $3 weekly. Children would normally remit all of their wages to their parents, or the wages might be paid directly to the parents.

It is difficult to put a monetary value on the host of activities that women routinely performed for their families and to which we commonly refer as housework. We base the price for housework on the lowest wages for full-time houseworkers in 1935, $863–$3,000 (Andrews, 1935: 74). Using the wages of a houseworker to estimate the value of housework clearly undervalues housework. A houseworker rarely performed the full range of activities that a housewife would. Furthermore, the wages paid to houseworkers never come close to a family wage in Binghamton during the time period under consideration. It is important to bear in mind that such domestic work is generally undervalued (NYSDL, 1971). Housework hours were derived from time budget studies and from consideration of other sources (Cowan, 1983: 159; Waite, 1928: 171).

Primary responsibility for housework would normally fall to the wife, a coresident female relative, or an older daughter. Children took on household duties as soon as they were mature enough to do them, and spent much of the time outside of school doing household chores. Men and teenage boys would rarely perform any of these duties. Virtually all of the E-J families had gardens either in their house lots or in fields provided by the company where they raised most of their yearly requirements for fruits and vegetables (Inglis, 1935: 194; BCOHP, n.d.). In addition to their gardens, they kept small stock in their yards, principally chickens, rabbits, and turkeys which provided a significant amount of the families' meat, and most or all of their eggs. Job assignment by gender and age-typing was least pronounced in gardening and small-stock raising, although women and girls tended to do housework in preference to tending gardens or small stock; conversely, men and boys would tend gardens and small stock in preference to doing housework. The exact distribution of these activities in a household depended on the size and composition of the household and changed as these characteristics of the household changed over time.

E-J built houses and sold them back to their workers on very favorable terms. Consequently home ownership among E-J workers in 1935 was approximately 75 percent, as compared to 45 percent among Broome County households in general. The males of the household performed the maintenance work on these dwellings. E-J houses varied in price from $3,000 to $4,000 in 1934, and the company deducted the mortgage payment (Inglis, 1935: 91). We valued home maintenance at 0.5 percent of the home's value (Waite,

1928: 166) and estimated a four-person household would be in a $3,000 home and an eight-person household in a $4,000 home.

For the most part, working-class families engaged in petty market production on a seasonal and/or sporadic basis. Most women sewed and mended for their families, producing a variety of items including most women's and children's clothing (Andrews, 1935: 391; NICB, 1926: 83). We have estimated the value of home sewing conservatively to equal 25 percent of the clothing budget given for the maintenance level. The women's sewing contribution equals half of the clothing required by the family, but the cash outlay for cloth and notions reduced the contribution to 25 percent. This would have been a strictly female activity.

Women engaged in some types of petty commodity production (i.e., sewing, baking, or laundry) on a regular basis. These activities were roughly equal in return, and personal preference played the biggest part in choosing one. We present laundry as representative and base our estimates of hours on doubling the laundry of a four-person household at the lowest hourly wage paid for housework (Andrews, 1935: 75). We applied these estimates to each family type.

We know that the adult males in some families produced wine and hard cider for consumption and sale, a particularly remunerative activity during prohibition. We have not been able to determine the contribution of this activity to household income either as a contribution to the consumption fund or as petty commodity production. Households would produce a batch of cider or wine and sell to other households and then at a later time buy these beverages from other households.

Almost all households kept boarders, often with two to a room. Boarding was an economic necessity for the households with space as well as for single working people. Binghamton newspaper ads indicate that boarders paid about $6 a week in the late 1930s. Care of boarders included meals and heavy cleaning. We use the estimate by Andrews (1935: 443) that each additional individual in the household added 6.6 hours a week to the housework chores, and apply it to boarders. Some households would not take in boarders when the household was at its peak in terms of size and productive power, but would resume taking in boarders as the children moved out, vacating space and reducing income. The care of boarders would have fallen most heavily on the adult or teenage female most responsible for housework.

Table 8. *Reconstructed patterns of household income in dollars, E-J workers,*
1935–40

Sources of	4-person[a]	%	6-person[b]	%	8-person[c]	%
Wages		41		52		63
Father	1,200	41	1,200	30	1,200	31
Mother			720	18		
Child			150	4	150	4
Teenager					1,080	28
Other						
Subsistence		35.5		30.5		35.5
Housework	863	29	930	23	1,000	26
Gardening	58	2	87	2	116	3
Small stock	85	3	127	3	170	4
Home sewing	47	1	70	2	94	2
Home maintenance	15	0.5	15	0.5	20	0.5
Market production		3		2		2
Laundry[d]	72	3	72	2	72	2
Rent	600	20	600	15	None	
Transfers						
Gifts	?		?		?	
Cortile	?		?		?	
Total annual	2,940		3,971		3,902	

Notes:
[a] 4-person household consists of father, mother, 2 children aged 8, 5.
[b] 6-person household consists of father, mother, relative, 3 children aged 11, 8, 3.
[c] 8-person household consists of father, mother, relative, 5 children aged 17, 14, 11, 8, 3.
[d] Additional market production options include produce, small stock, baking, wine/cider making, sewing.

Tables 8 and 9 illustrate the relationship of wage and non-wage income in Broome County working-class households of the 1930s. They show the contribution of different income forms in terms of their market price and labor time, and these tables identify the division of labor within households of different sizes and compositions. The tables show that, except in the largest households, wage income accounted for less than half of the labor time required for the household, and in the largest households the predominance of wages results from their having three or more individuals in the factories.

The three household compositions which we consider cover the

Table 9. *Weekly household hours, E-J workers, 1935–38*

	4-person[a]	%	6-person[b]	%	8-person[c]	%
Waged work						
Father	48	36	48	22	48	18
Mother			48	22		
Teenager					96 (2 @ 48)	37
Child			15	7	15	6
Other						
Total waged hours	48	36	111	52	159	61
Subsistence work						
Housework	50	38	57	27	64	24
Gardening	2.3	2	4	2	6	2
Small stock	4.5	3	8	4	10	4
Home maintenance	6	5	7	3	8	3
Child care	6.2	5	11.3	5	11.3	4
Total subsistence hours[d]	69	52	87.3	41	99.3	38
Market production[e]	3	2	3	1	3	1
Rent[f]	13	10	13	6	—	—
Total hours, of which:	133	100	214.3	100	261.3	100
Father	61.8					
Mother	71.2					
Per productive member[g]			56.6		43.5	

Notes:
[a] 4-person household consists of father, mother, 2 children aged 8, 5.
[b] 6-person household consists of father, mother, relative (other), 3 children aged 11, 8, 3.
[c] 8-person household consists of father, mother, relative (other), 5 children aged 17, 14, 11, 8, 3.
[d] Hours are adapted from studies conducted by Bigelow in 1953 and the US Bureau of Human Nutrition from 1926 to 1931 (cited in Vanek, 1973: 124). Our child care calculations include age-specific adjustments for the household sizes being discussed.
[e] The example we have used for hours spent in market production is the taking in of laundry.
[f] The example we have used for rent is spent on the care of two boarders.
[g] Productive members are: mother, father, other, teenager, working child.

majority of working-class households. Even though we know the four-person household of the cost of living studies would have been rare in the Broome County working class, we present this as the first of our three household composition types. The reason such a household would have been rare is revealed by the number of hours of work (133 a week) it would have taken to support this household (Table 9).

Based on census data and oral histories, we expect that the six-person household would have been the more usual working-class household. This household consisted normally of a husband, wife, three children (estimated as 11, 8, and 3), and an "other." The other would probably have been a relative, parent, grandparent, or sibling of the husband or wife. Usually, if this other was an aunt, mother, or grandmother of the husband or wife, the wife would enter the factory, leaving the children and house in her care. If the other was male or of the same generation as the husband or wife, the other would enter the factory, leaving the wife at home. In our analyses we have assumed the former situation. Advantages to this household type over the four-person household include a higher total household income ($3,971 a year) and less work for the members of the household (214.3 hours divided between three adults and an older child).

The eight-person household, although certainly not the norm, was common, and informants regarded a large household as optimal. Our model represents a large diversified household with a husband, wife, five children (estimated as 17, 14, 11, 8, and 3), and an other. These households would have been at their peak earning power in terms of wage income, and would have stayed at this level as long as two or more children who were old enough to work in the factory had not left the household. Some non-wage activities were dropped as the potential for wage income increased, so that the total income did not differ greatly from the six-person household. The real advantage in such a household lay in the number of hours of work involved for each member. We expect that the 261.3 hours required by this household would have been divided relatively evenly between the three adult members and the two teenagers.

Comparison of these three household types allow for a few generalizations concerning household income in Broome County during the 1930s. First, it is clear that the stereotypical four-person household would have been overworked, and that subsistence income would have been more important in this situation. In terms of monetary return per hour, non-wage work suffered in comparison to wage income, and increasing labor investment in non-wage work had diminishing returns. This reflected both the devaluing of non-wage activities and the small range of such activities possible with 50 × 150 foot house lots and limited access to petty market production. All households had a base of subsistence activities, most notably, housework, gardening, and small-stock raising, in which they engaged. Increasing the number of adult or teenage household members did not result in a significant increase in the time invested in subsistence activities, but did lead to a proportional increase in wage income. Such individuals were obviously more valuable than boarders who, as non-household members, were not obligated to pool incomes, and would therefore return much less to the group.

In our estimation, wage income rarely accounted for more than 60 percent of total income, and in many cases accounted for no more than 50 percent. These calculations definitely overestimate the contribution of wage incomes, since they assume full employment, although we know this was not the case. We were also unable to assign values to many non-wage activities, including a myriad of activities not necessarily available to a large number of households and having very small returns. For example, we know that eastern European women in one neighborhood would pick up pieces of coal dropped from the trains, as they walked home from work. Thus it is most likely that wage income accounted for less than half of the household income in Broome County working-class households.

The mix of income types in these households was not the result of random processes. Individuals might choose to take in laundry as opposed to baking bread, but the necessity for some such activity was determined by the other sources of income and the household size and age levels. Wage income remained the crucial nexus for the mix of incomes and was the largest single source of income. Reproduction required multiple wage earners in each household and residence in the city, and necessitated the inclusion of non-nuclear family members in younger households and the earliest possible employment of children in older households. Of course, someone (a female) had to stay at home to care for younger children and maintain a base of subsistence activities, including housework, gardening, and small-stock raising.

By 1958, the Broome County economy had undergone a number of changes. E-J remained the predominant employer, but its 45 percent share of the labor force represented both a relative and absoloute decline in the number of workers it employed. The company dismantled almost all of its welfare programs in the 1940s, and the declining prospects of the company were clear in the community. As E-J declined, the labor force in Broome County became more diversified, with growing participation in the manufacture of instruments and electrical equipment, and in the service sectors. Many former E-J employees faced the search for new jobs, and their children could no longer plan on moving into jobs with the company.

With the decline of E-J, the children of the 1930s found themselves in a dilemma. Most had not completed high school and therefore found it difficult to gain employment in the expanding and more highly paid firms, such as IBM. If they were lucky enough to obtain jobs, they found their advancement in the company blocked, a pattern described throughout the US at this time. This experience led them to emphasize education for their children. In 1950, 92.2 percent of those aged 14–15 in Broome County were in school and 84 percent of those aged 16–17. Between 1950 and 1960, the median school years completed increased from 9.8 to 10.9 years. Advanced schooling eliminated full-time wage contributions to the household by teenagers.

We see at this time a major shift in the ideology regarding children. Whereas in the 1930s the child was expected to serve his or her parents and substantially contribute to the well-being of the household, by the 1950s this relation was reversed, with the household serving the child and preparing the child for adulthood (Graebner, 1986; Ogburn and Nimkoff, 1955; Sears *et al.*, 1957). Expenditures on children began to exceed the amount they contributed to the household, and the majority of this burden fell on their mothers.

Adolescence had been "created" at the turn of the century as a way of prolonging childhood and postponing adulthood among the middle and upper classes (Graebner, 1986). At this time, an emergent child-centered ideology reinforced the importance of a nurturing home environment. This child-centered ideology with its concept of adolescence became a reality for the working class of Broome County only in the 1950s. The increasing significance placed on adolescence caused a decrease in children's contributions to the household's waged and non-waged income. Their labor contributions were limited, as advanced schooling entailed that more time be spent not only in school but also in other activities such as sports and school clubs (Bigelow, 1953: 16). Children continued to "help" with housework primarily by taking responsibility for cleaning up after themselves and doing dishes, but our interviews confirm other studies which indicate that they rarely participated in major housework activities such as heavy cleaning and laundry (Ogburn and Nimkoff, 1955).

Information on teenager employment is extremely difficult to obtain for all our time periods in Broome County, as elsewhere (Oppenheimer, 1982: 448). The percentage of teenagers (14–20 years) reported in the census as formally employed was 20 percent in 1960. The majority of teenager jobs in this time were part-time, often paid under the counter and poorly paid at that (NYSDL, 1967b). Teenagers assisted in mom-and-pop groceries, delivered papers, worked in gas stations, and in a variety of other unskilled part-time or irregular jobs. The majority of teenagers did not work or worked sporadically, and those who did retained control over their own income. The household benefited from such work only to the extent that teenagers assumed responsibility for buying their own clothes and other items, such as radios, records, and entertainment.

Broome County remained an area of high female labor force participation, with women comprising 35 percent of the labor force in 1960 as compared to the national average of 32.2 percent. This, however, represented a substantial drop from 45 percent of the labor force in the 1930s. The majority of working women continued to work in factories. We also observe an increase in the number of women engaging in part-time labor during this time period.

The national ideology of a family wage and the movement toward consumerism placed conflicitng demands on women. Women were expected to and did devote themselves to their children and to the maintenance of their home. They also had to respond to the perceived increased economic needs of the family. Yet women's employment was often cited as a factor contributing to juvenile delinquency (Keller, 1968; NYSCYD, 1956). Working mothers were under the extra pressure of being held accountable for their children's problems. Many attempted to meet these conflicting demands by working part-time jobs (NYSDL, 1967a).

There is some evidence to suggest a decline in household size and in the frequency of households containing non-nuclear family members. Overall, the percentage of persons living in households who were not members of the elemental family was 22 percent in 1950, and by 1960 was reduced to 13 percent. The inclusion of other family members to assist with the child care of working mothers or take the place of mothers in the labor force appears to continue, but at a lower rate.

The 1960 housing census indicates that most of the population resided in their own homes, only half of which were mortgaged. Nineteen percent of the homes in Broome County were two-family houses, down from 29 percent in 1940. It is not possible to state how many of these two-family homes were owner-occupied, but interviews with realtors active in the 1950s indicate that this was a frequent occurrence. The interviews with realtors and other individuals further indicate that it was common to rent the other half to kin. This would have made further income-pooling possible.

A number of non-wage income activities had either declined or virtually disappeared by 1955. In the 1950 census only 6 percent of the population in households in the Broome County area were "lodgers." The practice of keeping boarders appears to have declined, and with it both the income and additional housework generated by the practice. By this time, the practice of keeping small stock was also in decline. People were in addition no longer turning their lots into miniature farms. Gardening continued as one of the few subsistence activities to involve both husbands, wives, and children. Gardens were planted primarily to furnish fresh vegetables for summer eating and to provide quantities for the canning of family favorites such as pickles, jellies, and tomatoes. Buying in bulk from fruit and vegetable stands in the country became common, with the produce often kept in home freezers. The purchase and storing of food in this manner required ownership of both a car and a freezer.

Home economists encouraged such home production, but a "consumerist" attitude worked against it. Ads in the local papers reflect this consumerism, such as those advertising store-bought cupcakes which "taste so good that mother stopped baking." The practice of home baking declined during the 1950s. The baking of bread was virtually totally discontinued and the baking of specialty items, cookies, and cakes was less frequent than in the 1930s.

All indications are that the amount of time spent on housework did not significantly decline despite the acquisition of household appliances. Much of the savings in household time created by household appliances was accompanied by an increase in personal attention given to children, as well as in the standards of housework (Bigelow, 1953: 15; Ogburn and Nimkoff, 1955: 150). Studies show that, when the amount of time spent in housework decreased, this was generally due not to "labor-saving devices" but to a lowering of standards (Cowan, 1983: Oppenheimer, 1982; Berk and Berk, 1979). The practice of lowering standards did not occur very often until our later time period. In addition, the acquisition of appliances contributed to perceived increased cash needs of the household, which were strongly associated with women's willingness to enter the labor force (Vanek, 1973).

Non-wage activities declined in importance in the 1950s. The largest non-wage contributor, housework, remained unchanged but other non-wage activities, most notably the keeping of boarders and small stock, declined greatly (Table 10). The household appears to have become more dependent on the wages of a male "breadwinner" in the 1950s, but the family wage would have been a reality for a minority of working-class households, since 38 percent of the women were in the labor force, and at least 12 percent of working-class women were involved in part-time or irregular employment.

Table 10 summarizes the labor investments involved with households of different sizes and with different levels of female participation in the labor force. Because of the declining participation of children, particularly teenagers, the number of hours of work required of the parents did not change dramatically with larger household size, and in some situations rose instead of falling as it did in the 1930s. Also unlike the 1930s, the husband's labor contributions to the household consumption fund remained essentially the same regardless of the size of the family or the wife's labor force participation.

Comparison of Table 10 with Table 9 also makes it clear why the smaller four-person household with an unemployed wife was the ideal of the 1950s. The wife's labor in such a household in the 1950s was considerably less than for the same-size household in the 1930s, and compares favorably with the hours required of wives in larger households of the 1930s. This happens because the wife in the 1950s did not tend large gardens, small stock, and boarders, and did not take in either laundry or sewing. Furthermore, the discrepancy in the relative contribution between the wife and husband would have been less than two hours a day. We estimate the standard of living regarded as necessary in this period required an income of approximately $4,500 a year. With an average manufacturing wage of $4,000 a year, such an ideal situation was available through the

Table 10. *Household income in hours and dollars per week, 1955–60*

	Father: Metals and machinery Mother: Not employed				Father: E-J Mother: Services full-time				Father: Wholesale-retail trade Mother: Services part-time			
	4-person[a]	%	6-person[b]	%	4-person	%	6-person	%	4-person	%	6-person	%
Weekly hours												
Waged work												
Father	40	39	40	35	40	33	40	31	40	34	40	31
Mother	—		—		35	30	35	27	15	13	15	12
Total waged hours	40		40		75		75		55		55	
Subsistence work[c]												
Housework	48	47	46.5	41	35	29	39	30	48	41	46.5	36
Child care	8	.07	19.5	17	5	.04	8.5	.07	8	.07	19.6	15
Home maintenance	6	.05	7	.06	6	.04	7	.05	6	.05	7	.05
Total subsistence	62		73		46		54.5		62		73.1	
Total hours	102		113		121		129.5		117		128.1	
% Mother	55		58		62		64		61		64	
% Father[d]	45		41		38		36		39		37	
Hours: Mother	56.1		66.7		75.0		82.9		71.4		82.0	
Father	45.9		46.3		46.0		46.6		45.6		46.1	

WEEKLY INCOME

		%		%		%		%		%		%
Wages												
Father	263	49	263	50	240	42	240	45	157	34	157	35
Mother	—		—		102	18	102	19	—		—	
Teenager[c]									30	7	30	7
Subsistence[d]												
Father	42	8	37	7	46	8	26	5	42	9	37	8
Mother	211	40	205	39	159	28	139	26	241	53	235	52
Child and teenager	18	3	21	4	28	5	21	4	18	4	21	5
Total income	534		526		575		528		458		450	
% Mother	40		39		45		46		53		52	
% Father	57		57		50		50		43		43	

Notes:

[a] 4-person household consists of father, mother, 2 children aged 8, 5.

[b] 6-person household consists of father, mother, 4 children aged 14, 11, 8, 6.

[c] Teenagers worked but did not pool income.

[d] These wages and hours were taken from Gauger and Walker's 1981 study in Syracuse, NY. It appears that, although some of the work we have included as "home maintenance" in previous tables was omitted from their study, the total hours are close to those reported by Berk (1985).

wages of a single individual to a sizeable portion of the working class, but not to the majority.

Rising real wages made the majority of subsistence activities of the 1930s both uneconomical and unnecessary. The declining real price of goods made the returns from extensive gardening, small-stock raising, and boarders increasingly marginal, while increasing wages meant that the only way women could contribute significant cash income to the family was by obtaining waged work. In 1960, 33 percent of the married women in Broome County (USBC, 1960a) worked and would have found themselves in the situation of contributing 75 to 80 hours a week to the household consumption fund as opposed to their husbands' contributions of 45 to 50 hours a week.

In 1977, manufacturing continued to be the largest employment sector, with over half of the manufacturing jobs in "high tech" electrical instruments and machinery. These industries paid wages higher than the national averages. The largest employers were IBM, Singer-Link, and General Electric. Few women were employed in the high-wage industries, but were rather to be found in service-sector jobs paying below minimum wage (Coleman *et al.*, 1984: 25). In 1977, women constituted 43 percent of Broome County's labor force, with 50 percent of adult women employed, and 50 percent of married women in the labor force (USBC, 1980a).

Not surprisingly, the low-wage jobs also had the highest rates of part-time employment. Two-thirds of these industries counted more than half of their employees as part-time, or less than thirty hours per week (NYSDL, 1977: 26). The low-wage part-time businesses which relied most heavily on women were clothing stores, department stores, variety stores, and confectioneries.

Since part-time employment was defined as thirty hours or less weekly, a person might labor six hours a day, five days per week, and still be considered only a part-time worker. For the majority of women who worked this type of "part-time" job as well as for those in "full-time" employment, the additional work performed at home combined to present many women of the 1970s with the equivalent of two full-time jobs, or the "double day" (Berk, 1985).

Another factor to be considered here is teenage employment; yet once again little information is available. Census and Labor Department data from the area do not detail the jobs performed by youths, although they report that 40 percent of those aged 16–19 were in the labor force, up from 20 percent (aged 14–17) in 1955. Interviews with city officials, as well as with individuals who were teenagers or parents of teenagers in 1977, indicate that it was common for teenagers to have part-time jobs at one time or another. The jobs most often cited confirm New York State Department of Labor (1973b) records for teenage employment, and include fast-food work, clerking, and delivery. The jobs most likely to be available to teenagers are listed in the low-wage sector. A survey of Broome County businesses from the 1955 and 1978 city directories indicates a dramatic increase in such business establishments in the late 1970s, from 296 in 1955 to 554 in 1978, with a county population increase of only 987 people. The expansion of these types of establishments in the 1970s allowed dramatic increases in teenage employment since teenagers were both the primary employees and the primary consumers of their goods.

This did not necessarily account for all of the teenage employment. Many students worked below minimum wage, performing various tasks, and obtaining work through personal friends and family networks; babysitting, yard work, and paper routes were sources of cash for the younger teenagers and pre-teenagers.

By 1977, the combined forces of economic necessity and ideological shifts had resulted in a new household form and function. Changes in household membership followed trends begun in the earlier periods. Household size dropped from 3.81 in 1940 to 3.26 in 1960, and was down to 2.74 by 1980. The census category, household, refers to all individuals living under a single roof, and does not correspond to the concept of a household as an income-sharing group used in our study. During these time periods in Binghamton, most households in our sense shared a common dwelling; hence the decline in the census category probably also reflects a decline in the size of the income-sharing group. Non-nuclear family members who had comprised 13 percent of the persons in households in 1960 now constituted less than one percent.

There were increasing pressures on women to provide for the emotional, economic, and transportation needs of the family. Almost half the women in the Broome County labor force were mothers of children under age 6, up from 19 percent in 1960. Interviews with Broome County women helped shed light on the everyday practices of juggling job, housework, and children. Women reported that their part-time jobs allowed them to come home around the time that

Table 11. Household income in hours and dollars per week, 1977–80

Weekly hours	Father: Electrical equipment Mother: Not employed				Father: Non-electrical machinery Mother: Services full-time				Father: Wholesale-retail trade Mother: Retail clothing part-time			
	4-person[a]		6-person[b]		4-person		6-person		4-person		6-person	
		%		%		%		%		%		%
Waged work												
Father	40	35	40	32	40	30	40	30	40	31	40	29
Mother	—		—		35	26	35	35	15	12	15	11
Teenager[c]												
Total waged hours	40		40		75		75		55		55	
Subsistence work[d]												
Father	10.5	.09	10.5	.08	12	.09	8.5	.09	10.5	.08	10.5	.08
Mother	56	49	56	45	41	30	34	30	56	44	56	40
Teenager	7	.06	7		—		7	.05	—		7	.05
Child	—		10.5	.08	7	.05	10.5	.08	7	.05	10.5	.08
Total subsistence	73.5		84		60		60		73.5		84	
Total hours	113.5		124		135		135		128.5		139	
% Mother	50		45		56		51		55		51	
% Father	44		41		36		36		39		36	
Hours: Mother	56.8		55.8		75.6		68.8		70.7		70.9	
Father	49.9		50.8		48.6		48.6		50.1		50.0	

WEEKLY INCOME

		%		%		%		%		%		%
Wages												
Father[e]	90	59	90	55	71	40	71	38	65	42	65	39
Mother[e]	—		—		58	33	58	31	25	16	25	15
Subsistence												
Housework	49	32	48	29	36	20	40	22	49	32	48	29
Child care	8	5	20	12	5	3	9	5	8	5	20	12
Home maintenance	6	4	7	4	6	3	7	4	6	4	7	4
Total income	153		165		176		185		153		165	
% Mother[d]	37		41		56		58		54		57	
% Father[d]	63		58		44		42		46		43	

Notes:

[a] 4-person household consists of father, mother, 2 children aged 8, 5.

[b] 6-person household consists of father, mother, 4 children aged 11, 8, 5, 3.

[c] These hours are taken from Robinson (1977).

[d] Mother performs housework and child care; father performs home maintenance.

[e] Wages are from NYSDL (1977).

their children returned from school, so that they could drive them to lessons, sports, etc., take time off when children were ill, and change jobs more easily according to household demands. Children in the 1970s had more activities available than in previous times, and at younger ages.

The number of hours spent in housework (approximately 8–10 hours a day per two-child household) did not change significantly from the previous periods (Table 11), although the distribution of labor expended in certain tasks shifted. For example, less labor time may have been invested in such activities as laundry and dish-washing, but more was likely to be invested in the care of family members (Gauger and Walker, 1981). Informants speaking of this period note a decline in their housework standards. "When the kids were little I had more time, but then when I was working . . . Who cares? There's more important things to do. But when I was a kid, oh, the house was ripped apart from ceiling to floor [when being cleaned]."

A woman's employment status had little effect on her husband's participation in household work. Husbands would sometimes as-sume child care responsibilities in the evening while wives finished the housework. In addition to housework, subsistence activities included gardening and hunting. Generally speaking, women con-tinued to practice home canning and preserving family favorites that were either raised at home or bought in bulk. Gardening was an activity which still involved both wives and husbands. Men con-tinued with, and even increased, wildgame hunting, mostly seeking white-tailed deer. This activity was viewed, however, not primarily as a contribution to the household food supply, but as a leisure activity (Severinghaus and Brown, 1982).

Home sewing also continued, but savings varied per item. County extension agents estimated a saving of 50 percent on "special items," such as a wool suit, prom dress, or curtains, but nominal savings on such items as underwear, sleepwear, and daily wear. Women interviewed either had sewn for their families or had felt that they ought to have done so. All had tried, but as one woman put it, "I bargain-hunted, because I didn't have the time to sew."

Home maintenance was likely to occupy some time in the majority of households, as home ownership in Broome County was high. Census data indicate that 68 percent of occupied dwelling units were owner-occupied. The percentage of two-family homes was now lower (20 percent or less), as more new homes were built to be single-family dwellings. Two-family homes were less likely to have been owner-occupied and, when the other half of the home was rented to family members (perhaps only 19 percent of the cases), the rent was often below the going rate.

Two market activities appeared to have increased in importance since the 1950s – garage sales and child care. Garage sales increased as a cheap source of goods as well as for the non-reported income it garnered (Herrmann and Soiffer, 1984). The decreasing size of the household and the increasing number of women in the labor force required new patterns of child care. The number of women in the labor force with children under 6 jumped from 19 percent in 1960 to 49 percent in 1980. In the 1930s, when women took waged jobs, another household member assumed responsibility for child care, but in the smaller households of the 1970s that extra person was no longer available. The demand for child care outside of the household was met in Broome County primarily by women who took children into their homes, rather than by day care facilities. In 1980, at least 9,096 children under the age of 12 required either day care or afterschool care, and only 616 were cared for in commercial day care facilities, the remainder being cared for in the homes of individuals (Winckler, 1985).

Real income in Broome County as measured by the US Consumer Price Index rose only 26 percent from 1958 to 1977, as compared to a rise of 75 percent between 1936 and 1955. More importantly, real income remained flat from 1974 to 1977, and fell by 7 percent between 1974 and 1980 (NYSDL, 1973a; NYSDL, 1977). Households also incurred greater expenses, especially for education, since by 1977 the median level of education in the area was 12.5 years. Whereas a high school diploma had been required for employment in the 1950s, in the 1970s employment increasingly required at least some college or other technical training. Children's activities and demands on household resources increased.

Households responded to these increased needs by sending more married women into the labor force and allowing greater employment of teenagers. The wages of the wife were pooled with the household fund and, unlike the 1950s, were regarded as necessary for the survival of the household rather than as a means of purchasing extras. The teenager's wages benefited the household only obliquely as teenagers bought some of their own clothing and consumer goods.

The period of teenager dependency on the household established in the 1950s was lengthened and became an even more expensive drain on household income and labor, the cost of which was primarily carried by their mothers.

The increased commodification of goods and the time required for women in waged labor worked against a return to the unwaged activities of the 1930s. The ever-increasing requirements of education for children and the social institution of adolescence prevented households from relying on the contributions of teenage workers by the household. If teenagers entered the workforce without completing at least 12th grade, they would not be able as adults to reproduce the standard of living of their childhood households.

Comparison of Table 10 with Table 11 shows that there were no dramatic changes in the distribution of labor responsibilities within households between the 1950s and the 1970s. The proportion of households with working wives, however, increased significantly. In 1955, the average manufacturing wage was 89 percent of the amount we calculated as necessary for the socially determined cost of reproduction for a family of four. In 1977, we calculated this cost to be approximately $13,700 a year. The average manufacturing wage of $10,596 in that year accounted for only 77 percent of this total. The percentage of married women working in 1980 was 50 percent, up from 33 percent in 1960. The percentage of working women with children under the age of 6 jumped from 19 to 46 percent in the same period.

Over the period from 1890 to 1980, we can identify several cyclical patterns as well as constants and secular trends in householding practices in Broome County. Changes in the mix of household incomes is characterized by a strong secular trend toward increasing dependence on the wage, but cyclical shifts exist within this general trajectory. Household size has consistently declined through the period of our study with concurrent changes in composition. The role of women and children in householding has changed greatly through time, while the role of men has changed little. The cyclical rhythms that we see in the data appear to relate to A/B-phase fluctuations.

Real wages in the Binghamton manufacturing sector rose slightly from 1890 to 1910, leveled and fell in the 1930s, began a precipitous rise through 1973, but then fell from 1973 to 1980. With this general increase in real wages, wage income became increasingly important in the income mix. Against this general increase in wage income, subsistence activities normally referred to as housework remained amazingly constant, while other subsistence activities such as gardening and small-stock raising generally declined, although with some fluctuations. These subsistence activities increased in importance in the 1930s, declined greatly in the 1950s, and increased but remained minor in the 1970s.

Petty market production and marketing activities tended to increase with B-phases and decrease with A-phases, but the nature of these activities changed, and the overall trend was for them to decline. In the 1930s these activities were quite important and consisted of things such as baking bread for sale, taking in laundry, making pasta, and the like. In the 1970s, these activities were less important than in the 1930s but more important than in the 1950s. The major income sources of this type which we see today were garage sales and day care for children in private homes (Herrmann and Soiffer, 1984). Only the latter generated sufficient income to become a substitute for waged labor. The demand for the service results from increasing female participation in waged labor and fewer family members in the households to care for children.

Household size stayed relatively constant in 1890 to 1910, but decreased from 1935 to 1980. The biggest drop in household size occurred between 1930 and 1955, and there was no evidence of an increase by 1980. The number of boarders taken in by households generally declined from 1890 to 1930, then fell dramatically in the 1950s, and did not appear to have increased significantly by 1980. The combination of these trends led to a consistent decline in the number of individuals per dwelling unit from 1890 to 1980.

The participation of women and children in the wage labor force fluctuated over time, but the relationship of these activities to householding was not the same in each fluctuation. Participation of women in wage labor clearly increased in A-phases and declined in B-phases. The participation of children under age 14 declined with the passage of child labor laws in the 1920s. The participation of children aged 14 to 19 followed the same ups-and-downs as women's employment. After 1950, the teenagers did not pool much of this income with the household, most of it going instead to increase their own levels of consumption. Men's participation in wage labor remained very constant, and the pressures of A/B fluctuations were met by women and children shifting into wage labor in B-phases, and out of it in A-phases. Finally, the withdrawal of teenagers from income-pooling after 1950 resulted in a pronounced increase in the exploitation of women within the household in the late 1970s.

CHAPTER 4

Puerto Rico: from colony to colony

Maria del Carmen Baerga

The island of Puerto Rico was a Spanish colony from the fifteenth century to the very end of the nineteenth century. In 1898, as a consequence of the Spanish-American War, Puerto Rico became a "territorial possession" – a colony – of the United States. For the purposes of this analysis, we are considering Puerto Rico as a local region within the United States, at least after 1898. In 1917, Puerto Ricans were granted US citizenship. In 1952, Puerto Rico officially became a "Free Associated State" (Estado Libre Asociado), a kind of commonwealth with some political autonomy in local affairs, but subject to US federal law without congressional representation.

Throughout the nineteenth century, the island's economy was oriented toward export agricultural production, alternatively sugar and coffee. The last quarter of the century saw some growth and technological innovation of the sugar haciendas, but overall production languished under Spain's mercantilist restrictions. Coffee exports fared somewhat better, and expanded in response to European demand. Coffee production was based upon a mix of medium-sized haciendas, some of which incorporated technical innovations in the processing stage, and small-scale producers, using family labor in cultivation and harvest. By the end of the century, however, many small-scale producers had succumbed to competition and indebtedness and were gradually integrated as semi-servile labor in the haciendas (Dietz, 1986: 64–69).

Throughout most of the nineteenth century, landowners voiced complaints about the lack of workers for commercial production. By the last quarter of the nineteenth century, the practices of granting parcels of land to the worker and his family, as well as advancing part of the wage in kind, were the principal means of securing a workforce for commercial production. This not only provided the further exploitation of the workforce through indebtedness, but actually lowered the cost of labor. Once a worker moved within the domain of the hacienda or was advanced part of his earnings in subsistence articles (from the company store), he became tied to that particular landowner, and could not work for anybody else (Dietz, 1986: 48, 50). This meant being available to work whenever his services were needed, no matter the time, the place, or the season. Moreover, the wife and children were expected to assist upon request, both in the fields and in the landowner's household.

The structure of the hacienda provided work for entire families, with members dividing their time between production directly for the landowner and subsistence activities on the allotted plots of land. Women performed primarily reproductive tasks, for example, cooking, cleaning, taking care of the children, sewing, raising animals, and subsistence agriculture, among other things. Children started to work at relatively early ages – the 1899 census reported occupations for people 10 years and older – and the type of tasks they performed were fundamentally decided by their gender. Household monetary earnings were supplemented by some limited subsistence activities. Besides planting plantains and vegetables (*viandas*) around the house, workers kept animals like chickens, goats, and pigs for their own consumption. In the countryside it was common to find homemade goat cheese for household consumption (US Department of Labor, 1901: 416).

In 1899, nearly two-thirds of the wage labor force consisted of agricultural workers, of which women were less than one percent (Rivera, 1980: 48). Only 9.9 percent of the female population was engaged in wage labor, in contrast to 59.9 percent of the male population of the same age group (Picó, 1980: 24). More than three-quarters of the female labor force was composed of domestic servants. They worked as cooks, laundresses, seamstresses, and maids. Nevertheless, the real participation of women in commercial agriculture, as well as of other members of the household, has been concealed by the fact that during the nineteenth century the head of the household, usually a male, was considered the chief earner. Consequently, the transactions recorded in the hacienda account books only show payments made to the head of the household (Picó, 1986a: 12).

In addition to the wage and subsistence incomes, sources indicate the increasing importance of informal activities by the end of the nineteenth century. These were mainly casual activities to generate cash. In fact, the only way in which working-class households could have somehow eased the ties of indebtedness and patronage that linked them to the hacienda work regime was through the intensification of income-generating activities by the various members of the household (Dietz, 1986: 51). Women, for example, raised vegetables, fruits, and poultry, and made sweets which were later peddled by the children. Another source of income was the selling of eggs. This was a source from which money for groceries was largely derived. Likewise, even the humblest dwellings usually contained small hand-powered sewing machines, which were kept in active use for economic reasons (US Department of Labor, 1901: 396).

The core of the workers' households was formed by the parents and children, but the presence of other kin was common. The average household size was of 5.2 members. There were 115 families per 100 dwellings, a figure that suggests that a high percentage of the families had their own residence. This is not hard to believe if one takes into account that most dwellings were simply huts (US War Department, 1900).

Thus, by the last quarter of the nineteenth century, households began to depend increasingly on wages (mostly in kind although some cash was circulated) from the hacienda. Within this context, casual market activities were a source of income independent from the hacienda and a way to get cash and ease indebtedness. Although they were viewed by households as an alternative to the harshness of the hacienda regime, they actually fostered the existence of low wages in the haciendas. Landowners paid only one wage but appropriated in effect the labor of virtually all the members of the household. Furthermore, by providing the worker's household with a plot of land they secured a much better control of the labor force. Nonetheless, for the workers, these non-wage activities represented a way to avoid total subjection to the work regime.

The process of divorcing the direct producers from the land, which had begun in the nineteenth century, reached its climax in the first decades of the twentieth century. The years that followed the North American occupation of the island (1898) were marked by the sudden eclipse of the haciendas through the construction of large US-owned sugar *centrales* (Herrero, 1974). This meant that the workers faced not only the loss of employment but also the disruption of their subsistence arrangements that had constituted part of their wage relationship with the hacienda. Seeking work, families migrated to the areas in which plantations and *centrales* had been established.

The sugar industry employed predominantly male workers. It did not offer fixed wage employment, frequently hiring workers by the task. This depended on the size of the plantation, its location, and the type of work required (Silvestrini, 1979: 65). The industry was seasonal, providing work for only five-and-a-half months of the year. During the dead season almost everybody was unemployed. This created a very serious situation for those for whom the industry represented the main source of employment.

Coffee, tobacco, and citrus were also produced on the island, though on a smaller scale than sugar. These were also seasonal crops, and wage levels were even lower than those in the sugar industry. The tobacco industry had a considerable impact on the labor force structure since it was the first to incorporate thousands of women into the wage labor force. Tobacco was cultivated and then manufactured into cigars on the island. Women participated in the manufacturing phase, mainly as tobacco strippers. The industry reached its highest export levels in 1922. However, by the 1930s the market for cigars had shrunk considerably. The main reason for this decline was the competition with US-made cigarettes.

The needlework industry was also among the newly established industries, and by the 1930s had become the leading source of female employment. It began to produce on a large scale in the context of the First World War. During and after the war, it became very difficult for US East Coast department stores to obtain sufficient quantities of needlework from their traditional sources. Puerto Rico was an attractive alternative since there were thousands of poor women in need of cash income. Although some work was done in factories, the bulk of the work (95 percent) was performed by home workers (US Department of Labor, 1940: 6). Contracting involved a long chain of intermediaries (US investor to contractor to agent to sub-agent to worker). There were no written agreements for the stipulation of the commissions of these intermediaries, nor of the wage itself. Wages in the needlework industry were among the lowest on the island.

The world economic crisis of the 1930s ripened the set of contradictions underlying the Puerto Rican plantation economy. The local sugar industry grew in the shade of the North American market and its capacity for expansion was limited by this fact. Sugar prices in the international market had declined since the beginning of the 1920s, but the industry grew and maintained a high rate of profit until the 1930s. This expansion was attained largely through protectionist measures on the part of the US (Pantojas, 1985). However, in 1934, the US Congress passed the Jones–Costigan law, which imposed a reduction of 150,000 tons in the Puerto Rican quota for the US market. This reduction precipitated the collapse of the sugar sector, causing more unemployment and affecting small and medium sugar producers, usually Puerto Ricans, who depended on the large *centrales* for the grinding of their crops. The large *centrales* gave priority to their own cane and refused to grind other harvests. The Jones–Costigan law was a blow to the industry from which it never recuperated.

Wages became increasingly important for the workers' survival after 1898. The basic staples of the Puerto Rican diet – rice, beans, and codfish – were imported. Although nominal wages doubled, and in some cases tripled, during the years 1898–1920, such increases were canceled out by the tremendous increase in the prices of the basic necessities. According to Pérez (1984), real wages actually suffered a relative decline during this period. Not only did laborers suffer low wages and seasonal employment, they were simultaneously deprived of the access to the means of producing subsistence, the land (Hanson, 1955: 31). Under these conditions, the ways in which the working-class household eked out a livelihood changed significantly.

In 1910, approximately 82 percent of all the male population 10 years and over was employed (Diffie and Diffie, 1931). The economic situation compelled other members of the working-class household to look for wage work in the newly established industries. These were mostly daughters and female heads of households. Women's employment increased 61.2 percent during the years 1899–1910 (Rivera, 1979: 11). Most of these female workers were concentrated in the tobacco industry. In 1899, less than 2 percent of the tobacco workforce was constituted by women. This figure increased to 27.8 percent by 1910 and to 52.9 percent by 1920 (Quintero, 1982: 76). According to one study (Picó, 1986b), female tobacco workers tended to be younger, single, and had less children than other working women (laundresses, cooks, and ironers). Nearly 22 percent of the tobacco workers were heads of households, while 58.4 percent of them belonged to households headed by women. Close to 39 percent were daughters of the head of the household.

Most married women, however, stayed at their homes performing domestic tasks, taking care of the domestic animals, and the house garden. Seven out of every ten rural workers, aside from the ones who lived in the sugar *centrales* where there was no land available at all, had house gardens. However, these consisted of only two or three plantain or banana plants, some vegetables, and various medicinal herbs. Gardens were poorly cultivated and were estimated to have produced only one-third of their potential. Households did not have the means to buy seeds and tools. Also, most workers were reluctant to invest their time or labor in improvements to the land because they did not own it and could have been removed from it at any time (Puerto Rico, Departmento del Trabajo, 1914: 91). Commonly, working-class households kept chickens, goats, and pigs for their own consumption (USBC, 1910b: 56).

The general standard of living for working-class households worsened during the 1930s crisis. Most of the family income was spent on food, leaving almost nothing to cover other expenses like clothing and shelter. The average home of the Puerto Rican worker consisted of a small shack constructed from waste lumber and zinc or any other material that the members of the family managed to collect. The native-style hut, the *bohio*, fell into disuse during this period. They were easily destroyed by hurricanes, and the materials donated by the relief organizations for rebuilding were lumber and zinc sheeting (Puerto Rico, Departamento de Instrucción Pública, 1934: 31; Morales Otero and Pérez, 1941: 610). Although many workers owned the houses where they lived, they did not own the land where the houses stood. Others lived in houses provided by the sugar plantations for which they worked. This was the least desirable arrangement because losing one's job meant literally being cast out on the street. Lack of sanitary facilities and overcrowding character-ized these proletarian dwellings.

In a context of high rates of unemployment and underemploy-ment among men, of progressively diminished access to land, and of very low wages, the Puerto Rican worker had to make further adjustments to survive the problems posed by the economic crisis of the 1930s. As production declined in the sugar and tobacco industries during the 1930s, unemployment and underemployment multiplied among men. At the same time, the needlework industry showed its highest rates of exports during the same period (Zeluck, 1952). It was precisely during this decade that women's participation in the labor force showed one of the highest rates throughout the twentieth century (Baerga, 1984: 237). Men's participation (14 years and over) in the labor force decreased from 93.7 percent in 1910 to 79.4 percent in 1940, while women's participation (14 years and over) steadily increased from 15.1 percent in 1899 to 26.1 percent in 1930, decreasing slightly (to 25 percent) in 1940 (Vázquez Calzada, 1978: 96).

The great majority of the new arrivals to the workforce were married women. While the proportion of single women in the workforce actually decreased slightly between 1920 and 1935, the percentage of married women increased by 23.3 percent. In absolute numbers, the total of married women in the workforce doubled in this fifteen-year period (USBC, 1920b; USBC, 1930b; PRRA, 1938). This massive entrance of married women into the labor force in the 1920s and 1930s can be explained by the expansion of the needlework industry. Unlike the tobacco industry, the needlework industry utilized mainly home workers. This allowed many women to reconcile their domestic responsibilities with wage work, thus providing the household a much-needed cash income during the agricultural dead season. A study of the activities of mothers in rural Puerto Rico conducted in 1933 shows that their opportunities to earn money were very few and often restricted to the domestic sphere. The most common activities among the women surveyed were serving meals to boarders, sewing clothes, needlework, and laundry work (PR Departamento de Instrucción Pública, 1934: 50). These were all sporadic and poorly remunerated jobs.

Households in which the chief earner was employed in the sugar industry, in coffee cultivation, or the needlework industry generally had the largest number of wage earners per family (Perloff, 1950: 168). Men worked outside the household in agricultural tasks, while women remained responsible for the reproductive activities within the household. This type of arrangement was crucial for the functioning of the whole productive system. Women saw their jobs in the needlework industry as something that they could do in conjunction with their domestic tasks; something usually not possible in other types of employment. Their wages were considered to be something "extra" during severe economic hardship, as a complement to the supposedly principal earnings of the head of the household. In fact, however, they were much more than that. According to the Manning Report (Manning, 1934) on the needleworkers, 58 percent of the wage-earning households surveyed had received wages exclusively from home needlework during the week preceding the interview, a week during the agricultural "dead" season.

In addition, other supplementary informal activities were carried out by different members of the household to make ends meet. Men engaged in fishing, fishnet weaving, carpentry, construction work, and plumbing, among other things. Women were laundresses, seamstresses, peddlers, herb gatherers, cooks, or maids. Other subsidiary activities were gardening, raising animals, manufacturing and selling illegal rum, selling illegal lottery tickets, gambling, gathering medicinal plants and herbs, etc. (Mintz, 1974; Steward, 1956). Still, in spite of all this, the standard of living was quite low. The common diet consisted of coffee in the morning, codfish and vegetables (plantains or tubers) for lunch, and rice and beans for dinner. Milk was rarely consumed. Furthermore, a study shows that the diet of working-class families worsened toward the end of the 1930s (Morales Otero and Pérez, 1941).

The average family size in Puerto Rico according to the 1935 census was 5.4 members, with the small farmers' households being the largest (6.7) and the urban San Juan shanty town the smallest (4.5) (PRRA, 1938). Most of these households consisted of simple families (husband and wife, with or without children) usually with an additional relative or unrelated person. In each household there was about one person (0.9) in addition to the "nuclear" family. According to Vázquez Calzada (1978: 79), there were no significant changes in the family structure between 1899 and 1940.

Among the wage-earning households, the highest income is shown by urban working-class households, followed by households of the sugar-producing areas. Households in which the head worked for tobacco, coffee, and fruit farms showed the lowest incomes (Morales Otero and Pérez, 1937, 1941; Morales Otero, Pérez, et al., 1939; Pérez, 1939, 1942; Hanson and Pérez, 1947). Wage-earning households derived from 60 to 90 percent of their income from wages. Out of this total, the wages of the principal earner ranged from 45 to 70 percent of the total household income (see Table 12). In the case of the sugar area households, the contribution of the head remained more or less stable throughout the 1930s, although in terms of the percentage of the total income in wages this share actually increased toward the end of the decade. The reason for this increase lies in the considerable reduction in the wage contribution of the other members of the household between 1936 and 1940. In 1936, the wage contribution of the other members of the household accounted for about 18 percent of the total household income. However, this category plunged to 4 percent of the total family income in 1940 in the sugar area, the only area for which such data is available. It is no coincidence that during that same year the needlework industry began to decrease in importance due to the application of the minimum wage to home work (Hernández, 1983: 167). During the years 1936–40, both total household income and wages as a percentage of this total decreased among the sugar area households. In contrast, the category of "other earnings" increased by 164 percent (Morales Otero and Pérez, 1941: 607). It seems that the workers displaced from the needlework industry turned to informal market activities rather than subsistence activities.

Throughout the sugar crisis of the 1930s, the household wage component held steady due to the additional needlework earnings. By 1940, however, households were without additional wage opportunities and thus sought out other non-wage income activities. The progressive shift from subsistence, as a supplemental source of household income, toward informal activities or odd jobs, began as early as the last decades of the nineteenth century, but reached a peak during the crisis of the 1930s. The systematic decline in land available for subsistence production, together with the increasing monetarization of the economy, account for this fundamental change in household organization.

Unemployment among men grew steadily from the beginning of the twentieth century, reaching catastrophic proportions during the crisis of the 1930s, due basically to the collapse of the sugar economy. At the same time, there was considerable reduction in men's labor force participation during the same period. The fact that the overall rate of participation in the labor force remained stable between 1899 and 1940 (53.0 and 52.1 percent respectively) indicates that the decreased participation of male workers was matched by an increased participation of women in the labor force. Since women's hourly wages were generally lower than men's wages, this meant that either the female members of the household had to work more than their male counterparts to maintain stable household incomes,

Table 12. *Annual income of wage earners' families by source (in percentages)*

Area and year	Number of families	Total members of families	Wages of male householder	Wages of other members	Products sold or consumed	Other earnings
Tobacco, coffee, and fruit regions						
(total) (1937)	5,743	34,265	51.7	18.2	19.7	10.4
tobacco	2,567	15,690	45.2	16.5	27.6	10.6
coffee	2,488	14,200	58.6	20.0	12.1	9.2
fruit	688	4,375	53.4	18.6	15.2	12.8
– citrus	483	3,207	54.1	19.2	14.9	11.7
– coconut	205	1,168	51.6	17.1	15.9	15.3
Sugar cane						
(1936)	745	3,904	69.9	17.9	5.3	6.9
(1940)	1,027	5,462	69.8	4.2	7.8	18.2

Sources: Morales Otero and Pérez (1937, 1941); Morales Otero, Pérez, *et al.* (1939).

or the total household income decreased in the 1920s and 1930s. The falling standards of living suggest the latter. However, the wage contribution to the household, as a percentage of the whole, probably did not change from the 1900s to the 1930s, because of the incorporation of women into the labor force – single women at first, and later on married women. It was not until 1940, with the application of the minimum wage law to industrial home work, that the wage contribution to the household decreased.

Puerto Rican households did not accept passively the decline in their livelihood and conditions of work. During the first four decades of the twentieth century, the country faced many strikes, demonstrations, the burning of sugar cane fields, and other open signs of class struggle. A major economic transformation was indispensable. Some attempts to improve the precarious and potentially explosive situation of the island were made in the 1930s, through the extension of some New Deal programs to the island. However, the resources available were limited and their effects were hardly felt. Up to that moment, the island administration had been in the hands of US-appointed governors and locally elected legislatures, which served as biased arbitrators in the confrontations between labor and capital. The ascendancy to the political power of the Popular Democratic Party (PDP) in 1940 under the leadership of Luis Muñoz Marin, who had been educated in the continental US, marked a major political transition. The PDP's program was characterized by the massive intervention of the insular government in restructuring the economy of Puerto Rico.

Both Muñoz and the New Dealers in Washington agreed that industrialization was the only real hope for long-run economic development. As early as 1942, the government of Puerto Rico created the Development Company as well as the Government Development Bank. This was intended to attract capital investment in industry and business on the island. During the war years, the agency set up its own industries in order to make up for shortages and to promote economic ventures on the island (Wells, 1969: 145). This was a transitional phase that paved the path for the government's postwar developmentalist project promoted under the rubric of "Operation Bootstrap," a vigorous campaign on the part of the Development Company to attract private investment to the island. The government offered a series of tax exemptions as well as technical assistance, the training of personnel for the new factories, loans, and other financial subsidies (Morley, 1974: 224). Initially, light industry responded to the incentive program, producing mainly textiles and garments. By the 1960s, light industry began to decline as a consequence of the emergence of production sites like Korea, Taiwan, and other Southeast Asian countries (Rivera, 1986). Promotional efforts were then geared toward attracting heavy industry. Large mineral products firms like Union Carbide Co., Commonwealth Oil Refining Co., and Phillips Petroleum Co. were among the industries that took advantage of the Puerto Rican "bonanza." Later on, these were joined by pharmaceutical industries, motor vehicle plants, and electronics.

These were capital-intensive, export enterprises which, on the one hand, did not generate the necessary jobs to solve the unemployment problem of the country and, on the other hand, did not contribute to the overall economic development of the island since they exported most of their profits (Morley, 1974: 226). The result was a massive migration of working-class people to the United States. Without the emigration of thousands of Puerto Ricans to the East Coast of the US during the 1950s and the 1960s, the efforts of the reformist program of the PDP to raise the standards of living of the masses would have been minimal (History Task Force, 1979: 127–28).

Concurrently, the government implemented other measures to create the necessary infrastructure for industrial development as well as welfare reforms to calm down the restless population. For example, the privately owned water and electric power systems were consolidated under a unified public system that offered a better service at lower rates. A public transportation system with low rates was also created. The public school and higher education systems were expanded and improved. New programs of financial aid and scholarships were made available to poor students. In terms of health care, great efforts were made to eradicate the main causes of death during the 1930s. Also, child welfare programs, milk stations, prenatal clinics, dispensaries, and public health units were created or expanded, in both rural and urban areas.

An important factor that helped the Puerto Rican government move ahead with the developmentalist project was the vast economic aid that the island received from the United States in the form of grants, loans, credits, guarantees, services, and particularly, commercial and fiscal privileges. Federal funds sponsored directly and indirectly many of the island's social services and public works.

Also, they stimulated the development of the economy through expenditures for defense, among other things.

The implementation of the different programs and reforms described above served a double end. On the one hand, it raised the standard of living of the population and, as a matter of fact, answered many of the petitions that the working class had been making during the four previous decades. On the other hand, it created the necessary infrastructure for the development of large-scale industry on the island. This included not only the creation and expansion of material facilities, but also the creation of a labor force in accordance with the new needs of industrial capitalism. The economic expansion of the island during the 1940–72 period was quite impressive. While the economy grew at an annual rate of 10%, the standard of living more than tripled, and personal income increased from $213 in 1940 to $1,113, measured in 1954 constant dollars (Kreps, 1979: 687).

The US-subsidized Puerto Rican government touched the lives of most of the population in numerous and varied ways. For one thing, the occupational structure was transformed completely. Agricultural jobs, once the work of the majority, accounted for only 7.9 percent of the labor force in 1972. By that year, 19.3 percent of the labor force was in manufacturing, 18.3 percent in trade, 17.8 percent in government, and 17.1 percent in services (de Jesus Toro, 1982). The expansion of the governmental sector and the service sector, along with the creation of new avenues for social advancement such as the Veterans' Administrations facilities (for Puerto Ricans who had fought in the Second World War and the Korean War) as well as financial aid for training and higher education, created a whole new middle stratum that was clearly distinguishable from the working class. Poor people witnessed the progressive regulation of their lives by the government through the establishment of innumerable welfare programs like social security, subsidized housing, maternal and child welfare services, vocational rehabilitation of the handicapped, social and economic rehabilitation for those on relief, and institutional and other types of care for the aged, the blind, and the disabled.

Working-class households in the 1940–72 period were less beset by the problem of low wages than during the previous periods. Earnings in the newly created spheres of employment were three times higher than earnings in the rapidly disappearing agricultural and home needlework occupations. The problem that faced many households now was the lack of members with the proper skills to take advantage of the opportunities that the new economic order was offering. In sum, in the 1920s and 1930s there were more people employed but at lower wages, while in the 1950s and 1960s there were fewer people employed, but at higher wages.

Total employment decreased during the 1950s by 51,000 jobs. 47,000 of these were lost in agriculture, trade, and personal services. However, the unemployment rate showed a reduction, corresponding to a decrease in the rate of labor force participation, down from 55 percent in 1950 to 47 percent in 1958. The young and the aged, women with small children, and adults without education or training who could not secure a job among the new opportunities, dropped from the labor force. Many male adults migrated to the United States. Others either went back to school or took advantage of the welfare programs. Along with the unemployed, most dropouts were being supported mainly by the employed members of their households (Committee on Human Resources, 1959).

In 1953, 60 percent of all heads of houshold were wage-earning employees, 20 percent worked on their own account, and the remaining 20 percent were either out of the labor force or unemployed (Puerto Rico, Departamento del Trabajo, 1960: 20). According to a 1953 study (Committee on Human Resources, 1959), households with an income higher than $1,000 per year were considered to have escaped the rigors of extreme poverty. According to this standard poverty line, 43 percent of all households lived in extreme poverty in 1953.

The great majority of households below the poverty line were not suffering from the unemployment per se of its members. Their low income was related to the fact that their members were outside the labor force (female heads with small children, old or disabled people) or were still linked to low-paying jobs (e.g., in agriculture). These households tended to have fewer employable adult members than the ones above the poverty line.

More than 50 percent of the unemployed lived in households above the poverty level. The great majority of these households had one, and in many cases, more than one, wage earner upon which the unemployed could rely. Most of the people employed in the industrial sector belonged to households above the poverty line. On the average, these households tended to be composed of more adult members than the poor ones, and enjoyed a higher rate of schooling. Higher household incomes were achieved by preserving family links of adult members with at least some education. By the same token, a major cause of low income was lack of education. Most of the households in the lowest income level had only one full-time worker, who was unable to earn more than minimal wages (Committee on Human Resources, 1959).

For the households below the poverty line (see Table 13), income in kind in the form of lodging, food produced and consumed, medical services and clothing, among others, compensated for the low income in wages. Also, cash gifts from persons outside the home were important sources of income. These came almost always from relatives and attested to the importance of preserving family ties in the process of adapting to the industrial society. It seems that people who were enjoying the higher income power of the new job opportunities shared their good fortune with their less fortunate relatives. Households above the poverty line (where most unemployment was found in 1953) made up for the loss of income provoked by unemployment with income derived from family business and from military payments. Military pensions were relatively large and placed quite a few families into higher-income brackets. Benefits to the veterans allowed many to go back to school or to set up a small business (Quintero, 1978: 66).

The decade of the 1960s was one of further economic development. Most of the growth in employment between 1940 and 1970 actually took place in this decade. Also, this period showed the lowest rates of unemployment: 10.9 in 1964 and 10.0 in 1969 (Kreps, 1979: 590). As may be expected, the wage component of the household total income increased during this period (see Table 14). The prosperity of the "Puerto Rican model" was short-lived, however. Unemployment constituted a problem during the whole expansion period, but reached catastrophic proportions after 1970. This was due to the fact that, although the industrial program succeeded in creating 117,000 jobs during the 1941–77 period, this increase did not make up for the loss of jobs in the agricultural sector and for the natural growth of population. Between 1940 and 1976, population in Puerto Rico increased at an average annual rate of 1.5 percent while employment augmented at a rate of 0.8 percent (Kreps, 1979: 691–92). Furthermore, the petrochemical industry, for which massive investments in the necessary infrastructure had

Table 13. Sources of income for different-income households, Puerto Rico, 1953

Sources of income (percentage of households in each category)	Households earning 60% or less of the poverty level 19.0	Households earning 60 to 100% of the poverty level 24.0	Households earning 1–2 times the poverty level 37.0	Households earning 2 times or more the poverty level 20.0
Wages and salaries	39.9	56.6	57.4	53.2
Self-employment	4.4	2.9	3.2	3.7
Family business	6.8	7.5	14.6	12.5
Military services	1.8	2.3	6.8	5.2
Persons outside the family	10.4	10.8	7.4	3.6
Social security	—	—	—	—
Public assistance	9.0	2.0	—	—
Rents	—	—	—	1.3
Sale of food	—	—	—	—
Single payments	2.0	2.0	1.8	1.5
Income in kind	24.0	11.0	6.0	3.0
Other	—	2.5	—	14.5
Total	100.0	100.0	100.0	100.0

Note: — = less than 1%.
Source: Committee on Human Resources (1959).

Table 14. *Sources of income for households (in percentages), 1953, 1963, and 1977*

Sources of income[a]	All households			Wage earners' households		
	1953	1963	1977	1953	1963	1977
Wages and salaries	57.1	69.9	51.4	73.0	82.4	74.1
Professions and trades	4.8	4.1	6.1	3.5	2.3	6.6
Non-incorporated business	16.7	10.0	5.4	6.1	2.1	1.7
Military service	6.2	1.8	2.3	4.6	1.2	0.5
Social security	0.3	3.4	11.0	—	2.7	2.6
Food stamps	n/a	n/a	7.0	n/a	n/a	7.0
Other	14.9	10.8	16.8	12.8	9.3	7.5
Total	100.0	100.0	100.0	100.0	100.0	100.0

Note: [a] Income in kind not included.
Sources: Puerto Rico, Departamento del Trabajo (1959); Clapp & Mayne (1980).

been made, foundered in the energy crisis of the mid-1970s, which made Puerto Rican refined oil much too expensive to compete in the world market (Rivera, 1986). Return migration from the continental US, as a consequence of the general crisis, worsened the unemployment situation in Puerto Rico. Since the beginning of the industrialization program, the government tried to deal with the problem of unemployment in two concrete ways. In the first place, they launched a population control campaign which involved the large-scale sterilization of women in their reproductive years. Secondly, they encouraged the migration of the so-called surplus population. During the 1950–70 period, the massive migration of thousands of working-class families contributed to a decline in the unemployment rate. But this trend was reversed in the 1970s, posing a further burden to the already precarious job structure.

Another noticeable characteristic of the period of industrial development was the steady decline of the rate of labor force participation. From 1950 to 1976, labor force participation declined from 54.6 to 42.0 percent. This contraction may be attributed to men, whose participation rate plunged from 79.8 percent in 1950 to 59.4 percent in 1976 (Vázquez Calzada, 1978: 96; Kreps, 1970: 591). Women's participation rate remained more or less stable during the same period (30 percent in 1950 and 26.1 percent in 1976).

The trend toward an increased dependence on wages was brought to a sudden halt by the crisis of the 1970s. Unemployment nearly doubled between 1969 and 1976 (10 to 19.9 percent) (official figures as quoted in Kreps, 1979). In 1972, 45 percent of the unemployed belonged to households in which no other members were employed, 35 percent were in households with only one other member employed, and only 20 percent in households with two or more members employed (Puerto Rico, Oficina del Gobernador, 1974).

By the same year, only 26.3 percent of the households had two or more members employed, 48.4 percent had one member employed, and 25.3 percent of the households either had all of its members out of the labor force or unemployed. These figures attest to the precarious condition of most households in the 1970s. A 1977 study (Clapp & Mayne, 1980) reported that 44 percent of all households had no members working (an increase of nearly 75 percent in five years), 41 percent had one member working, and only 15 percent reported having two or more members employed.

Table 15. *Household sources of income (in percentages), 1977*

Sources of income (percentage of households in each category)	Low-income 32.6	Medium-income 35.9	High-income 31.5
Wages and salaries	13.4	45.9	59.6
Social security	34.7	17.1	4.8
Food stamps	27.6	11.9	1.7

Source: Clapp & Mayne (1980).

The extent of the crisis is attested by the increasing number of heads of households who were being affected by the lack of job opportunities. While in 1970 only 6.7 percent of the household heads were unemployed, by 1976 this figure more than doubled to 15.8 percent (Kreps, 1979: 595). In 1977, one study estimated that around 52 percent of all heads of households were either out of the labor force or unemployed (Clapp & Mayne, 1980: xiv). This meant that, of all heads of household, from 16 to 20 percent were unemployed, while 22 to 30 percent were outside the labor force.

Personal income showed a sharp decline in 1973 and 1974, although the Kreps report pointed out that there was no further deterioration up to 1977, the year in which the report was written. The gap between structural unemployment and diminished agricultural activity on the one hand, and the high cost of living and a more or less stable personal income on the other, was narrowed by a massive infusion of federal transfers into household budgets. In the 1970s, there were various income support programs in existence on the island. The four major ones were unemployment insurance, social security benefits, public assistance cash payments, and food stamps.

According to a study of family income and expenditures in 1977, social security and food stamps were the second and third most important sources of income for the household (Clapp & Mayne, 1980). For all families, wages and salaries constituted 51 percent, social security payments 11 percent, and food stamps 7 percent of total household income. If we examine these figures by income groups, the role of transfer payments seems even more important (see Table 15). For households located at the bottom of the income scale, social security was the principal income source, followed by food stamps, accounting for 62 percent of the total household income. For the households located at the middle of the income scale, social security and food stamps accounted for nearly 30 percent of total household income. Only for the households located at the top of the income scale did food stamps and social security represent a mere 6.5 percent of total household income. The declining importance of wages as a principal source of income for the household contrasts sharply with the data for 1953 and 1963, in which wages and salaries constituted the most important source of income for all income groups. It is evident that one of the principal strategies utilized by the Puerto Rican households to confront the chronic malady of unemployment in the country has been to make maximum use of the available public assistance. The great magnitude of federal transfer payments to poor families indicates the institutionalization of unemployment on the part of the federal and local governments.

Although personal income has shown a great increase in the last thirty years, poverty is still widespread in Puerto Rico. Various studies have demonstrated that the cost of living is higher in Puerto Rico than in the continental US (Kreps, 1979: 688). Most of the products found on the island are imported and that makes them more expensive than on the continent. Moreover, one must bear in mind that Puerto Rico imports not only commodities from the continental US, but also its standard of living. The high rate of mobility of the Puerto Rican population between the island and the continent, plus their exposure to mass communications (cable TV, commercials, magazines, movies), have effectively spread the idea of the American Dream within the Puerto Rican population. In 1975, 62 percent of all the island's residents, or 57 percent of all families, were poor according to the US official poverty measure (Kreps, 1979: 687). In this sense, transfer payments have not resolved the problem of poverty on the island, which were related fundamentally to structural unemployment.

In summary, the main feature of the island's labor structure throughout the twentieth century has been its inability to absorb the majority of the able working population. This fact, along with the proliferation of low-wage types of employment, has put an enormous pressure on the working-class household while risking the daily and generational reproduction of the working population. Responding to this situation, working-class households have resorted to different strategies at various points in time. These have included the multiple wage earners, subsistence and cash-generating activities, migration, and dependence on transfer payments, among others. The progressive intervention of the government in the lives of the Puerto Rican people after the 1930s, far from improving their quality of life, has disrupted the traditional networks of mutual aid among the members of the household and fostered dependence on federal funds from the United States. None of these strategies have resolved the problem of poverty on the island.

While previously people tended to depend upon the other members of the household for their subsistence, the US federal government has increasingly assumed that role. Families have become smaller in the last forty years, due to the marked reduction in members other than the couple and their children. In a context of high unemployment, high cost of living, and little agricultural activity, members beyond the family nucleus had become a real burden. The number of children born to the families has also been reduced. While the participation of men in the labor force has decreased sharply in the last forty years, women's participation increased slightly. Furthermore, the relative economic power that women have achieved after the Second World War, together with the increased importance of government transfers, have rendered them more "independent" from men. This fact is clearly demonstrated by the high divorce rate existing on the island and the growing presence of female-headed households – around 20 percent in 1980 (USBC, 1980b).

Food stamps and social security have become a way of life for many households in the last two decades. This has had very profound implications for the way of life of the Puerto Rican people. The government has assumed the role of the "provider," as many find welfare payments more reliable than the husband's paycheck. Unfortunately, federal funds are not a real alternative since they have never covered people's needs adequately. This is readily confirmed by the high rates of poverty among female-headed households. Furthermore, federal funds are constantly threatened by the conservative postures of the US government. In this sense, the 1970s crisis differed from the crisis of the 1930s in terms of the exhaustion of the traditional alternatives to which the members of the working-class households have resorted historically. It is in this context of poverty and of the dissolution of the traditional networks of mutual aid between individuals that current problems like the rise in criminality and of illegal economic activities that have character-ized the Puerto Rican society in the 1980s have to be studied.

III

Mexico

Introduction

Lanny Thompson

Throughout the nineteenth century, Mexico was a peripheral region of the world-system. The Mexican economy suffered from a dependence upon the production of silver for export, the scarcity of credit, the lack of technical innovation, and the absence of anything resembling an integrated national market. In the cities, the guild system deteriorated, but the factory system was still in its most incipient stage. Agriculture was dominated by large "feudal" estates juxtaposed to subsistence-oriented peasants, although in many areas small-scale independent producers rivaled the larger estates (Cardoso, 1983). It is not at all clear that Mexico shared the mid-century (1848–73) expansion of the world-economy and the first three-quarters of the nineteenth century are generally considered to be one long period of economic stagnation in Mexico (López Cámara, 1984; Padilla, 1968; Rodríguez, 1983).

The latter half of the "great depression" of 1873–96 in the core areas witnessed important institutional changes in Mexico, especially during the 1880s, followed by strong economic growth from roughly 1890 to 1910. The downswing of the 1880s in the United States, France, and Great Britain led to the investment of foreign capital in Mexico, especially in the railroads. In turn, the development of extensive railways, actively promoted by the government, served as a major economic catalyst and was associated with an eventual expansion of exports as well as the nascent integration of the domestic market. Foreign and national capital was also invested in mining, which expanded its export production, and in manufacturing, oriented to a growing, and increasingly integrated, domestic market. Even though the railroads did not constitute a "leading industrial sector" sufficient to fuel an industrial "take-off," other manufacturing sectors – iron, steel, sulfuric acid, and textiles – showed rapid growth rates from 1890 to 1910 (Rostow, 1979: 499).

In the countryside, that supposedly "archaic institution," the hacienda, responded to both internal and external markets by expanding production, as did the smaller estates and farms. The consensus seems to be that economic growth was slow, but significant, in the 1870s and 1880s, while rapid and sustained growth occurred in the 1890s, and continued almost ten years into the new century (Cardoso, 1983).

The exceptional economic growth of the 1890s slowed just a few years into the new century and ended abruptly with the outbreak of the Mexican Revolution in 1910. This was followed by a long period of overall stagnation, marked by short, sporadic recoveries in different sectors during the early 1920s, with stronger indications of recovery and growth evident in the following decade. During the 1930s, the Mexican state undertook a program of land reform and industrialization designed to develop the national market and strengthen its position within the world-economy. The nationalization of the petroleum industry in 1936 provided the state with hard currency to further its strategy of import substitution. The Mexican economy began its "take-off" stage in 1940, with fairly steady industrial growth up until around 1970 (Rostow, 1979: 491–99). It was during this period of sustained growth that Mexico attained its status as an industrialized semiperiphery (Gereffi and Evans, 1981).

During the 1970s, the Mexican state sought to diversify industrial export production, utilizing direct foreign investment and loan capital, as well as its petroleum revenues, to finance the development of internationally competitive industries. Nevertheless, the end result has been an economy plagued by severe trade imbalances, by growing indebtedness, difficulties in local capital formation and by rampant inflation accompanied by a series of currency devaluations. Government austerity measures and political repression contributed to the decline in the standard of living of the working classes. At the same time, the links with the domestic US economy have become even stronger, stimulated by wage differentials between the two countries. On the one hand US enterprises have established border industrialization projects, and on the other hand, Mexican laborers have migrated, both on a permanent and seasonal basis, to seek work in the US (Cockcroft, 1983; Gereffi and Evans, 1981).

Historically, there has been very little legislation that explicitly directed itself toward internal household matters. The state policy after the restoration of the republic in 1867 was a continuation of the liberal principles expressed in the constitution of 1857. The official position was that there was no legal or economic basis for legislation directly affecting the standard of living of the working classes. Instead, the government should "contribute to the improvement of the condition of the worker by indirect means," namely, "the preservation of peace, the promotion of industry and the investment of capital, national and foreign ... and the assurance of national credit" (Romero, 1975: 83–84). Indeed, the government was quite active in promoting economic growth, chiefly through the development of an extensive railway system and the support given to the national credit bank. The maintenance of political stability during the regime of Porfirio Diaz (1876–1910) provided a favorable context for the expansion of commerce and investment. As the state attempted to promote economic growth by putting market forces into play, households were left alone to bear the brunt of these changes. The "preservation of peace" under the Diaz regime included the repression of the workers' organizations and the frequent use of state violence to break up strikes.

As a result of the revolution, labor legislation was introduced to protect the rights and living standards of laborers. The newly adopted constitution of 1917 included ample rights and protection for labor, which were extended even further in subsequent legislation. Laws were passed governing working conditions, and the employment of women and children. Labor unions became official bodies, closely aligned with the government's party. The "family wage" was guaranteed by the constitution and, in 1934, the legal minimum wage was established. In practice, it has never constituted a wage sufficient to maintain a family.

In addition to labor legislation, the amount and proportion of the federal budget devoted to "social expenditures" has increased fairly steadily since the late 1920s, although it has remained low proportionally when compared to core countries. The bulk of these expenditures have been allocated for basic services, especially education. In addition, programs designed to help provide low-cost housing, introduced in the 1920s, have slowly evolved over the years. Social security programs were first established for government employees in 1925, and thereafter expanded to other occupational groups. In the mid-1960s an official agency was established to buy basic foodstuffs at high prices from the rural areas, and sell them at low prices in the city. In 1974, price controls were established for basic consumption items, in an effort to guard the purchasing power of the wage in the face of inflation (Hewitt, 1977). Despite the widespread need for social welfare and public health programs, for housing, and for water and sewage facilities, these have never occupied a significant share in national budgetary considerations (Wilkie, 1970: 156–76).

Regardless of the ample constitutional concessions to labor, in practice only a minority of workers, those in key industrial branches, actually reaped the benefits of such progressive legislation. In addition, government spending has helped increase the size of the middle class employed in official agencies, banks, or enterprises. Thus, social policy has had some impact among organized industrial laborers, government employees, and among the middle class, especially in Mexico City. But despite efforts to guarantee basic levels of consumption through the legal minimum wage, social expenditures, and later, price regulation, these measures alone have not been enough to raise a family above poverty, even according to the government's own standards. In the countryside, social and labor legislation remains practically a dead letter for the bulk of rural laborers. On balance, the government's social programs have had much less effect on households than the economic programs (Wilkie, 1970).

In the countryside, the support for the 1910 Revolution was based primarily on the land issue. A massive land reform did not come until the 1930s, but when it did it had a substantial effect upon the incomes of rural households. The government established an *ejido* system of localized administration of nationally owned land, through which households gained use rights to small parcels of land. Eventually the land reform affected one-quarter of the nation's entire surface area and provided more than one-half of the rural population with access to plots of land, which were used for subsistence and market-oriented cultivation (Whetten, 1948). The immediate result of the land distribution was to raise peasant incomes, and to hold back a tide of city-ward migration. However, after the 1950s the economic context had changed and these small parcels became overcrowded, impoverished backwaters sending forth a steady stream of migrants.

If the years from 1917 to 1940 were the era of social legislation, then the years between 1940 and 1958 were marked by a return to a strong emphasis on economic development undertaken by private enterprise with a strong measure of government participation. Subsidies for private investment were granted by the government in conjunction with infrastructure development. Public policy was crucial in creating the economic climate and support for private investment in manufacturing, while key sectors, electricity, petroleum, and the railroads, were nationalized and transportation and communications were developed. On balance, however, Mexico has managed to achieve its rapid industrialization with an absolute minimum of public expenditure (social, economic, and administrative), even when compared with other countries of Latin America (Reynolds, 1970: 269).

The 1950s and 1960s were marked by an emphasis on general economic development as the most efficient way to improve the standard of living, but not to the exclusion of social legislation. Since the 1970s, this social legislation has proved to be insufficient (or a dead letter) to deal with the overwhelming economic difficulties. Indeed, the demands of workers, students, and peasants were increasingly met with political repression and austerity measures (Cockcroft, 1983). Despite the increasing involvement of the state in social welfare issues, its positive effects on household incomes have been dubious. The "welfare possibilities" of the Mexican state "lie outside the policy boundaries" compatible with the promotion of national capital accumulation, the attraction of direct foreign investment, and the payment of the debt service (Gereffi and Evans, 1981: 57). Some have concluded that state involvement in social welfare allows greater political control over the populace, but has not actually improved the social conditions of the laborers to the same extent (Eckstein, 1977).

CHAPTER I

Mexico City: the slow rise of wage-centered households

Lanny Thompson

Throughout the latter part of the nineteenth century, the workforce in Mexico City can be conveniently divided into three basic groups. First, there were the common laborers. They were employed as unskilled labor in workshops, as day labor on construction sites, and as factory operatives and outworkers. Secondly, there were the skilled artisans working for wages, who maintained a status somewhat higher than common laborers. Thirdly, there were those who offered goods and services in the marketplaces, in the streets and plazas. These were petty merchants and sellers of homemade products, and those offering personal services. Included among this group were the independent artisans who operated family workshops, or had been reduced to hawking their products on the street. During the 1890s, the demand for common labor of both genders increased, due primarily to the expansion of large-scale textile and tobacco manufacture, and to the boom in construction. The demand for skilled male laborers increased slightly. In contrast, opportunities for petty market activities were reduced as commerce came to be taken over by larger establishments and merchants.[1]

Women made up better than one-third of the workforce in Mexico City from the middle of the eighteenth century to the beginning of the twentieth. Women were already quite active during the mid-nineteenth century in numerous occupations and trades, with domestic service representing only one-third of women's employment. With the decline of the guild system, women had expanded their activities in small-scale production, commerce, and services. An "industrial" census of Mexico City of 1879 shows that, of all the persons employed in factories and workshops, 28 percent were women, 13 percent children, and 59 percent men. Likewise, the census of 1895 shows that women made up 27 percent of those employed in "industry." What was exceptional about the 1890s was that women, as well as men, were drawn into wage employment by the development of larger productive and commercial establishments, which employed them in factories and workshops as well as outworkers in their own homes.[2]

The wages paid to common day labor did little more than provide for the daily costs of the worker, and they could not have supported a family of four. Comparing the customary wages with the cost of living one can conclude that from 2 to 2.5 times the wages paid to common day labor was the minimum income necessary to support an average-sized household. Market earnings were equally low and more irregular and did not usually surpass the wages of common day laborers. The better-paid artisans could have managed on roughly 1 to 1.5 times their customary wage, but were never far from the destitution of the poorest whenever unemployment, sickness, or other calamity struck. Nominal wages increased fairly steadily during the 1890s, but so did prices. Laborers did not experience any significant improvement in their living conditions; there is indeed reason to believe that they worsened.[3]

The customary earnings provided an extremely low standard of living, satisfying only the "animal necessities," as one critic expressed it (Guerrero, 1901: 154). In other words, it approached a physiological minimum. The US Consul reported that the "average scale of living is lower than among any class we know of in the United States, not excepting the free negroes in the Southern States" (US Bureau of Foreign Commerce, 1885: 116). Families of laborers were poorly fed, clothed, and housed. Their diet consisted primarily of tortillas, beans, and *pulque* (a fermented drink), and only occasionally included meat, eggs, or milk. Their lodging consisted of a single damp room, sometimes shared with another family. Their possessions were limited to a few basic kitchen items (*metate, ollas*), and rushmats (*petates*) placed on the ground for bedding. Neither beds, tables, nor chairs were customary. The poor sanitary conditions and high mortality rates led one author to call Mexico City the "most unhealthy city in the world" (Pani, 1917: 7).

Given the wages usually received, the households of common laborers would have needed to pool their incomes to maintain even a minimum standard of living. Indeed, the municipal census of 1882 shows that the average number of persons with remunerative occupations per household was 2.3 among the common laborers. Almost three-quarters of households included two or more earners;

one-third of the households were composed of three or more laborers. These figures confirm that a single laborer could support himself or herself and about two children, but not an entire family. An indication of the importance of income-pooling is the high rate of employment among women. Married women made up almost one-half of all women with occupations. Indeed, we find that married women were in fact more active than either single sons or daughers in the households of common laborers. In addition, about 20 percent of these households were headed by women.[4] This pattern was different from both the countryside, where women seldom worked for their own wages, and from the urban pattern developed during the 1930s, when married women would for the most part drop out of the labor force.

A working-class newspaper of the 1880s explained why women labored in the following way. Only in those families where the men enjoyed a sufficient salary were the women dedicated exclusively to domestic life and did not enter the factory or workshop. However, among the "multitude of working families," employment was only seasonal, or was poorly paid, so that male incomes could not cover the basic necessities. In these cases, "the women are obliged to work in the workshops to help sustain the family, and the brothers are also urged to fulfill their duty, so that the incomes balance with the expenditures." Nevertheless, this income deficit was "permanent and terrible" (CEHSMO, 1975: 154).

We should not assume, however, that households were pooling wage incomes exclusively. The importance of Mexico City as a commercial center meant that many households found the opportunity to gain incomes from the market. Petty commerce and personal services were widespread activities in Mexico City, and independent artisans had been generally reduced to hawking their products in the streets and marketplace. Incomes from marketing were a very important addition to wages among the households of laborers. In the municipal census the instances are common in which persons listed as "merchants," or otherwise involved in commerce or personal service, lived in the same households as day laborers or even skilled artisans. This was the case for washerwomen, tortilla makers, sweets sellers, and so forth.

In Mexico City, subsistence activities were largely limited to unpaid domestic activities that provided no real alternative to money incomes. These activities were dependent on, even limited by, the presence and need for money, and the custom of buying ready-made products for immediate consumption. This was especially the case for the food consumed daily by the popular classes. It is doubtful, given the overcrowded conditions in the city, that households were able to prepare meals regularly, much less raise gardens or small stock, except those who lived on the outskirts. The municipal census shows that most households inhabited single rooms, and many were homeless altogether. The numerous women occupied as tortilla sellers indicates that women's role in the household was not centered around the making of the tortilla as it was in the country. The *taco*, made from the tortilla and a multitude of different fillings, was commonly consumed on the street and in small *fondas* by all members of the popular classes (Poniatowska, 1982).

One estimate of the market value of domestic activities may be constructed using the wages paid to maids or cooks. If we assume that one person was available more or less full-time for domestic work, then this contribution would be equivalent to the wages paid to common labor. It is doubtful, however, that much time was devoted to domestic activities. Common laborers simply did not have the resources to set up "housekeeping" or practice "home economics" in the middle-class sense. Instead, they lived in "subsistence-poor" households with a limited domestic life.[5]

These data suggest a rough equivalence of the wages of common labor and of market earnings. Domestic activities were circumscribed by the lack of resources. These were the households of common laborers, or petty merchants and those employed in the service trades. The money incomes were usually earned by earners of two or more incomes; thus the incomes of the head of household probably did not exceed 50 percent of total money income. Therefore, the majority of households during the 1880s were composed of roughly equal proportions of wages and market income, provided by men, women, and children. What emerges is a picture of households in which virtually all those capable of earning money incomes did so. These households were what today would be called "marginal."

At least two important variations existed. First, skilled artisans earned better wages, even though they still counted on income from other members of the family. As a general rule, they retained a status only slightly superior to common laborers, and only an elite maintained very high income. The households of artisans frequently included members employed as common laborers, and resided in close proximity to poorer households. Nevertheless, the households of artisans were composed of fewer employed persons, with the average being 1.9 per household. Generally, they did not send quite as many of their members into the workforce. The additional workers must have been necessary to surpass the poverty level when there was employment, and to survive when there wasn't. The head of household may have contributed two-thirds of the money income, supplemented by the earnings of a spouse, son, or daughter.[6]

Secondly, laborers employed in poorly paid positions in large (sometimes industrial) establishments tried to arrive at a minimum family income level with a second source of income. They show a very high household participation, frequently with three or four members employed. In many households all of the adults and older children registered an occupation.[7] These households were extremely wage-centered, with a very limited domestic life. One indication of this is the sheer amount of time spent in the factory, from ten to twelve hours a day. There must have been precious little time for even the most basic of domestic tasks including the preparation of meals. There is evidence as well that child care was a persistent problem, with women bringing their children to the workplace. One observer noted in 1893 that most of the women employed in the tobacco trades were married women with children. These women would bring their children to the factory where they were cared for by a matron in a separate room. When girls were 13, they could begin working for wages with their mother (Bancroft, 1893: 234). A "nursery" was not always supplied, however. There is no image more striking than that photograph of a seamstress working at her sewing machine in a crowded workshop as a woman overseer stands behind her giving instructions. This seamstress, in the middle of her work, has a suckling child at her breast (Acevedo, 1982).

Unfortunately, there are no direct household data for the turn of the century. Nevertheless, one can infer the results of the economic expansion using the three household types developed above. As large-scale production and commercial establishments grew in importance in Mexico City, two separate tendencies can be hypothesized. First, among the households of the common laborers and of the skilled artisans the proportion of wages increased, as wage employment expanded and market earnings declined. Secondly, many households were converted into the wage-centered, subsistence-poor proletarian houshold, as entire families were drawn directly into large-scale production or into production "put out" by large establishments. These two tendencies do not represent a radical break with household patterns that already existed in the 1880s, but they did become more common. Contemporary social critics complained that the industrialization of the 1890s had swelled the ranks of the poorly paid laborers and paupers (Guerrero, 1901; Lara y Pardo, 1908).

As we have seen, households were generally composed of multiple money earners, had very low levels of consumption and a limited domestic life. These households were most frequently composed of nuclear families. Even so, one common way to promote income-pooling among these three household types was the expansion of the household to include non-kin members. The most frequent method of expanding the family structure was through the addition of persons of the same generation, that is, laterally. This usually meant the addition of brothers or sisters, and sometimes non-kin as well, with or without families of their own. The addition of persons with no obvious kin relation was rather frequent in the city and it was not at all uncommon for non-related simple families to share a lodging. When families were expanded across generations, they were most frequently of the ascendant type, that is, with the younger generation holding authority. The most frequently found example was a widow or widower living with one of their married children. These variations in the expansion of family structures varied considerably with those of the countryside, which were usually expanded in a descending fashion and rarely included non-kin members. The so-called traditional patriarchal "extended" family was not often found in Mexico City among the working classes.[8]

At the same time, a rather large proportion of families were lacking a nuclear component. When the homeless (and also domestic servants) are added to these, the presence of single individuals or less than nuclear groups becomes quite large. Many laborers were not fortunate enough to receive stable wages and were reduced to utter poverty and homelessness. The census of 1900 showed that 14 percent of the population surveyed in Mexico City lacked "a permanent home" (González Navarro, 1974: 1, 143). The infamous "leperos" of Mexico City were vagabonds that lived in the streets and were blamed for most of the crime (González y González *et al.*, 1956). One contemporary author reports that hundreds of vaga-bonds were periodically rounded up and deported from Mexico City to serve as laborers on plantations in the south or to serve in the army (Guerrero, 1901). It would seem that many laborers failed to obtain stable employment and to maintain households at all.

Both the tendency to expand the family structure of the household and the frequent failure to maintain a stable household at all seem to have the same cause, low wages.[9] It seems that while there existed a certain economic necessity to expand the family group, at the same time the situation of low wages and widespread commodification made family formation more flexible and ad hoc. Low wages made the sharing of income necessary, but domestic work and life was rather minimal. This made the family ties much more fluid and more tenuous. Very low wages tended to reduce laborers very much to individual earners, in the sense that among many households every member needed to work, if at all possible. In other words, wages frequently covered only the daily reproduction of the laborer who earned them.

Such very low wages tended to promote flexible family structures, ones which came together to share the costs of housing and food, and to pool incomes and resources, but were also easily rearranged. To the extent that wages were reduced to the amount sufficient for the simple daily costs of the laborer, a stable family, reproduced generationally, was more difficult to maintain. Low wages, which represented a monetary advantage to the employers, were possible precisely because laborers lived in households where they pooled their income and expenses. But the lower the wages, the weaker and more tenuous was the family structure. The dialectic of the urban household was that the more laborers were forced into employment the weaker the household structure.

As we have seen, to have multiple money earners in the household was the solution to inadequate wages. But this strategy came up against a serious obstacle, the falling demand for labor. From the early 1900s through the 1920s, laborers suffered from both a contraction of the labor force and rampant inflation accompanied by falling real wages. The downswing provoked social chaos and political rebellion precisely because the usual household strategies had been exhausted. More wages, that is, wage earners, were needed to supplement the household budget, but less employment was to be found. The influx of landowners into Mexico City may have provided more opportunity for domestic and personal service, but many were reduced to begging and prostitution. One contemporary study showed that most prostitutes came from the households of urban laborers hit by hard times (Lara y Pardo, 1908).

In the face of the sheer impossibility of resolving the crisis of reproduction through income-pooling, the response on the part of households was political. The growing presence of wage-centered households associated with large-scale production led eventually to a successful labor movement, requiring not only wage earners, but wage-centered households. This distinction, between those individuals who might earn wages, and wage-centered households, is extremely relevant for explaining the very different political responses of urban and rural laborers, and the general failure of the unification of both movements. Wage labor was used extensively upon haciendas before the revolution, but households had not yet become wage-centered. They were still composed of significant proportions of subsistence and market income. The revolution in the countryside, exemplified by the Zapatista movement, was directed at the restoration of land, not toward wage increases. In contrast, in Mexico City, where the wage-centered, subsistence-poor, household was prevalent, the labor movement was organized around securing a better wage as well as ending abuses at the workplace.

Even among the urban laborers, distinctions are found. During the 1880s the working-class movement was led primarily by small artisans and consisted in mutual aid societies aimed at assisting small-scale production and providing social security. By the 1890s, the working classes found a new expression, the strike aimed at higher wages and better conditions of labor. The first movement was associated with artisans struggling against the waging of their employment; the second movement was associated with those laborers already dependent upon the large-scale enterprise. A reasonable hypothesis would be that the first group lived in households that showed some diversity, combining wage and market income, while the second group lived in more wage-centered households. The organized labor movement that proved to be successful was composed of members of wage-centered households.

Census data shows that the proportion of persons economically active actually contracted up through the 1930s and expanded only slightly during the 1940s. Above all, it was married women who left the labor force, although child labor also diminished, while schooling increased. During these years, the rate of women's participation in the paid labor force was the lowest in the entire study period. The data also show that since the 1940s there has been a steady rise in the employment of women, especially during the decade of the 1970s. The rate of women's participation from 1895 to 1980 shows a rather symmetrical "long wage": relatively high during the 1890s, falling gradually until 1940, and then rising steadily up to 1980.[10]

As a result of the organized labor movement, salaries for industrial laborers improved dramatically during the 1930s. The late 1930s and the early 1940s were probably the best and most optimistic years in the entire history of the industrial proletariat. Nevertheless, these relatively high real wages of the late 1930s were to be eroded by inflation beginning in 1945, remaining relatively low during the 1950s. Thus real wages actually fell during the period of rapid growth, at least for the better-paid laborers. Wages may have improved slightly for the lower-paid groups, thus lessening the income differential between the two groups. Real wages begin to show an improvement in the beginning of the 1960s, but it is not until the late 1960s that real wages for industrial laborers once again reach the 1939 level (Bortz, 1987; Everett, 1980). During the mid-1970s real wages increased, but after 1979 have suffered from inflation and general economic crisis (Gregory, 1986).

Despite the improvement of wages, a consistent feature of the industrial wage has been that by itself it cannot usually provide a basic standard of living for the household, even during periods when real wages have been the highest. The legal minimum wage has never constituted a "family wage" and this has been a consistent observation since its establishment in the mid-1930s.[11] Nevertheless, when compared with the nineteenth century, the wages normally paid seemed to have covered a greater portion of the socially necessary costs of reproduction. In addition, the standard of living had improved considerably. Food consumption and clothing improved, and standards of personal hygiene went up. New domestic goods, furniture (tables, chairs, beds), and kitchen items (stoves), and eventually the radio and television, entered the household budget (Hewitt, 1977).

The 1930s are marked by the ascendancy of two important groups in the urban workforce: the modern industrial proletariat, and the middle class employed in service and professional occupations for private companies or for the government. The growth and concentration of the industrial proletariat in Mexico City was quite dramatic during the twentieth century. In 1895, the industrial proletariat constituted only 14 percent of the urban population, but due to the industrial expansion of the 1930s this figure had reached 39 percent by 1940 (Iturriaga, 1951: ch. 3). In 1960 almost 39 percent of Mexico's entire industrial labor force resided in Mexico City (Wilkie, 1974: 44). The middle class rose from about 30 percent of the urban population in 1895 to 35 percent in 1940, most of which were "white collar" employees in business, industry, and government (Iturriaga, 1951: ch.3).

From a population of less than half a million during the first decades of this century, Mexico City grew to about one million inhabitants by 1930, almost tripled by 1950, and reached 8.5 million by 1970. During the decade of 1940–50 rural migrants accounted for almost 75 percent of Mexico City's population growth (Muñoz *et al.*, 1982: 9). Many of these immigrants joined the ranks of the poorest paid, which constituted better than one-half of the urban population, including the lower strata of industrial laborers and service employees (Wilkie and Wilkins, 1981). The poorly paid common laborers and self-employed, the so-called "marginals," have thus maintained a persistent presence in the urban landscape since the nineteenth century. In contrast, the independent artisans of the nineteenth century have practically disappeared.

A rough summary estimate of the stratification of industrial laborers around the estimated poverty level, derived from different studies around 1970, would be that 20 to 30 percent of the industrial laborers earned less than the legal minimum wage, and thus much less than the poverty level. From 40 to 65 percent earned one to two times this minimum, or just at the poverty level, and 10 to 20 percent earned more than twice the legal minimum wage, somewhat better than the poverty level. Thus, it would appear that only about one-quarter of the industrial laborers earned a wage that was near or slightly better than a family wage; the great majority earned much less. When we consider all those who worked for wages, the situation was even more desperate. The legal minimum represents the *lowest* salaries paid in large- and medium-scale industry where the workers were well organized, but it was commonly the *highest* salary for unskilled workers in services, commerce, and small workshops

(Everett, 1980: 116). Those earning less than the minimum wage, or its equivalent in market earnings, constituted more than half the urban workers in Mexico in 1970 (Wilkie and Wilkins, 1981).

The weight of the principal wage income was greater in the household budget of industrial laborers of the 1940s, when compared with their counterparts of the nineteenth century. Wage earners were better able to provide for their families even with a shorter work week. The budget surveys show that the principal wage covered a much larger proportion of the necessary income than earlier. According to budget studies done in 1934 and 1941 the principal wage income of the head of household constituted 71 to 76 percent of the total money income of the household. This was supplemented by additional income from the breadwinner (4 to 6 percent) and by contributions of other unspecified household members, equivalent to 19 to 20 percent of the total. Over 90 percent of combined household income were from wages.[12]

There is an apparent paradox. On the one hand, wages and working conditions were much better by 1940; but on the other hand, income shortfalls were still present and the practice of multiple earners prevalent, although less so. Like their counterparts of the nineteenth century, industrial laborers still lived in households of multiple wage earners. Of the households surveyed in 1934, the average was 1.6 earners per household: skilled workers averaged 1.5; the semi-skilled, 1.6; and the unskilled, 1.8. Of all households, 53 percent had only one person occupied, the remaining 47 percent were composed of more than one laborer. Among the skilled laborers only 39 percent of the households had two or more persons employed, while among the unskilled 62 percent were composed of two or more laborers (Bach, 1935).

The explanation of this apparent paradox is twofold. First, households were larger, yet composed of fewer occupied persons. Thus, even though the practice of multiple earners was still prevalent, the "earner ratio" increased substantially.[13] Secondly, the standard of living had improved dramatically when compared with the nineteenth century, even though households still sought living conditions better than the customary wage could provide. The budget study of 1934 showed that 32 percent of the households had total incomes greater than the amount needed to live in "conditions of comfort and hygiene" (Bach, 1935: 21–22). It is unlikely that many attained this income from a single wage earner per household, but these households were no longer "subsistence-poor."

It would seem that the improvement in wages and in the standard of living among the industrial working classes was associated with an intensification of unpaid domestic work by women. Labor organizations and government agencies alike simultaneously promoted the "family wage" for men and "homemaking" for women. Writing in the official publication of the *Secretaría de Trabajo y Previsión Social*, one author argued that, when women worked outside the home, the proletarian family suffered "notorious damage." The woman, he wrote, should devote herself to being "wife, mother and housewife," while the man "works and produces" (Ibarra, 1946: 36). Toward this end, the government of the Federal District established "women's work centers" (*centros femeniles de trabajo*) where they were taught the basics of homemaking (González Navarro, 1974: I, 204). The first direct observations of household activities, done by Oscar Lewis in the 1950s, indicated that mothers dedicated most of the day to domestic work, usually helped by their daughters (Lewis, 1959).

Furthermore, housing increasingly became a political issue during the twentieth century, beginning with rent strikes and demands for rent control in the 1910s and 1920s, followed by land occupations and the growth of working-class neighborhoods (*colonias proletarias*) in the 1930s and 1940s. An important feature of these working-class neighborhoods was that much of the housing was self-constructed. This self-provisioning of housing signified an increase in unpaid work for both men, who were charged with construction and repair of the dwellings, and women, who were charged with maintaining them and making up for their inadequacies (González Navarro, 1974: I, 155–214).

Although women's workforce participation began to increase again during the 1940s, the participation of proletarian wives and mothers remained low for at least the next thirty years. In 1970, after the head of household, sons were the most active, constituting 20 percent of the economically active household members. They were followed by other male relatives (12 percent), daughters (9 percent), and other female relatives (8 percent). Wives constituted only 4 percent of economically active members of households, and they were active in only 11 percent of all households surveyed (García *et al.*, 1984: 21). A later study found that these women dedicated most of their time to domestic activities. Those households with the greatest amount of domestic work were precisely those proletarian households composed of large nuclear families in which the mother was not employed. The time spent in domestic work might be as high as 72 hours weekly, equal to 1.5 times the normal industrial work week. The author concluded that when the household had sufficient income to purchase a variety of commodities, then domestic work increased.[14]

Thus, the households of industrial laborers around 1940 and thereafter were significantly different from those of the previous century. They lived in wage-centered households in which the head of household provided around three-quarters of the money income, although multiple earners continued to be an important strategy. These households had an expanded domestic life, based fundamentally upon the activities of women. At least one woman, most likely wife and mother, dedicated most of her day to cooking, cleaning, and to the care of children, as well as to shopping, sewing, and mending, often with the assistance of daughters or other family relatives. This work was undertaken under very adverse conditions often lacking even the most basic services of running water, indoor plumbing, adequate drainage or even electricity. This scarcity could be compensated only by the long hours that women dedicated to domestic work.[15]

In contrast to the skilled laborers, many unskilled laborers continued to be employed at far below the socially necessary wage in the small-scale competitive sector. This often took the form of "self-employment" in marketing activities or petty commodity production. This is commonly known as the "informal sector." Budget studies show that the poorest stratum showed the most diversification in income sources, combining both wages and market incomes. One study showed that among the "self-employed" in Mexico City, 51 percent of household income was from wages, with the remaining income from "enterprises" (38 percent) or "investments" (11 percent) (Banco de México, 1966: 251). Another study found that those earning one-half or less of the minimum wage received 42 percent of their income from wages, 45 percent from "enterprises," and 12 percent from transfers, with 1 percent from "other" sources (Hernández and Córdoba, 1982: 87). Therefore, compared with the households of skilled laborers, these unskilled, "marginal" households had a greater percentage of income derived from market sources. These households combined roughly equal proportions of wage and market income, contributed by various members.

These figures probably overestimate the weight of market income, since many of these activities are "disguised" wage activities. For example, what at first appear to be independent sellers or "self-employed" construction workers are actually working for small businessmen, or even larger companies. Domestic outwork may also be confused with market earnings because of the payment of piece rates. Indeed, the distinctions between wage, market, and subsistence income become blurred at this level. Domestic activities also are frequently combined with market activities, for example, in the case of raising animals or preparing food for sale. While part of the product is sold, part is reserved for the family.

It is precisely these poorer households that show the highest rate of female participation, including married women, as well as female heads of household. The need for money income was so urgent that such activities assumed a very high priority, and in fact may have cut into the time devoted to subsistence work. Even though the harsh conditions of poverty required more subsistence work, the necessity of money often meant that women actually reduced their domestic activities in order to seek wages or market income. If there was no one else to take over these tasks, for example, a mother or a daughter, they were simply curtailed. Among the poor households in which women were forced into wage employment, often in the form of outwork, the time spent in domestic tasks was among the lowest. Among these households domestic work constituted from 12 to 48 hours per week, in general only about 54 percent of the normal work week in industry. The extreme poverty of some households preempted domestic work, due to very low consumption and the necessity to devote more time to money-earning activities: their time spent in domestic work is low because their consumption is low (de Barbieri, 1984: 184–86).

The household of the unskilled, "marginal" laborer bears a striking resemblance to the household of common laborers during the nineteenth century. Nevertheless, the proportion of such households seemed to decline during the 1930s and 1940s as they were transformed into more wage-centered structures. With the downswing after around 1970, this transition slowed, and perhaps reversed itself slightly. It is most probable that the late 1970s and

1980s brought with them a relative "marginalization" of many of the proletarian households: increased use of multiple earners in general and a higher female employment in particular; declining domestic work and consumption; and a slightly higher proportion of market income in the household budget. Indeed, a study based upon a 1977 survey found that among those households earning from 1.5 to 2 times the legal minimum wage (the condition of the majority of the industrial working class) they received 76 percent of their income from wages, 20 percent from market earnings, and 4 percent from transfers (Hernández and Córdoba, 1982: 87).

The middle-class households were a new type emerging after about 1940. Those surveyed in the 1950s had a higher average income, and higher education than the other groups. It is interesting to note that even though the standard of living, in terms of housing, nutrition, and other expenditures, is much higher than that of the manual laborers, it is attained only through the use of additional money earners, especially women. Among the middle class, the average number of economically active persons per household was two, usually a man and his wife. These households have the highest rates of women's participation, and it is among these households that wives were the most active. But unlike the women of the marginal sector, they were employed in the formal sector, as secretaries, nurses, teachers, and in professional jobs.

Furthermore, the time devoted to unpaid domestic work was less. An important reason for this is that they could afford to hire domestic service, chiefly from the ranks of the marginal households. Almost one-half of these households counted on domestic servants, even though the cost of servants for all households equaled only about 5 percent of the household budget (Barba de Piña Chan, 1960). Depending on whether the wives of the middle class were employed or not, domestic work equaled 69 to 123 percent of the industrial work week. The cases in which the domestic work was the lowest were those in which the wives worked and hired paid domestic service; while the cases in which the domestic work was the greatest were those in which the wives did not work, and had children (de Barbieri, 1984: 235–37). The middle-class household is thus especially important in understanding women's economic participation: not only do they *send* women into the labor force, they actually *employ* other, poorer women. The increased participation of women after 1950 is apparently associated with the expansion of the middle-class household, on the one hand, and the persistence of the marginal household, on the other.

Historical and cross-sectional comparisons of the family composition of the proletarian, marginal, and middle-class households are wrought with methodological difficulties. Concerning the kin structure of proletarian families during the 1930s and 1940s there is almost no information available.[16] The budget survey of 1934 noted the presence of "other relatives," presumably due to the "typical Mexican phenomenon" in which "sisters, aunts and grandmothers live together with the family" (Bach, 1935: 24–25). On the average, 23 percent of the households contained "other relatives" in addition to the head of household, spouse, and children. As one might expect, skilled laborers showed lower figures (15 percent), while the unskilled showed higher ones (33 percent). By 1970, the "relatives" were still an important addition to the household labor pool among manual laborers, constituting 20 percent of those earning money income (García *et al.*, 1982).

The problem of small, subsistence-poor households, evident in the nineteenth century among laborers, seems to have diminished corresponding to rising wages and improved public health. Although multiple earners continued to be a strategy throughout the twentieth century, domestic work and life has increased in importance and the average family size has increased dramatically.[17] The evidence suggests that family size increased because households had more children, not because they had expanded their kin composition. Infant mortality rates, as well as general mortality rates, fell dramatically (Cook and Borah, 1971; González Navarro, 1974). Nevertheless, the continued practice of expanding the family in various ways in order to promote income pooling indicates that low wages continue to be problematic. For example, Lomnitz (1975: 104) found that marginal households were still characterized by "extreme fluidity" in household formation, including a wide variation of less-than-nuclear, nuclear, extended, and multiple families.[18]

In conclusion, the secular trend in Mexico City has been toward the gradual waging of households, without, however, the disappearance of the marginal household, composed of a mix of wage and market income earned by different members of the domestic group. The nineteenth century saw the gradual decline of the guilds in Mexico City, accompanied by an increase in wage labor combined with petty marketing and production activities. In this context, the employment of women increased, showing a significant increase mid-century, lasting through the 1880s. With the expansion of large-scale production, especially during the 1890s, many households became highly wage-centered, composed of multiple wage earners, but with a restricted domestic life. The majority of the households of urban laborers, however, were still composed of a varied mix of market incomes and, increasingly, wages. During the economic expansion, laborers were beset with the problem of extremely low wages, with extremely poor standards of living combined with tenuous household formation and restricted domestic life.

The immediate effects of the Revolution of 1910 are unknown, but the subsequent reforms led to rising wages, during the 1920s and especially the 1930s. Households became increasingly wage-centered, which led to an increase in unpaid domestic work. Households of the new industrial proletariat enjoyed better standards of living and were larger in size, but continued to send out multiple wage earners, although less so. During these years, the employment of women fell. This trough of women's employment was associated with the period of relative prosperity for the industrial working class and the emergence of wage-centered house-holds with an expanded domestic life. Wage levels and the standard of living improved significantly. This was accompanied by an expansion of unpaid domestic activities as women left the labor force and domestic consumption increased, the net result being that the subsistence income of this new waged household was greater than those of the wage-centered household of the nineteenth century. Market income tended to decrease both absolutely and proportion-ally to wages. The middle class also began to grow during this period.

Nevertheless, the rise of the industrial proletariat and the middle class did not absorb the marginal households, which have shown a remarkable persistence since the nineteenth century, even during the period of rapid industrialization and expansion, 1940–70. The downswing of the 1970s was marked by an expansion of activities of the small-scale competitive sector, but now much more dependent upon capital than earlier. As a result, "informal" production and market activities have become less and less an independent house-hold activity and more and more a kind of wage employment. The gradual increase of women's employment during the period of economic growth, and the rapid increase of female employment during the 1970s were apparently due to the marginalization of the households of laborers. This has meant the diversification of varied income activities of several members in order to maintain only a minimum standard of living. In the face of declining wages and meager market earnings, more household members, especially women and children, sought employment. On the one hand, this promoted large families in order to augment the household labor pool, but on the other hand, their poverty meant limited consumption and a tenuous domestic life.

NOTES

1 The preceding summary is based on my reading of de Gortari (1982), González Navarro (1957), and González y González *et al.* (1956). This study does not include households of the middle and upper classes, and thus omits live-in domestic servants as well.

2 This summary is based upon Arrom (1985), the "industrial" census of Busto (1880), and upon data published by the research group at El Colegio de México (Rosenzweig, n.d.). "Industry" does not necessarily refer to mechanized factories, but also to various workshops and to a variety of trades. It is a mistake to say that, with the industrialization of the 1890s women left the home or domestic service directly to enter the factory, as some authors suggest (Vallens, 1978).

3 These estimates are based upon wage rates published by Busto (1880) and Romero (1898), compared with the cost of living derived from reports of the US Consul in Mexico City (US Bureau of Foreign Commerce, 1882, 1885), of the Secretaría de Hacienda (1911), and reprints and facsimile editions of working-class newspapers. For a complete discussion of these sources, see Thompson (1989: 69–76).

4 *Padrón de la Ciudad de México*, 1882. The data are from all those households (n = 171) containing persons listed with unskilled occupations residing in cuartel mayor 7, menor 29, manzana 229 (primera parte) and cuartel mayor 5, menor 18, manzana 159.

5 This estimate, which includes the imputed value of room and board, is based upon my reading of Romero (1898). For a comparison of middle-class and working-class norms with respect to domestic life, see US Bureau of Foreign Commerce (1882, 1885) and Motts (1973).

6 *Padrón de la Ciudad de México*, 1882. The data are from households (n = 46) that contained persons with skilled occupations residing in cuartel mayor 1, menor 1, manzana 11 and cuartel mayor 2, menor 7, manzana 66. This sample is different from the preceding one of common laborers due to the better occupational status of the head of household and the better area of the city. Still, 26 percent of these

better-off households contained additional members employed in common labor or marketing.

7 *Padrón de la Ciudad de México*, 1882. These households contained persons employed primarily in the tobacco and the textile industries, residing in cuartel mayor, 7, menor 29, manzana 229 (primera parte) and cuartel mayor 5, menor 18, manzana 159.

8 Complete nuclear families (a couple, with or without children) were found about 50 percent of the time. In blocks of poorer households the proportion was closer to 40 percent. Various expanded family situations were found in 30 percent of the cases: (a) extended families (with additional members) were 16 percent; (b) multiple-related families (two or more simple families) were 6 percent; and, (c) groups of non-related simple families, 8 percent. But almost 20 percent were less than nuclear groupings: (a) truncated simple families (parent missing) were 10 percent; (b) small non-family groups, 2 percent; and (c) single persons 8 percent. The data are from the *Padrón de la Ciudad de México*, 1882, cuartel mayor 7, menor 29, manzana 229 (primera parte), which contains households (n = 335) of the three main types discussed above. Family size for this sample was 3.6.

9 Another factor would be the very high mortality rates. In Mexico City the yearly average mortality rate from 1895 to 1903 was 48 per 1,000 inhabitants. Pani concluded that Mexico City had the highest mortality rates in the world. He blamed the poor diet, the inadequate housing, and the absence of sanitation (Pani, 1917: 8–13). In other words, these high mortality rates can be traced to low wages.

10 For a complete discussion of the evidence for this pattern, see Thompson (1989: 63–67).

11 The level and the adequacy of the legal minimum wage has been widely disputed. Various studies during the 1970s have found that the cost of the most basic standard of living (as established by official criteria) was equivalent to from 1.7 to 1.8 times the legal minimum in Mexico City (Juárez, 1984; Murphy and Selby, 1981). This figure can be considered to be an adequate estimate in the absence of a detailed historical study.

12 In 1934, a budget study was done among 281 households of industrial laborers of Mexico City. In 1941, the study was repeated among 1,140 households of industrial laborers in various cities of central Mexico. Both studies yielded practically identical results. The findings were reported in the *Anuario estadístico de los Estados Unidos Mexicanos* (Dirección General de Estadística, 1941, 1943) and in Bach (1935). For a complete analysis, see Thompson (1989: 213–17).

13 The "earner ratio" is the ratio of household size with respect to the number of regular money earners. In 1882, the ratio was 1.6; in 1941, 3.4. This comparison is based upon data from a block with a high proportion of textile workers in 1882 and the budget studies of industrial laborers in 1941. This first figure suggests that in 1882, one

laborer supported 1.6 family members, roughly him or herself and another person. For the second date one laborer supported 3.4 family members, him or herself and 2 to 3 others.

14 The time spent in unpaid domestic work was greater among the working class than the middle class, greater in the nuclear families than the extended ones, greater among women who did not have paid employment than those who did, greater among those who did not hire paid domestic service than among those who did, and greater among those who had children than among those who did not (de Barbieri, 1984: 202, 232–33).

15 At the national level the number of homes without either water or drainage actually increased in absolute and relative figures between 1939 and 1960. As late as 1970, 45 percent of the population of Mexico City did not have a bathroom with running water (González Navarro, 1974: I, 170–72).

16 By the 1970s there was more information, but of dubious utility. For example, one study (García *et al.*, 1982) found only slight differences among the families of "manual laborers," "non-manual laborers," and the "self-employed." The authors' emphasis upon the occupational category of the (male) head of family was an unfortunate choice for the study of income-pooling arrangements.

17 The average family size increased rapidly during and after the 1930s, averaging 5.2 members among industrial laborers in 1938 and 5.4 in 1941 (Dirección General de Estadística, 1941: 771; 1943: 989–94). By 1963, the families of industrial laborers averaged 6.0 members (Banco de México, 1966: 102–04). A 1970 survey found that average family size was 5.7 among manual workers, 5.3 among the self-employed, and 4.9 among non-manual workers (García *et al.*, 1982). In the poorest neighborhoods, family size was even greater, averaging between 6 and 7 members (Sierra, 1962: 89).

18 She found the following distribution of family types: 19 percent less-than-nuclear; 52 percent nuclear; 10 percent extended; and 18 percent multiple. When families were expanded, there was a tendency toward lateral expansions.

CHAPTER 2

Central Mexico: the decline of subsistence and the rise of poverty

Lanny Thompson

Throughout the nineteenth century the vast majority of the agricultural labor force employed by the estates of central Mexico consisted of temporary wage laborers, who worked only during the peak agricultural seasons, about six months out of the year. Most of these laborers were residents of small settlements (*pueblos* or *ranchos*), more or less independent of the large estates.[1] The "debt peon," who was permanently tied to a large hacienda, represented only a very small minority of the agricultural labor force. For the most part, laborers were recruited through wage advances made in cash or kind, but in general, payments were quite low. In addition, tenancy and share-cropping were frequent arrangements between the estates and temporary laborers. These laborers were dependent upon the estates, were often indebted, and were usually required to perform some wage labor in exchange for their access to the land. Furthermore, the more that the estates could extract surplus production, by means of rents and shares, the more peasants were obligated to work for wages. Throughout the 1880s and 1890s, the estates, responding to growing markets, sought to expand their landholdings and recruit more wage labor. Both of these ends were achieved precisely by expropriating village residents and smallholders of their lands. Many of these then became tenants and sharecroppers dependent upon the estates; others became wage laborers (Katz, 1974; Warman, 1976: 53–89).

The agricultural labor force was almost exclusively male, including boys who would accompany their fathers and earn one-half the adult wage. Women rarely participated in wage labor in agriculture, and did not find much wage employment of any kind in the villages and small towns of central Mexico. In 1895, when central Mexico (excluding Mexico City) was predominantly rural, women constituted only 12 percent of the economically active population, and those were certainly employed in the larger towns and cities.[2] Although the references are few, they are consistent in placing emphasis upon the fundamental role of women in domestic activities, rather than in wage labor.[3] Busto wrote in 1880 (I, 7), "Women are rarely employed in agricultural work; their duties are domestic ones, and to bring the laborers' food to the field." Even though this statement is true, it is a gross understatement, as we shall see.

In agriculture, nominal wages were fairly uniform throughout central Mexico and remarkably stable throughout most of the nineteenth century, perhaps rising very slightly around 1890 and again around 1900. Real wages may have increased slightly during the 1890s, but fell steadily after 1900. Wages were paid in cash, although the use of scrip was common, as was payment in corn rations, especially among the resident laborers. As a whole, wage rates were extremely low by urban standards. Compared with the wage levels in Mexico City, the rural wage was equal to, or even less than, the lowest wages paid to common urban laborers.[4]

Despite the very low wage rates in agriculture, the practice of multiple earners was not as prevalent among the rural households as in the city. The evidence from one village in 1868[5] shows that the majority of households (68 percent) had only one laborer, most of the remaining households (22 percent) having two earners, usually composed of a father and his single son.[6] Sons might begin laboring alongside their fathers as early as age eleven or twelve and would earn half the adult wage (González Navarro, 1957). In this village, not one single woman held status as a wage earner, and other sources confirm this pattern for the rural areas in general (Warman, 1976; Menegus, 1980). On average, only 1.2 persons per household declared a regular occupation, and yet these households were somewhat large, consisting of 4.6 members. Apparently, one laborer, working roughly six months during the year, could provide the bulk of the wages necessary to support himself and three or four household members. This rural employment pattern departs significantly from that of Mexico City, in which one finds the regular practice of multiple earners, including women, far more widespread.

Although wage rates were very low, contemporary opinion, at least from the 1860s until the 1880s, held that wages were *sufficient* in the countryside to maintain peasant families reasonably well-fed.[7] One observer reported that the rural population could maintain themselves "healthy and robust," thanks to their cultivation of corn, beans, and chile, which they pursued with "admirable perseverance" (Bustamante, 1861: 58–59). Another observer noted that wages were "high," but even so, during certain periods during the year it was difficult to obtain laborers. The local population was "content to live from corn, beans and legumes, and fruits" and had few additional needs that could only be obtained by money (Sartorius, 1870: 194). He explains that, "The people of the indigenous villages are limited to the sowing of their very simple food, and are occupied a few days per year as day laborers, only in order to buy a few yards of cloth, to pay ecclesiastical and municipal fees, and to get drunk" (Sartorius, 1870: 191).

Wages were "sufficient" because of the predominance of subsistence goods in the household consumption pool. Subsistence activities were so widespread throughout the countryside that, in numerous areas, they constituted practically an alternative to wages, at least to the extent that estate owners and government officials were concerned about labor shortages. In the 1870s and 1880s, labor shortages were reported in many parts of central Mexico and throughout the Republic. For estate owners and government officials it was a paradox that, although there was no lack of population, there were labor shortages. They attributed this to the "backward" subsistence economy of the indigenous peoples, to their "indolence, drunkenness, and lack of initiative." In fact, the relative independence of the laborers from the wage, and thus, too, its "sufficiency," was the result of the widespread access to lands used for subsistence cultivation. This access to land was frequently guaranteed by the communal land tenure of the villages, or alternatively through smallholdings. Those who found abundant labor in their locale attributed this to the scarcity of land, or its poor quality (González Navarro, 1957: 143–49; US Bureau of Foreign Commerce, 1886).

It would seem that villagers guarded a certain standard and style of living at once at odds with the estates, yet never isolated from them. To some extent wage labor, and even indebtedness, were necessary to maintain the subsistence orientation of the community. Nevertheless, the evidence shows that the villagers maintained a certain bargaining power, probably up until the 1890s in many areas (Bazant, 1973). This "subsistence-centeredness" meant a relative independence from wages, provided by the access to grain. In this way the villages and the estates existed in "precarious equilibrium" (Warman, 1976: 76).

Women's unpaid activities were an essential complement to subsistence cultivation, undertaken primarily by men. Whole corn, whether it be from the cornfield (*milpa*) or received in kind from the estates, was decidedly not a meal. It had to be transformed into tortillas and combined with beans, chile, and various other vegetables, tubers, herbs, and cacti. After the grain had been separated from the ear, it was soaked in lime (the mineral) to soften it. It was then ground by hand on a stone *metate*, water being added to make a thick dough. The tortillas were then formed by hand, one by one, and cooked on a clay or metal *comal* over a flame. The preparation of tortillas in the traditional way took from four to six hours per day. Women frequently arose before dawn to begin their work. They were also responsible for carrying the midday meal to the men in the fields.[8]

In addition to tortilla making, women were responsible for a number of domestic tasks, such as general cleaning, washing, and sewing. They would also carry water and collect fuel. In addition, they would raise pigs and chickens and cultivate minor fruits and vegetables. In many areas women specialized as well in various "home industries" such as spinning and weaving cloth, and making clothing, pottery, or other goods for sale. As one observer noted, "When not cooking or grinding, the woman mends the scanty clothing, or does some light work in the field, or manufactures something for sale ... " (Bandelier, 1884: 142). In sum, women occupied themselves in a wide range of domestic activities, including some agriculture, animal raising, and handicrafts. Adult women were helped by their daughters and by their young sons, at least until they began to accompany their fathers to the fields. "Only the men were permitted the vice of leisure" (González, 1979: 68).[9]

Market activities were also an important source of rural household incomes. Villagers would generally trade among themselves, also taking their agricultural products to nearby towns and cities, but it is doubtful that much money changed hands. A variety of handicrafts produced by men and women were offered, depending upon local specializations. Textiles were among the most common handicrafts, as were leather products, including shoes and saddles. The weaving of cane and reeds into hats, baskets, and beds was also important as was the making of various pottery. Towns also depended upon villagers for a steady supply of wood and charcoal for fuel. In most areas marketing constituted an exchange of surpluses from subsistence-oriented production, as well as a variety of specialized handicraft products. These market incomes probably tailed behind wages in importance as a general rule, even though in some of the commercialized regions small-scale producers were more market oriented (Bandelier, 1884; Starr, 1900; Nutini and Isaac, 1974).

As subsistence production lowered the socially necessary wage, it also provided an alternative to the wage. This contributed to rural labor shortages, in some areas as late as the 1880s (US Bureau of Foreign Commerce, 1886). During the economic expansion, however, the estates gained control over and squeezed subsistence production in order to extract more surpluses in the form of wage labor, shares, and rents. There is some evidence that household members sought wages more frequently, but it is doubtful that the waged employment of women increased, with some localized exceptions (Warman, 1976; Katz, 1974; Menegus, 1980; González Montes, 1986). The amount of wages in the budget increased slightly in absolute terms, much more so in relative terms. It is certain that the amount of subsistence returns declined both relatively and absolutely. In many cases, households were cultivating the same lands as before, but now having to give up shares, or pay rents (Platt, 1942). There is no evidence that the new demand for labor provided either employment or wage income sufficient to make up for the loss of subsistence income. The estate may have needed more labor, but the seasonal nature of the employment did not change. The increase in wages did not make up for the loss of subsistence. Market income probably declined with the economic upswing as industrial goods out-competed handicrafts, especially textiles. As a result, the standard of living declined.

The "traditional" rural family is usually considered to be a shifting stem structure, formed through patrilocal marriage. According to an accepted model, families generally went through a stage in which a son married, and then continued to live with his father for a period of one to five years. If there were more than one son, this stem structure would shift from son to son. Finally, the surviving parent would form a part of a son's family (frequently that of the youngest). Thus, while the majority of families appeared to be nuclear at any one time, almost all families went through a multiple, and then an extended, phase (Nutini et al., 1976; Arizpe, 1984).

The evidence from a village census of 1868 provides some support for this generalization. The extended family was found in 10 percent of the residences, usually composed by the addition of a widowed parent to the household of a married son. The multiple family was found in 13 percent of the residences, usually composed of a "patriarchal" family, that is, a married son living in his father's residence. However, the simple family seems to have been more prevalent (74 percent) than might be expected.[10] For the most part, then, these were nuclear families, consisting of a couple, usually with children. Even though "households" were fairly well defined by a common hearth, they were embedded in kin networks at the community level. This particular village apparently had an ample land base, which may have promoted the early formation of separate residences.[11] The average size of the domestic unit was 4.6, somewhat larger than in Mexico City at that time, but smaller than rural families of 1940 and after.

Family composition may have changed somewhat as households lost their access to subsistence and became more dependent on the estates. There are some indications, although not conclusive, that the domestic unit expanded to include a wider kin network. In 1889, there was a census in a village[12] which lay directly adjacent to an hacienda. Of all households, 60 percent were composed of simple families, 24 percent of extended families, and 16 percent of multiple families. This pattern conforms closely to the "traditional pattern" described by anthropologists, which may be less "traditional" and more a response to relative land shortages or the private ownership (or control) of land. Population growth during the period, along with the expansion of family structure, also suggests that there may have been a small increase in family size. The average size of the domestic unit was 4.8.

By the 1890s, the balance between wage labor and subsistence had been upset by the expansion of the estates. However, with an economic downturn at the turn of the century, the income-pooling strategies of households were exhausted. Despite the increased importance of wages, rural households had retained a strong subsistence orientation through tenant and sharecropping arrangements. The revolution in the countryside was precisely a resistance to wage labor and a bid to institute autonomous subsistence cultivation. The response to the crisis of subsistence was political and the revolution in the countryside sought one basic goal – the return of lands to the villages. Thus, the income orientation of the household influenced the direction of the political struggle. Unlike those urban laborers who lived in wage-centered households, the rural laborers continued to live in subsistence-oriented households, despite the fact that they worked for wages on an ever-increasing scale. One should also note the "historical and moral element" of the struggle: the indigenous villages were more rebellious than the mestizo smallholding areas of more recent settlement. Resident laborers either sided with the estates or were absent from the rebellions.

After the outbreak of the revolution most of the commercial agricultural production was disrupted and the estates were abandoned in the central zones. As commercial production was disrupted, the labor force contracted and so the extent of wage employment decreased. In order to survive, cultivators returned to subsistence agriculture, as well as to hunting, and gathering wild plants. We know very little about the period, but it is safe to say that subsistence cultivation, and perhaps marketing, increased during these years, while wage employment declined. Overall, the years from 1910 to 1917 were extremely difficult ones in the countryside, marked by fighting and famine. The rural population diminished; households decreased in size and were generally broken apart. The remnants of domestic groups were combined to make ad hoc structures with various kin and even non-kin members (Womack, 1970, 1978; Warman, 1976).

In contrast, the 1920s were years of recovery from the destruction wrought by the revolution. Cultivators slowly regained lands that had previously been taken by the haciendas and began to restore production of their basic staple crops. During the decade of the 1920s the land devoted to corn increased slowly, but surely. Land distributions proceeded very slowly during the 1920s and early 1930s, but households managed to occupy unused lands without formal possession. Production expanded even faster than the population, and so the standard of living improved (Warman, 1976). Households increased their subsistence and their marketing income. The labor force expanded somewhat and wage rates showed marked increases. The overall tendency, especially after 1920, was an increase in the proportion of subsistence and market income, while the proportion of wages declined.

The real wage in the countryside climbed quickly throughout the 1920s and remained high during the 1930s, showing significant gains until the early 1940s when the cost of living outran nominal wage increases. Even with the noteworthy advances in the wage rate in the countryside, reformers maintained that rural laborers continued to live in desperate poverty due to the inadequacy of rural wages. According to national averages the agricultural daily wage was only 32 percent of the daily wage in industry in the 1940s (Fernández y Fernández, 1946). It is doubtful that wages alone were able to provide much more than the barest minimum in the countryside, even during the period of rising real wages. If there were significant improvements in rural standards of living this was due to the land reform, which would provide rural households with supplementary incomes.

The land reform, undertaken primarily during the 1930s, significantly decreased the number of landless rural laborers and created a large group of *ejidatarios*, who gained access to nationalized *ejido* lands administered at the village level. Iturriaga (1951) estimated that, in 1895, agricultural laborers made up 78 percent of the rural population. By 1940, however, the land reform has reduced the landless laborers to 60 percent, and increased *ejidatarios* to 25 percent of the rural population. Paré (1977: 68–95) presented comparable statistics: in 1930, 68 percent of those active in agriculture were landless laborers, but by 1940 this figure had been reduced to 50 percent. In this way, the land reform has been credited for slowing down the process of proletarianization and holding back the migration to the cities.

Those who managed to gain access to land, especially the *ejidatarios*, did not return to the "subsistence-centeredness" of the previous century. Beginning in the 1930s the same harvest that had sufficed to maintain a family in 1925 "ceased to give." In other words, it failed to cover all the income necessities of the family. The problem was neither small harvests nor land shortages; indeed during the 1930s harvests were better and more land was available than ever before. The "crisis of traditional cultivation" was, simply put, a lack of money; not of land, not of product. While corn continued to provide much of the grain needs of households, it was failing to cover their additional money needs. Not only did everything cost more, but norms of consumption were changing. More manufactured items entered the household budget (Warman, 1976: 175–205).

The household's response to the crisis of traditional cultivation was both the commercialization of their product, and the increased participation in wage labor. In other words, households responded through a diversification of their income activities. Besides cultivating the cornfield (*milpa*) they introduced various commercial crops and at the same time frequently sought work as day laborers. The new activities demanded more work and new resources that were organized in a different way, and that were added to the traditional activities. This expansion of activities was possible through the increased number of household members. The households did not become more specialized; rather they increased the variety and complexity of their activities. These new activities were aimed at obtaining money, and as a consequence the consumption patterns have changed, expressed in the growing acquisition of manufactured goods and the relative reduction of subsistence cultivation (Warman, 1976: 305–06). Among these households significant income came from each of the main sources: 57 percent of all income came from wages, followed by market income (32 percent) and the imputed value of subsistence cultivation (11 percent). The activities of additional household members contributed as much as 29 percent of the total income, mainly from wages.[13]

Money income became increasingly important for all rural households during the 1930s. Even though the number of landless laborers decreased due to the land distributions, those with access to land, either *ejidatarios* or smallholders, marketed their production on an increasing scale, while at the same time increasing their participation in wage labor. In contrast, subsistence cultivation decreased, at least in relative terms. The general consensus among anthropologists has been that subsistence agriculture provides at most one-half of the community's grain needs throughout rural central Mexico. While the absolute levels of subsistence production have remained stable since the 1930s, they have declined rapidly as a proportion of all income (Belshaw, 1967; Warman, 1976: 229–30; Dinerman, 1978; Nutini and Isaac, 1974; Arizpe, 1973). In 1970 those households possessing less than 4 hectares of land (64 percent of all "peasant" households) produced annually the value of no more than one-half the annual legal minimum wage in the countryside, which is about 25 percent lower than in the city (Schejtman, 1982: 109–14). Assuming two wage earners, the value of subsistence cultivation and marketing could not have exceeded 20 percent of all incomes. Indeed, most budget surveys have shown that subsistence cultivation accounts for 10 percent or less of total income (Banco de México, 1966; Secretaría de Programación y Presupuesto, Mexico, 1981).

Increasingly, the search for wage incomes has led to migration. Arizpe's (1980) monograph on migration clearly demonstrates that, in the village where the *ejidatarios* were land poor, a "relay" migration took place, in which fathers, sons, and daughters migrated at different stages of the family cycle to maximize the household's labor pool in a manner such that, during the entire life cycle, there were usually at least two members migrating. Depending upon the domestic cycle, there are from 1 to 5 persons employed in wage labor in the household, so that 3 or 4 sons or daughters were needed to contribute income. This seems to indicate an increase in the number of wage earners per household, especially compared with the nineteenth century. Thus, we find not only that households began to send more labor into the market, but that this labor was increasingly women, especially daughters.

Since 1940, the expansion of the virtually landless rural population reasserted itself, despite the previous land distribution. Budget studies done around 1940[14] show that the households of agricultural laborers received almost 75 percent of their total income come from wages, and almost 20 percent from marketing. The imputed value of subsistence cultivation constituted only 5 percent of the total income. They had little or no access to land, although they might have made use of the house plot to raise animals or plant fruit trees or vegetables. In this way they managed some subsistence food production and marketing. Handicrafts might also have been a source of market income (Mendieta y Nuñez, 1938). Rural laborers did what they could to supplement their wages, but in the absence of land, the income gap forced them to curtail consumption. It seems that, above all, low wages meant a very low standard of living. The rural proletariat were the poorest of the poor in Mexico.

According to these budget studies, among landless agricultural laborers, the principal wage equaled about 60 percent of the total money income; a full 40 percent of the money income came from sources other than the wages earned by the head of household. For the most part, this additional income was earned by other members of the household, either as wages or from marketing. Although the budget studies did not specify exactly which members were contributing the additional money income, from other sources we know that sons, and increasingly daughters, contributed wages, while above all it was mothers that contributed the market income. The head of household also had small additional earnings from marketing.

The census, and even family budget surveys, affirm that rural women were still not highly active in waged activities. The positive relation between size of locality and the employment of women is very clear (Ruiz, 1978). Although women still did not find much employment in the rural areas, increasingly rural women migrated to the urban areas to find work (Arizpe, 1984). Thus, one finds a general increase in women's employment in central Mexico. Furthermore, the census is quite misleading because we know from ethnographies that women were busy marketing and occasionally doing agricultural tasks. They were not, however, very active in agricultural wage labor, except in the most wage-centered house-holds in the zones of highly commercialized agriculture, where they labor with other family members (Maldonado, 1977).

In the countryside women spent long hours in unremunerated domestic tasks: they made tortillas and prepared food; they cared for children, educating them and supervising them when they were old enough to help with the work; they cleaned, mended, and often made, clothing; they carried water and frequently gathered firewood to be used in preparing meals. Women managed to fill out the day with domestic and other unremunerated tasks. They usually raised domestic animals, such as chickens, turkeys, and pigs, and grew fruits and vegetables on the house plot; they frequently gathered wild food, herbs, and medicinal plants, depending upon local conditions; in many villages women also made handicrafts, such as clothing, blankets, embroidery, or pottery. Women frequently helped with light field work during harvest or whenever extra hands were needed. They also participated a great deal in markets, selling their own products, those of the family, or "retailing" products. While an older women marketed various products, daughters, or sometimes daughters-in-law would cook and clean the house. For this reason one usually found more than one adult woman in the household.[15]

At first glance, the principal activities performed by women seem unchanged since the nineteenth century. Nevertheless, upon closer examination one notes that the crisis of traditional cultivation has affected the work of women too. The tortilla provides an interesting point of departure. The stone *metate*, which kept women busy grinding corn about two hours per day, was being quickly forsaken in the 1930s for the commercial mill. Here women could take their prepared corn to have it ground for a small fee. The tortillas continued to be cooked at home. This seemingly small change was not insignificant, especially when we consider it to be only the beginning. After around 1940, the completely homemade tortilla has been gradually supplemented by the mill-ground dough, the commercial tortilla and by bread, except in the most isolated areas.[16]

The importance of the change seems to be twofold. First, the use of the mill represented a cost where previously there was none. The cost increased further if ready-made tortillas or bread were purchased. Secondly, being freed from the lengthy daily task of grinding corn, women were available for other activities. Lewis (1963: 98–100, 108) associates the widespread use of the corn mill with the increased time spent by women in marketing (both buying and selling). Thus, it appears that subsistence work had been slightly curtailed, while marketing activities had become more important. This shift is not recorded in census data because marketing is not usually considered to be the primary occupation. From the studies of Lewis we can conclude that the time spent in marketing, both buying and selling, has increased; that the *nixtamal* mill facilitated market activities; and that daughters were important contributors to domestic work.

In the countryside, women continued to be involved in subsistence, and devoted much more time to it than did men.[17] It is very difficult to establish a precise percentage for these tasks, because of the lack of integrated studies that either estimate the value produced by all household members, or construct time allocation tables for entire households. Subsistence has come to depend more and more on money income, and despite the long hours contributed by both men and women, subsistence in no way provided an alternative to money, as it did to an extent in the nineteenth century. The time spent has remained very high, although the character and valuation of such work has changed considerably. Standards of living have changed rapidly since the 1930s, taking on a more urban, commodity-based norm. The satisfaction of these new standards meant the participation in the national market, obtaining money income and purchasing manufactured products. Rural residents thus became more dependent on commodities to supply food, clothing, and domestic goods. But since the terms of exchange did not favor agricultural products, especially corn, the satisfaction of the most basic necessities, such as nutrition, became increasingly problematic (Hewitt, 1977: 70).

Thus, after 1940, proletarianization in the countryside has taken three distinct paths in central Mexico. The first of these paths was the development of the households combining wage and market earnings supplemented by subsistence. The land distributions resulted in a highly diversified wage/market household, which gradually incorporated more wage income and, to a lesser degree, market income. The proportion of subsistence income has consistently deteriorated since around 1940, even for those households with access to land. The use of multiple wage earners (sons first, then daughters) became generalized. As a result, the wage composition of households increased. They were large households, somewhat expanded. The tide of urban migrants came in large measure from these households.

The second of these paths was the extension of the relatively wage-centered proletarian household. Since 1940 the numbers and percentage of landless grew steadily, and by 1970 almost 60 percent of those active in agriculture were landless laborers (Bartra, 1974; Paré, 1977). Even though wages made up the greatest proportion of household income, marketing activities frequently provided an important supplement. Some subsistence production, although minimal, was common. These rural proletarian households were composed of multiple earners and represented a major source of seasonal labor migration.

Finally, proletarianization has taken place through permanent urban migration. This signified a transformation of rural-type households to those of the urban type (both proletarian and marginal). Laborers migrated to two major zones nationally: to the northern areas; and to Mexico City. The rapid growth of Mexico City, and of other major urban areas in central Mexico, has been fed by a steady stream of migrants from the rural areas. During the 1940s, 73 percent of the population growth of Mexico City was accounted for by rural migrants; during the 1950s, 44 percent; and during the 1960s, 46 percent. This urban migration indicated a massive proletarianization of rural residents. In 1930, 68 percent of the economically active population in Mexico was employed in agriculture; by 1970 this figure had been reduced to 39 percent, even though the absolute numbers of those engaged in agriculture continued to increase (Muñoz et al., 1982: 9; Paré, 1977: 90).

Perhaps the most noticeable change in rural families was that family size was large in 1940 and growing consistently throughout Mexico (Cook and Borah, 1971). This was associated with a population boom unparalleled in the history of Mexico. In general it has been those households with some access to land that are the largest, with the completely landless households being the smallest. We can conclude that from 1930 to 1970 the proletarian households had grown to be from 5 to 5.5 members, while the combined "wage/market" households of small-scale cultivators had grown to be from 6 to 6.5 members on the average. Estimates vary according to different budget studies, but the overall average must be around 6.0, with the proletarian family being less, and the wage/market family greater, than this average.[18]

This increase in family size was not necessarily the result of an expansion of the family structure, but rather of an increase in the number of children. Generally speaking, the nuclear family has been the most commonly found form, around 64 percent of the total (Lewis, 1963: 60). Nevertheless, these figures hide the fact that throughout the entire life cycle practically everyone lives at one time in an extended or multiple family. This occurs at two points: the first when the son brings his new bride to live in his father's house; the second when his own sons bring their wives. The waging of households and the practice of labor migration are apparently associated with larger families (averaging 6.8), but fewer expanded families (19 percent), according to Arizpe (1980). Nevertheless, Nutini *et al.* (1976) found that labor migration could actually strengthen the stem family, but apparently with the simultaneous presence of subsistence cultivation. Among *ejidatarios* producing for the market, families were smaller (averaging 6.2), and more expanded in structure, with extended families constituting 33 percent of the total. Sons and daughters also migrated but to a smaller degree, since they were needed above all in the agricultural work of the household (Arizpe, 1980). The practice of patrilocal marriage has not disappeared in the countryside. It appears to be weakest among the land poor, and strongest among those who retained lands that provide a greater proportion of money and subsistence. It appears then that the diversification of income (i.e., the case of the wage/market households) has led to larger, somewhat expanded families. Those more market-oriented households are somewhat smaller, but more expanded. The proletarian households were of an intermediate size and less expanded.

In conclusion, the waging of rural households occurred in alternating phases of expansion and contraction. During the 1870s and 1880s, subsistence income was of central importance to rural households. Subsistence cultivation was so widespread throughout the countryside that, in numerous areas of central Mexico, it constituted practically an alternative to wages, at least to the extent that estate owners and government officials were concerned about labor shortages. Households were subsistence-centered, with additional wage and eventually market income. With the expansion of demand for agricultural products during the 1880s and especially the 1890s, estate owners consciously sought to deprive rural residents of their independent land base in order to secure an ample and cheap labor force. This resulted in falling subsistence returns for households, which were not made up by the slight increase, absolutely and relatively, of wages in the income pool. Market income also fell, both relatively and absolutely. Overall, the levels of consumption fell. The Revolution of 1910 and the consequent economic depression brought about a contraction of the labor force and a renewed emphasis on subsistence and probably an increase in marketing income as well, due to the disruption of commercial production on the estates and the recovery of village lands. Subsistence cultivation and, increasingly, market income gained importance during the 1920s, and were further promoted by the land reform of the 1930s. Since the 1940s, the overall trend has been marked by an expansion, in absolute and relative numbers, of the landless proletariat, an increase in the wage composition of the households of cultivators, and by the continuing process of proletarianization through urbanization. In the face of persistently low wages, and falling subsistence cultivation, the importance of multiple wager earners, and of supplementary market incomes, became increasingly important among rural households. By the 1970s, the effectiveness of land distribution had reached its limits, and subsistence income was reduced to being a mere supplement to wage income.

NOTES

1 This chapter attempts to make generalizations concerning central Mexico as a whole. Nevertheless, one should recognize certain differences

between the predominantly indigenous areas and the mestizo ones. The former were characterized by villages (*pueblos*) with communal tenure, but private usufruct rights. The latter were characterized by small-holders living in small settlements (*ranchos*).

2 In contrast, the official rate for Mexico City that same year was 35 percent, almost three times as high. See Rosenzweig (n.d.).

3 Many observers described marriage rituals in which men and women would act out their respective roles in the household. The rituals for women centered upon the making of tortillas and the bearing of children. See Bustamante (1861), Starr (1900), and León (1943).

4 This generalization is based on the figures published by Rosenzweig (n.d.), and were compared with other accounts, such as Katz (1974) and Fernández y Fernández (1946). The real wage trend is an estimate based on cost of living indexes derived from urban prices and consumption patterns, which are not a good indication of rural ones.

5 *Padrón del pueblo de San Andréz Acatlán y su congregación de San José* (Veracruz, 1868). The village consisted of 130 dwellings. This municipal census was part of an incomplete national census, attempted by the Ministerio de Fomento. A photocopy of the census was available in the Biblioteca Orozco y Berra, Mexico City.

6 A few households (4 percent) had three employed members, and the rest (6 percent) declared to have no employed persons.

7 More recent scholarly opinion, while perhaps more balanced, does not really contradict this view of the sufficiency of the wage, at least before the 1890s: see Bazant (1973), Cross (1978), Warman (1976), González y González (1956). The well-known criticisms of the rural conditions made by Molina (1909) and Cabrera (1975) reflect the situation of the early 1900s.

8 Bandelier (1884) and Starr (1900) offer direct observations of food and its preparation during the nineteenth century. Twentieth-century descriptions of tortilla making in the traditional manner are found in Redfield (1949) and Lewis (1959, 1963).

9 See also the descriptions provided by Warman (1976), González y González (1956), Whetten (1948), Redfield (1949), Lewis (1963, 1959), Ramos and Rueda (1984).

10 A small number (1.5 percent) were less than nuclear groups, with the remaining 1.5 percent composed of households including persons unrelated by last name (*apellido*).

11 The evidence for these statements is the following. The *pueblo* of San Andréz Acatlán included a smaller *congregación* of San José of recent origin; all of the residents of the *congregación* named as their place of origin the *pueblo* of San Andréz Acatlán. All of the households of the *congregación* were composed of nuclear families. Other authors argue that in the traditional village, household usufruct rights to land were granted through the village, not through the father (Powell, 1974;

Bandelier, 1884). Powell (1974) found that only 3 percent of the families consisted of parents with married children.

12 *Padrón del pueblo de San Marcos Necoxtla* (Puebla, 1889). The village consisted of twenty-five dwellings. The population of the adjacent hacienda San Andrés was originally included in this census, but the records for all but two households have been destroyed. This municipal census was part of an incomplete national census, attempted by the Secretaría de Fomento. A microfilm copy is available in the library of the Museo de Antropología, Mexico City.

13 These figures represent a typical combination of incomes compiled from various descriptive and quantitative sources, especially the budget studies published by the Dirección General de Estadística (1943) and the Banco de México (1966). For a detailed analysis, see Thompson (1989: 283–89).

14 In 1939, 1940, and 1941, budget studies were carried out among rural laborers, sharecroppers, smallholders, and *ejidatarios* in the states of Jalisco, Guanajuato, Michoacán, and Aguascalientes. The results were published in the *Anuario estadístico de los Estados Unidos Méxicanos* (Dirección General de Estadística, 1941, 1943).

15 The studies of Lewis (1959, 1963) show that women's work daily took as much as 23 to 24 hours divided among 2 or 3 women, i.e., a mother and her daughters. In addition to this, male children might be entrusted with the care of domestic animals and with carrying water. Belshaw's (1967) study confirms the long hours spent in domestic work. His examples ranged from 15 to 16 hours with one woman working, to 22 to 30 with a mother and her daughter occupied. The study by Beals (1970) found that women's domestic tasks ranged from 5 to 10 hours a day, but the author admitted that many tasks, such as marketing, went unreported. Other descriptive evidence can be found in Arizpe (1973), Taggart (1975), and Alonso (1984).

16 Some evidence of this process has been compiled by Thompson (1989: 296–99).

17 Lewis (1963: 155) estimated the time spent in the cultivation of one hectare to be 48 "man days" yearly for plow culture, and 143 "man days" for hoe culture.

18 The budget studies of 1941 found the average family size to be 5.4 among the rural laborers and 5.9 among the *ejidatarios*. In 1963, the family size among laborers was found to be 5.5, among the "self-employed" 6.3 (Banco de México, 1966). In the early 1970s, the average family size among the *ejidatarios* was found to be 6.6, and among the rural laborers, 4.9 (CDIA, 1973: 307). Arizpe (1980) found the families of *ejidatarios* to be between 6.2 and 6.8. In 1977, it was found that families headed by those employed in agriculture averaged 6.0 (Secretaría de Programación y Presupuesto, México, 1981: 67).

IV

Southern Africa

Introduction

Mark Beittel

In the late nineteenth and early twentieth centuries, the huge expanse of territory which is now known as the region of southern Africa was incorporated into the periphery of the world-economy. In the middle decades of the twentieth century, South Africa, one state in this region, became part of the semiperiphery of the world-economy. Each of these transformations had far-reaching effects: the former established southern Africa as a major supplier of minerals – diamonds, gold, and copper; the latter established South Africa as the most highly industrialized country in all of Africa and as the dominant political power in the region.

The primary locus of these transformations was the Witwatersrand (or Rand), which until the mid-1880s was a sparsely populated and isolated strip of the interior. Initially developed as a mining complex, and subsequently as a center of manufacturing, finance, and commerce, the Rand attracted immigrants not only from throughout the region but also from the far corners of the globe. The expanding labor force relied simultaneously on periodic waves of White and Black permanent settlers, and on the establishment and maintenance of a coercive system of oscillating migration for Africans.[1]

The racial divisioning of the labor force provided the foundation upon which South Africa's system of racial domination was built. Yet it would be specious to interpret the history of the region solely in terms of White versus Black, for there has been a considerable degree of differentiation and segmentation within each racial group. The introduction of apartheid policies in South Africa, for example, was not only a measure taken to protect White workers from Black competition, but also a means to satisfy the rapidly changing and at times conflicting labor requirements of South Africa's White farmers, industrialists, and mine owners.

189

Prior to around 1870, the only parts of southern Africa which were fully incorporated into the world-economy were the coastal colonies of the British and the Portuguese. For centuries these outposts had served as way-stations for ships and as suppliers of agricultural products. In the interior, independent African and Afrikaner farming communities were still free of the grip of colonial rule, and were only tenuously connected by trade relationships to the world-economy. From the 1860s onwards, however, the discovery and subsequent exploitation of precious mineral resources drove the process of incorporation forward, and the whole social and political landscape of the interior was altered: new production processes were implanted; colonial and settler political authority was extended and deepened; the form of labor exploitation and the organization of rural social structures were radically changed.

On the Rand itself, the effects of the discovery of a sizeable outcrop of gold-bearing reef in 1886 were dramatic. Within the short span of twelve years, an area which had been occupied previously by a few simple farms was transformed into a mining complex producing no less than 27 percent of the world's total gold output. By the First World War this figure had risen to 40 percent and during the 1920s it actually exceeded 50 percent (Transvaal Chamber of Mines, 1937). Though the gold mining industry on the Rand went into decline in the 1940s, far more gold has been removed from the Rand than from any comparable place on earth.

At the time of the initial gold discoveries, the Rand was part of the territory of the Afrikaner-controlled South African Republic. As the scale and potential wealth of the mineral deposits became apparent, the Republic threatened to eclipse the wealth and power of the neighboring British colonies. This situation eventually led to the South African War (1899–1902), which the British won. The Rand and its surrounding countryside was then administered as the Transvaal Colony until 1910, when four of the British colonies in southern Africa were amalgamated into the Union of South Africa. A series of developments in subsequent years strengthened the Union's autonomy and, in 1961, South Africa declared itself a Republic.

Johannesburg, situated at the midpoint of the gold reef, is the nerve center of the transformations that have occurred on the Rand. While today it is the hub of a vast conurbation of industrial zones, business districts, and segregated residential areas, just a century ago it was a mining camp which few thought would acquire any permanence. Far from following the fate of other frontier mining outposts, Johannesburg was guaranteed enduring centrality in the development of southern Africa by the large deep-level mines that were required to exploit the gold. Yet a second great transformation emerged even here with the implanting of industrial production.

The disruptions in the world-economy caused by the First World War allowed South Africa to embark on a program of import substitution. While the onset of the depression hampered this process, the 1932 decision by the Union government to abandon the gold standard for its currency, an act which effectively increased the price of gold, not only launched a renewed round of expansion in the gold mining industry but also stimulated large-scale investment in manufacturing. By the beginning of the Second World War, it was already clear that South Africa was well on its way toward joining the ranks of the industrializing, semiperipheral states.

During the war, the cutoff of imports and the production of war materials spurred the growth of South Africa's metal and engineering industries, and for the first time the value of the country's manufacturing output surpassed that of both mining and agriculture. This marked just the beginnings of a long period of absolute and relative growth in manufacturing as well as of expansion in all sectors of the economy. But the overall trend was not without significant interruptions: a serious recession in the early 1960s was caused by the international outcry over the Sharpeville shootings and a resulting loss of confidence by investors. As a result both of the tough measures adopted by the government to crush political opposition and of the massive inflow of foreign capital, the period between 1963 and 1973 was marked by a spectacular rate of economic growth.

The effects of the contemporary global Kondratieff B-phase began to be felt throughout southern Africa in the mid-1970s, and were exacerbated in South Africa itself by the crisis invoked by the Soweto uprising and by the victory of liberation movements in Mozambique and Angola. Nevertheless, the soaring price of gold during the late 1970s sheltered South African industry and the initial downturn was followed by a spectacular boom. However, this proved to be short-lived; by the mid-1980s the South African economy was in deep trouble, while the regime was confronted by the most serious political challenge ever mounted by the Black majority.

The development of the Rand as an urban-industrial complex has always rested upon deep relationships with rural southern Africa. The surrounding countryside has provided the sinews of the Rand's labor force and the markets for its services and manufacturing output. These complex relationships have varied over time in substance and direction, and no single rural area can possibly be considered typical of the processes at work over the course of the last century (Martin and Beittel, 1987). Nevertheless, it is clear that the study of labor force formation on the Rand cannot be restricted within its own boundaries. In recognition of these realities, we have examined one rural area long entangled in the development of the Rand – Lesotho, a small mountainous country completely surrounded by South Africa. Forged as a nation in the nineteenth century during the conflict between African communities, the Afrikaner settlers, and the British colonizers, Lesotho's present boundaries were set in 1869 as the British colony of Basutoland. In 1966, when it achieved independence, it changed its name.

Economic life in Lesotho has been bound up with that of South Africa since the mid-nineteenth century. Indeed, until the early 1960s Lesotho was presumed to become part of the territory of South Africa by almost all observers, and in particular by British and South African statesmen. This supported the promotion of open economic ties between the two areas, setting Lesotho apart from some of the other labor-supplying territories in the region. This is why today, no less than fifty years ago, its economic life remains interwoven with that of the powerful surrounding neighbor.

In southern Africa, state policies and administrative mechanisms have had a decisive impact on emerging household structures. During the nineteenth century, regional governments were extensively involved in mobilizing and channeling flows of waged labor. They used a variety of methods to force African men onto the labor market: the dispossession of African lands through conquest, the introduction of individual land tenure, the imposition of taxes payable in cash, and the enforcement of vagrancy laws. In South Africa, during the twentieth century, restrictions on African access to agricultural land have played a continuing role in maintaining the supply of labor. The Natives' Lands Act (1913) sharply restricted the number of African squatters on White farms and provided that Africans could not buy or obtain title to land outside of "scheduled areas" (then commonly known as the "reserves," more recently as the "Bantustans" or "homelands"). At the time of the Act, such "scheduled areas" comprised a mere 7 percent of total area of country; in 1936, amending legislation brought this figure to approximately 13 percent. Despite tremendous overcrowding on these lands, however, not even all of this quota has ever actually been in the hands of African owners.

The mobility of African labor has long been controlled by a complex body of legislation and administrative machinery known as the pass system. The origins of the system can be traced back to the eighteenth century, when the function of passes was to tie servants to masters and prevent the formation of a labor market. During incorporation, the system was adapted to suit the mining industry's need for cheap labor, and passes were used to promote organized labor recruitment, enforce employment contracts, as well as prevent the permanent settlement of workers and their dependents in mining districts. Following the First World War, the pass system was reorganized in an attempt to limit the pace of African urbanization and to protect the supply of rural labor for White farmers. After the Second World War, the function of the system was again modified to suit the needs of the growing manufacturing sector while protecting the interests of White farmers and mine owners. Until they were abolished in 1986, the pass laws played a crucial role in differentiating urban African workers into groups of temporary migrants and residentially stable urban dwellers (Hindson, 1987).

A host of other state measures were directed at establishing segregation in urban areas and, most importantly for the Rand, at requiring Africans to reside in municipally owned and rigidly administered townships. The Natives (Urban Areas) Act (1923) established the basis of residential segregation by prohibiting the sale of land in urban areas to Africans. During the 1920s and 1930s, sanitation and slum clearance measures were used to relocate Africans dwelling in inner city areas. From the 1940s onwards, the authorities increasingly took measures against the large communities of African squatters that had settled on the outskirts of major towns. The Group Areas Act (1950) provided for the establishment in cities and towns of specific areas for exclusive occupancy by a particular racial group. It gave the government the power to force the members of a racial group not designated for occupancy of a specific area to sell their property to those of the "right" one, and to compel the displaced tenants to move into areas proclaimed as their "group area."

State efforts to regulate mobility and residence have had tremendous effects on African households, most notably in terms of dividing families, obstructing urbanization, and increasing the cost of living. In the name of sanitation, slum clearance, and upgrading, as well as group areas and segregation, millions of Blacks have been coerced into moving from one urban area to another or else "endorsed out" of urban areas altogether. In the latter process many families have been forcibly divided, as only some members qualified for "exemptions" were allowed to remain in urban areas while others did not. Many people have stayed illegally, but their lack of documentation has sharply disadvantaged them from obtaining what is, for Black workers, well-paying and steady employment. Moreover the fact that municipal townships are almost always located far from the places where Africans must go to work has undoubtedly increased the cost of living.

The electoral victory of the Nationalist Party in 1948 formalized and extended racial discrimination. The Population Registration Act (1950) provided for the classification of the entire population according to ancestry, appearance, and general acceptance by the community. This was the basis for enforcing a whole range of racial legislation, including such "petty" apartheid measures as segregated amenities and prohibitions on "mixed" marriages and "inter-racial" sexual relations, to the "grand" apartheid scheme of dividing the territory of South Africa in a way that would assure continued White control over the state apparatus.

One of the central planks of the National Party's apartheid program was that separate, self-governing states should be formed for Africans in the Bantustans. The Bantu Homelands Citizenship Act (1970) dictated that every African would become a "citizen" of the Bantustan to which the state decreed they were attached by birth, domicile, or cultural affiliation, even if they had never visited, let alone resided, there. So, as the Bantustans were declared "independent" or "self-governing" by the central government from the mid-1970s, their inhabitants were deprived of their South African citizenship. In this way the government sought to create a residual "White" South African state with no African nationals. Consequently the millions of Africans who continued to live and work in South Africa were to be considered aliens, and would not be able to claim political rights.

The policy of depriving Africans of their South African citizenship should be seen as an attempt to create what the government hoped would be an internationally acceptable system of migrant labor. While no country other than South Africa has recognized the legitimacy of the Bantustans, the system has served to strengthen the hand of the state in preventing the relocation of rural households in urban areas and in reinforcing the disabilities of rural migrants in the urban labor market. In 1986, under mounting political pressure, the government passed the Restoration of South African Citizenship Act, which made it possible (though difficult) for certain categories of Africans who had lost South African citizenship to regain it.

Many pieces of legislation directly affected the prospects of wage employment on a racial basis, while others impacted it in less direct ways. The "colour bar" and "civilized labor" policies both limited African employment opportunities: the former by restricting certain specific jobs to Whites, primarily but not exclusively in the mining industry; the latter by promoting the replacement of Black workers by Whites in state employment. Other state policies and administrative mechanisms blocked or hindered Africans from obtaining skilled employment, and undermined the bargaining position of Black workers in the labor market. Suffice it to mention the many restrictions placed on Black trade union activity.

The state also limited Black participation in market activities. Of crucial importance has been the Group Areas Act (1950) which, in addition to strengthening residential segregation, also restricted commercial activities along racial lines. Blacks were barred from owning shops or businesses in "White" areas, being permitted only to operate as hawkers. But even this activity was subject to licensing by local authorities, who frequently restricted it. Other market activities were directly banned by the state or the state regulated them in ways that sharply reduced their profitability.

In South Africa, there has never been even the pretense of equality in social services, and this undoubtedly has exacerbated racial differences in household structures. For instance, unequal educational facilities have restricted employment opportunities for Blacks, and the system of state transfer payments has powerfully reinforced racial discrepancies in household income. Since the 1930s, social welfare provisions have provided best for the section of the population least in need of such services, the Whites, while granting those in the greatest need, the Black population, only minute levels of support. An integral part of the Bantustan policy has been to shed responsibility for African welfare to the Bantustan "governments," a means employed by the South African state to deflect growing political demands for increased social services.

NOTE

1 In this section, the term "Black" is used collectively to denote those people of African, Asian, and so-called Coloured descent, while the term "White" is used to refer to those people of British, Afrikaner, and other European descent. The more specific terminology – e.g., "Africans" – is used where a narrower meaning is intended.

CHAPTER I

The Witwatersrand: Black households, White households

Mark Beittel

The proposition that the households of the urban working class in South Africa are sustained solely by wages has long beeen contradicted by evidence of non-wage sources of income. Over half a century ago, for example, the members of the Native Economic Commission contended that "the urbanized Native is dependent for the support of his family purely on his wages," but noted that men's wages were so low that "most Native wives in urban areas have to do something to supplement the family income" (Union of South Africa, 1932b: 78, 140). Nonetheless, more recently, the proposition has been advanced anew by radical scholars such as Wolpe, who maintains that a large and growing proportion of urban Africans have become "fully dependent upon wages for subsistence" (1972: 444). Still, the conflicting evidence persists, and it is time to appraise the proposition in light of the historical pattern of household formation in South Africa's industrial heartland.

The incorporation of the Rand into the capitalist world-economy as a mining complex entailed massive immigration by both Whites and Blacks. In 1887, the population of Johannesburg and the surrounding mining camps was only around 3,000 people (Johannesburg Sanitary Department, 1896: vi). Less than a decade later, over 100,000 people resided within a three-mile radius of Johannesburg's Market Square. The Rand was a center of attraction to men in the prime of their working lives to the extent that in the mid-1890s, the disparity between the number of men and women was higher than 2:1 among Whites and 30:1 among Africans (see Table 16).

During this period, the mining industry shaped all facets of life and effectively dictated the pattern and conditions of employment. This is hardly surprising, since a huge proportion of the Rand's labor force was directly employed by the mines or in ancillary industries.

Table 16. *Composition of the population on the Witwatersrand, 1896–1980*

	1896	1911	1936	1960	1980
Total population (in 1000s)	102	496	1,017	2,210	3,713
Proportion African	42%	56%	56%	60%	61%
Proportion White	50%	39%	40%	35%	33%
Proportion Asian and Coloured	9%	5%	4%	6%	6%
African population (in 1000s)	43	279	571	1,317	2,276
Men	40	(255)	435	633	1,045
Women	1	(11)	76	330	670
Children (under 15 years)	1	(13)	60	353	561
Ratio of men to women	32:1	(23:1)	5.7:1	1.9:1	1.6:1
Proportion of children	2%	(5%)	11%	27%	25%
In the labor force					
African men	n/a	n/a	(>425)	614	867
African women	n/a	n/a	(<38)	163	382
Labor force participation rate					
African men	n/a	n/a	(>95%)	97%	83%[a]
African women	n/a	n/a	(<50%)[b]	50%	57%
White population (in 1000s)	51	193	402	773	1,209
Men	26	81	149	259	427
Women	12	52	142	267	444
Children (under 15 years)	13	59	111	247	337
Ratio of men to women	2.2:1	1.6:1	1.1:1	1.0:1	1.0:1
Proportion children	26%	31%	28%	32%	28%
In the labor force					
White men	n/a	n/a	134	225	348
White women	n/a	n/a	37	91	193
Labor force participation rate					
White men	n/a	n/a	90%	87%	81%
White women	n/a	n/a	26%	34%	43%

Notes:

It is widely acknowledged that the South African census has substantially under-counted Africans over the years. Changes in the boundaries of census districts have necessitated the construction of a definition of the Rand that is not strictly comparable over time; for a variety of reasons labor force participation rates for Africans must be considered approximate. Nevertheless, the figures indicate major trends. Figures in parentheses are estimates; 'n.a.' means that information is not available and no reasonable estimate could be made.

[a] The apparent sharp drop in the labor force participation rate between 1960 and 1980 reflects some real changes – a decline in the relative proportion of male migrants on the Rand and longer school attendance in part – and, evidently, some change in the manner in which the figures were compiled.

Whites occupied virtually all jobs requiring skill or authority, while Africans were mostly employed as unskilled laborers. African men were also extensively engaged as domestic servants. White women who were employed worked as nurses, housemaids, and cooks in the households of the well-to-do and in boarding houses and hotels. They provided other paid services for the male population as well. One estimate is that no less than "10 per cent of all white women over the age of fifteen in Johannesburg were prostitutes" (van Onselen 1982a: 104).

The pattern of wage levels was established by the mining industry, where there was a tremendous gap between the cash earnings of migrant African laborers and those of skilled White workers. Africans earned on average about £3 a month, less than 15 percent of average White earnings (Transvaal Colony, 1903: Exhibit 1; Zuid-Afrikaansche Republiek, 1897: Statement 7). It has been asserted that the pound-a-day standard for skilled White miners on the Rand established them as "the money wage leaders not only in South Africa but, probably, also in the world" (Golding, 1976: 81). The scarcity of skilled workers, coupled with their crucial organizing role in the labor process, bid up wage levels for the skilled segment of the labor force.

By the mid-1890s, only a small proportion of immigrant White workers were prepared to commit their families to a life in the interior of southern Africa. In 1897, less than 13 percent of White

Notes to Table 16 *(cont.)*

[b] Though based on employment figures for the Rand in 1936, this figure is somewhat misleading. The relatively large number of African women working as domestic servants and living on the premises of their employers at this time makes it appear as if there was a fairly high labor force participation rate for all African women. This was probably not so for urban-based women, most of whom worked in domestic service on only an irregular or part-time basis and lived in African residential areas. Other evidence indicates that there was a sharp rise in the labor force participation rate for African women between the 1930s and the 1950s. Note also that there was a huge growth in the number of African women in the labor force between 1936 and 1960.

Sources: Johannesburg, Sanitary Department (1896); Union of South Africa, Census Office (1912); Union of South Africa, Office of Census and Statistics (1938b, 1942); Republic of South Africa, Bureau of Statistics (1968b); Republic of South Africa, Central Statistical Services (1985).

mine employees were married and had their families living with them, while 33 percent were married but had their families living abroad (Union of South Africa, 1913: 12). Though many factors may have discouraged men from bringing or establishing families on the Rand, the single greatest obstacle was probably the extra-ordinarily high cost of living. Even after Johannesburg was con-nected by rail to the coast in the 1890s, the cost of food, clothing, and rent were much higher than on the coast or in Great Britain (Golding, 1976: 27, 47).

Under these conditions, it was mostly well-paid, skilled White workers that were able to establish urban households during the 1890s. These households, typically composed of a nuclear family, relied on women members with the assistance of a "houseboy" for domestic work. Although they were highly dependent on the income derived from a man's wage, they would commonly take in a lodger to help make ends meet (van Onselen, 1982b: 3). It should be emphasized that no more than 10 percent of the total labor force of the mines were accommodated in households of this type by the mid-1890s. The vast majority of mine workers lived as single men on the Rand, usually retaining links to households located elsewhere in southern Africa or in Europe. Single White mine workers either shared houses with other White men (often hiring a "houseboy" to undertake their domestic chores), lived as lodgers with White families, or took up residence in the many boarding houses which sprang up specifically to fill their needs. African workers were housed largely in barrack-like compounds, a system that had first been established in the diamond mines at Kimberley, but which was rapidly adopted by the Rand's mine owners as part of their strategy for controlling African workers.

Following the unification of South Africa in 1910, the first national census enumerated the population of the Rand at just under a half-million persons. Among Whites, the ratio between men and women had fallen to 1.6:1, while among Africans it remained very high (at least 23:1). The decline in the ratio for Whites had occurred primarily after the Anglo-Boer War (1899–1902), as growing numbers of Afrikaner families fled from the rural devas-tation caused by the effects of the cattle disease rinderpest, from the military actions of the British during the war, and from recurring drought. Gradually the main source of White immigration to the

Rand had shifted from skilled foreign workers to dispossessed Afrikaner farmers.

While the Rand's labor force had grown markedly in size, its composition remained fundamentally unchanged. The pattern of wages continued to be set by the mines, where the gap between average White and African earnings was greater in 1913 than it had been in the 1890s. While the nominal wage for skilled White workers had not significantly risen since the 1890s, its value increased nearly 50 percent as the cost of living on the Rand was reduced and brought more into line with coastal prices (Golding, 1976: 185, 207). By contrast, African wage levels fell both for mine laborers and domestic servants (van der Horst, 1971: 205; van Onselen, 1982b: 20–21).

Comparing the 1910s to the 1890s, a considerable shift is notable in the residence pattern of White mine employees: the proportion of those who were married and resided with their families rose to 42 percent, while just 8 percent were married but had families living overseas (Union of South Africa, 1913: 12). Skilled workers increasingly abandoned the inner city boarding houses and established themselves in family households in White working-class suburbs. The urban household type associated with these workers was becoming more widespread and financially secure, thanks to the decline in the cost of living and the ability of skilled workers to defend their wage levels through collective action.

Budget studies of "artisan" households established that the wage of a single male worker could cover the cash requirements of a hypothetical White family on the Rand adequately (Aiken, 1907; Transvaal Colony, 1908; Transvaal Chamber of Mines, 1914; Union of South Africa, 1914). Aiken, who was sympathetic to the plight of White workers, viewed the pound-a-day standard as a "never-ceasing effort for the family man to keep his expenditure within his income" (1907: 7–8). The Transvaal Chamber of Mines, however, staunchly maintained that a White "artisan" on the Rand earned a real wage higher than his counterpart did in the industrialized countries (with the possible exception of the United States), and enjoyed "a higher standard of existence" (1914: 313–14). The Chamber offered two pieces of evidence in support of this claim: the typical household budget of a White "artisan" on the Rand, compared to its British counterpart, showed that there was very little

household income in addition to the wage earnings of the male
worker; the widespread practice of keeping servants sharply differentiated South African from British habit. In considering this evidence,
the Economic Commission observed that "convention half ordains
that every family should have at least one native servant, whether
the family is of the servant-keeping class, according to English
standards, or not." The Commission concluded that "a native must
be reckoned as a part of the artisan's actual cost of living in South
Africa – one might even say as a part of his necessary cost of living in
a not overstrained sense" (Union of South Africa, 1914: 22).

The bargaining power of skilled White workers – their relative
scarcity, their key role in production, plus their organizational
skills – allowed them to carve out and defend a high standard of
living, not only in comparison to African laborers but in comparison
to their counterparts in core areas of the world-economy. The urban
household type associated with these workers was heavily dependent
upon the wages of a single male earner; the only other significant
source of cash income was rent paid by lodgers. This practice
remained a crucial form of income for widowed or divorced women –
in this sense, it continued to be an important source of income for
many White households over the course of their lifetime. However, it
declined over time and the proportion of household income derived
from wages tended to increase. By the 1910s, the households of
skilled White workers probably received at least 90 percent of their
cash income from a man's wage earnings. They typically were
composed of a nuclear family, and enjoyed the full-time services of a
"houseboy."[1]

While the households of skilled White workers constituted the
main urban household type formed during this period, other Whites
and Blacks lacking the skills to command higher wages were flocking
onto the Rand. In the volatile colonial context of the Transvaal, it
was the status and demands of "poor Whites" – primarily Afrikaners
fleeing deteriorating rural conditions – which at this time posed the
gravest social threat to the colonial order. "Poor Whites" were
unable to compete effectively with African migrants for unskilled
work. The wages offered for this kind of labor were so low that urban
life on a so-called "civilized" standard would have been impossible
to realize. The alternative was to identify non-wage niches in the
Rand's growing economy and carve out a precarious urban existence as small-scale brickmakers, as providers of animal-drawn

transport, or as participants in the lucrative trade of selling liquor to Blacks illegally. The latter activity alone reportedly provided a living for as much as 10 percent of the "poor White" population (Lewis, 1984: 25).

Prior to the First World War, the numbers of Africans who came to work on the Rand grew quite quickly, but few of them established what could be considered permanent urban residence. Undoubtedly many factors contributed to this pattern of labor force formation, yet no single one was as important as that of the continuing access to rural lands by Africans. However, since this also served to constrain the supply of African labor to White-owned capitalist enterprises, pressures inevitably mounted on Africans to migrate permanently to town, with the result that the pace of African urbanization began to accelerate.

After the First World War, the concentrated demand for consumer goods provided by an expanding urban population, and the growth of an engineering and metal industry to service the mines resulted in the Rand becoming the main center of manufacturing in South Africa. In contrast to mining ventures elsewhere in Africa, gold mining on the Rand was matched by investment in manufacturing and the development of a diversified infrastructure. This served to promote further the Rand's position as the commercial and financial center of the region. In other words, South Africa had "found its Ruhr" (Freund, 1989: 91).

By 1936, the population of the Rand had grown to over a million persons and there had been significant demographic changes. The ratio of men to women had fallen to 1.1:1 for Whites and had narrowed to less than 6:1 for Africans. The latter development reflected a massive migration of African women onto the Rand since the First World War. Clearly the number of African families resident in urban areas had grown dramatically since the 1910s, as indicated by a sharp reduction in the male-to-female ratio and by the growing proportion of the African population under 15 years of age.

Substantial changes in African residential patterns also occurred. Vast numbers of African men and women continued to be accommodated in rooms or shacks behind the White homes in which they were employed as domestic servants, while tens of thousands of male migrants lived in single-sex hostels on mine, municipal, and private property. But in addition to these forms of accommodation, there were several types of residence which offered urban Africans the possibility of family life. During and following the First World War, many made their homes in the inner-city slum yards of Johannesburg and other Rand towns. The government, however, was implacably hostile to these yards and sought to relocate urban Africans to newly created municipal townships, located far outside town centers and subject to much stricter forms of control.

Large numbers of Afrikaners also continued to migrate from rural areas onto the Rand. The "Poor White Problem" remained a subject which attracted public attention through the mid-1930s. Many "poor Whites" congregated in racially mixed, highly congested slums. Others were successful in finding a "sitting place" in periurban areas where they could find larger plots, cultivate gardens, and keep a few animals (Carnegie Commission, 1932: 220–21).

During the 1930s, the labor force participation rate for both African and White men was high. The principal source of employment for African men remained the mining industry, which relied almost entirely on migrants for the African component of its labor force. African men residing in urban areas were much more likely to work as laborers in industry or commerce. Many more White men were engaged in manufacturing and construction jobs than were employed in the mines, but in contrast to African workers, most of them lived with their families. They continued to occupy all skilled and supervisory jobs, most semiskilled jobs, and some legally protected unskilled positions as well.

The labor force participation rate was much higher for African than for White women, reflecting the growing number of African women who had gone into domestic service. A large proportion of White women were engaged in what the census called "household duties at home," and thus not considered to be "in the labor force." Employed White women were concentrated in commercial, clerical, and manufacturing jobs. Afrikaner women constituted a sizeable portion of the labor force in the expanding garment and food-processing industries.

The Board of Trade and Industries argued that the wage structure of South Africa was "peculiar":

Whereas in the Western World the spread between the highest and lowest rates of wages is usually about 30 percent, and seldom more than 50 percent, in the Union it is several hundred percent. The skilled craftsman in many industries earns as much in a day as the unskilled workman does in a week. (Union of South Africa, Board of Trade and Industries, 1945: 43)

Given the divisioning of labor, this huge differential of course coincided with race: African laborers earned in a week roughly what White employees earned in a day. Figures for the mid-1930s indicate that African men in industry and commerce were making about £4 a month, while White male employees were making at least £25 (Union of South Africa, Office of Census and Statistics, 1938a; Hellmann, 1948). Skilled White workers and supervisors earned much more.

White women's wages were much lower than those of White men, but much higher than those of African men. During the early 1930s, the average rate of wages for White women in the garment industry was a little over £7 a month, which was less than half of the prevailing manufacturing wage for Whites (Pollak, 1933). Employment opportunities for African women were limited to domestic service, where cash earnings amounted to between £1 and £2 a month (Hellmann, 1948; Union of South Africa, 1946).

The household type associated with skilled White workers and, by the 1930s, with a growing number of White supervisors of African labor was initially established before the First World War. There is little reason to suspect that its composition or income-pooling practices changed markedly during the interwar period. A report on White households in 1921 concluded that "it is clear that the average household of the Witwatersrand area was the *family* (as distinguished from the *household*) of husband and wife with one or more children – the husband a breadwinner and the wife performing household duties at home" (Union of South Africa, Office of Census and Statistics, 1921: 176). The majority of White households relied on a single "breadwinner," and only about 10 percent of White households hosted a boarder or lodger. Fifteen years later, a budget survey found that White households in the income bracket of a skilled worker were almost completely reliant on the wage or salary of male "head of household" (Union of South Africa, Office of Census and Statistics, 1937). The budget survey also indicated that the majority of these households employed domestic servants. In this regard, one prominent historian has observed:

Even as a skilled worker of the United States did not regard his motor-car as a luxury, so was the South African skilled worker inclined to consider native help for the grosser tasks of the home as a necessary part of the cost of living. Unique amongst the skilled workers of the Empire, the South

African artisan revealed his especial rank by being himself a frequent employer of labor. (de Kieweit, 1957: 209)

While the depression had a short-term impact on the households of skilled White workers, it hit much harder those of "poor Whites." White men without skills, argues Brink, "had to compete on an already oversupplied white labor market to find employment, and within the field of unskilled labor had to face competition from a much larger and cheaper black labour force as well" (1986: 2–3). Lack of employment opportunities for White men in urban areas drove the daughters and mothers of "poor White" families into the wage labor force. As the Carnegie Commission noted: "The earnings of the girls are of great importance to the poor family; particularly in the cities the family forms the wage-earning unit" (1932: xxiii; see also p. 184).

In the early 1930s Pollak found that, contrary to popular opinion, White women factory workers made substantial contributions to the income of their households. Women who were married or divorced but living with families usually contributed their entire wage to the household consumption fund; on average this amounted to nearly 64 percent of these households' total income. Daughters on average contributed two-thirds of their wages to the household consumption fund; this represented about 23 percent of these households' income. Pollak determined that, in 40 percent of the households investigated, women were the chief wage earners, though their wages were often supplemented by the earnings of younger brothers or sisters (1931: 579–81).

Two variants of an urban "poor White" household type were common during this period. In the inner city slums, where the more destitute "poor Whites" congregated, the cash component of household income was primarily derived from wages, much of which was earned by women. In the periurban areas, "poor White" households were able to acquire a small plot of irrigable land and meet a sizeable portion of their subsistence needs as well as perhaps to sell their surplus production. "But generally," the Carnegie Commission notes, "all these people are regularly employed in town, and travel to and from by motor bus or bicycle or suburban train" (1932: 221). This variant of the "poor White" household type was still essentially wage-centered but would have relied to a significant extent on subsistence production and, probably, on some market income.

Major governmental efforts had been made since the late nineteenth century to elevate the circumstances of "poor Whites." These policies, in conjunction with the economic boom that followed South Africa's departure from the gold standard in 1932, transformed the urban "poor White" household type. New opportunities were made available for unskilled White men, and the households of "poor Whites" became more like those of skilled Whites, although with a somewhat lower standard of living. This was compensated for in many cases by the wages earned by working wives and daughters, whose labor at first in factories and later in offices and shops allowed these households to consume at a "civilized" level.

By the end of the interwar period it is appropriate to think of a single general type of urban White household. While graduated by income level, most White households could afford a comfortable, or better, standard of living on the income of a single male wage earner. Most White households could readily afford the services of at least a part-time domestic servant and the employment of full-time maids was very common. Some White women continued to work for wages, allowing their households to consume at a higher level than would otherwise be possible. The White household type was probably 90 percent reliant on wages to cover its cash requirements, though these wages could variably be earned by a single male or by multiple earners. The main deviation from this household type would have been the small and declining number of White households in periurban areas which were able to supplement wages with agricultural earnings.

Even in the midst of the depression, "poor Whites" on the Rand were few in comparison to the vast number of poverty-stricken Blacks. Moreover, by the mid-1930s the conditions were significantly improving for "poor Whites," while they were deteriorating for urban Africans. In 1937, a Johannesburg City Councillor declared that nearly 100,000 Africans lived on the Rand "without visible means of subsistence" (Phillips, 1938: xxiv). Several years later a committee made up of prominent government officials reported that urban Africans suffered from overcrowding, malnutrition, lack of sanitation, and widespread unemployment (Union of South Africa, Department of Native Affairs, 1942), while a government commission concluded that 87 percent of the African households on the Rand lived below the "Poverty Datum Line" (Union of South Africa, 1944). The combined effect of these conditions was extraordinarily high morbidity and mortality rates. In 1940, for instance, the infant mortality rate for Africans in Johannesburg was 580 per thousand, more than ten times the comparable figure for Whites (Koch, 1983: 158).

It was under these harsh conditions that an urban African household type was established on the Rand. Its most striking feature was the low level of wages on which it was based. As the Economic and Wage Commission observed:

The urbanized native ... who has lost all connection with his pastoral origin and become detribalized, is in the same position as the white wage-earner. He finds the cost of living high, since he has to conform to urban requirements as to housing, clothing and transportation, and to pay urban prices for food; while the level of wages he is likely to receive is kept down in the neighborhood of the standard set by natives from reserves, living in compounds and working to supplement their agricultural livelihood. (Union of South Africa, 1926: 37).

A series of studies subsequently demonstrated that the average wages of a male worker would cover only a fraction – from one-half to two-thirds – of the "necessary" expenditure of a hypothetical urban African family.[2]

Hellmann's fine study of Rooiyard, an urban slum yard in Johannesburg under threat of removal, addressed the crucial economic problem of how urban residents could survive on low wages during the mid-1930s. She determined that the income of a male wage earner was "too low to meet such expenditure as [was] considered essential for healthy well-being"; in fact she argues that such income was not even sufficient "to meet actual expenditure, which ... often falls far short of the stipulated essential expenditure" (1948: 37). Hellmann persuasively demonstrated that the key to urban survival for African households was women's work: "Under tribal conditions that Bantu woman was an economic asset; on her work in the fields the family was dependent for its subsistence. In an urban area, such as Johannesburg, she is of no less importance, but the nature of her work has changed" (1948: 37). Hellmann showed that by far the most substantial cash contribution by women residing in the slum yards was obtained from brewing and selling beer, and not from wages.

"Practically every woman" in Rooiyard was involved in this illegal activity, and any woman who refused to participate was considered to be a "bad wife" (1948: 24, 40). Africans "eat from beer," said one brewer, and Hellmann estimated that a woman could make anywhere from £1 5s. to £4 15s. per month by selling beer to the many African men that lived in town without wives to brew for them. The vital importance of beer as a source of income for urban women can be gauged by comparing it to the average £4 a month earned by male laborers and the approximately £1 a month earned by women in part-time domestic service. All other "legitimate" sources of women's income – laundry work, hawking, and dressmaking were common – yielded far less cash. Nevertheless, taking in laundry from White households had several advantages over domestic service and, though it yielded only about £1 a month in income, it had become a widespread activity by the 1930s (Hellmann, 1948: 38; Union of South Africa, 1944: 11–12). The main advantage of laundry work was that it was done at home in the yards or townships, and hence allowed women to keep an eye on children, engage in beer production, and to be free of the immediate supervision of employers. Like domestic service, washing for White households had been an occupation for African men prior to the 1920s while it became an important source of income for African women during the interwar years (Beavon and Rogerson, 1986a). Declining returns probably account for the "feminization" of both activities.

Earnings by children and rent from subtenants were among the other resources available to some urban Africans, but it is unlikely that yard-dwellers derived regular income from these activities. Hellmann found that many women in Rooiyard had "back-door husbands" from whom they regularly received gifts (1948: 89). Also prostitution was undoubtedly widespread. On the other hand, some women were able to decrease significantly their household's cash requirements in lieu of making money; domestic servants, for example, not only ate meals at work but received or stole food and clothing to bring home with them.

The composition of the urban African household type that was taking form was both variable and fluid. Hellmann maintains that the essential core of urban income pooling was a man and woman, with or without children. "A woman's beer profits and her husband's wages are usually merged," she found, and "the wife controls the joint fund" (1948: 51). In many cases the man and woman who pooled incomes were not married – by either customary, Christian, or civil rites – while in other cases hybrid forms of rites emerged, coupled with the exchange of *lobola*, a "bride price" formerly paid in cattle and now in cash. The distinctly urban practice of *vat en sit* – men and women living together because they had children – was apparently common, and Koch argues that it "was clearly the crucial means whereby the informal production of the yards and income from formal employment were harnessed together to provide for the working class family's subsistence needs" (1983: 162). Hellmann notes that most Rooiyard families included children but many had been sent to live with rural relatives. Women too were likely to spend stretches of time in the countryside, particularly during the harvest season. Urban households were also enlarged by "visiting" rural kin who might stay for lengthy periods of time and participate in income-pooling.

In testimony before the Native Economic Commission during the early 1930s, the Union's Director of Native Labour was of the opinion that in Johannesburg "it would probably be true to say that a minimum of £6 (per month) in the way of income is essential for the well-being of a Native family of four persons" (Union of South Africa, 1932b: 208). Taking this figure of £6 a month as a hypothetical minimum level of expenditure for an African household, a figure 50 percent higher – i.e., £9 a month during these years – can be usefully thought of as a sustainable minimum level of expenditure – a more adequate portrayal of the cost of generational reproduction.[3] On this basis, we can make some calculations about the proportion of household income derived from wages and market sources: the average £4 a month wage of an African male laborer would cover only 67 percent of the hypothetical minimum level of monthly expenditure, while the balance would have to be made up by a woman's earnings. Given the limited opportunities for, and the constraining effects of wage employment, there were basically two alternatives for African women: combining earnings from laundry work and brewing – perhaps £1 a month from each activity; or risking police interference and brewing on a larger scale. In either case, the hypothetical minimum level of expenditure could have been met only by adding a woman's market income (33 percent of the total) to a man's wages (67 percent of the total).

The average wage of an African man would cover only about 44 percent of the sustainable minimum level of household expenditure; a woman's income from taking in laundry would merely boost this figure to 56 percent. But if a woman worked very hard and risked brewing on a large scale, she might be able to match a man's wages, and together they could cover 89 percent of the sustainable minimum level. It is, however, unlikely that this level of activity could have been regularly maintained. A more realistic estimate of the monthly contribution from the different income sources might be: £4 (50 percent) from a man's wages; £3 (40 percent) from a woman's brewing activities; £1 (10 percent) from a shifting variety of other sources. The total income of £8 a month by this reckoning is probably high in comparison to actual levels but would still be a full £1 a month short of covering the sustainable minimum level of expenditure.

It is unlikely that most African households were ever able to earn, let alone to earn consistently, the sustainable level of £9 per month. The result was widespread deprivation and debt, even among those households which included a steadily employed man. Moreover, a heavy burden was placed on the adult female member, who not only was responsible for housework and child care activities but was relied upon to close the huge gap between the male's wage and the household's expenditure.

The downward pressure on African wage levels exerted by the system of oscillating migration assured that the urban African household type formed during the interwar years had to pool wages with income from other sources. While much variation no doubt existed, it seems that transfer payments – mostly *lobola* payments and gifts – were either infrequent or irrelevant, while rent income and subsistence production were severely constrained by the crowded conditions of slum yard life. The main source of non-wage income was derived from market activities, which in urban areas served a function in some ways analogous to agricultural production in the countryside. Even if the primary source of non-wage income was beer brewing by women, this household type had to engage in a range of other income-generating and expenditure-reducing activities. The members of such households were able to carve out at best a marginally sustainable level of urban existence, and lived in constant peril of both unemployment and police harassment.

After the Second World War, the Rand served as the core of a vital and expanding industrial complex in the southern Transvaal, while Johannesburg served as the commercial and financial center of the region. By the 1960s, mining had been eclipsed by both manufacturing and commerce as the main contributors to the

Rand's gross products. This shift in the Rand's economy is evident in the findings of the 1960 population census: a large proportion of African men was still classified as laborers, but they were mainly located in secondary industries and commerce rather than in mining. Changes in manufacturing production processes were creating a new layer of semiskilled operative positions increasingly filled by African men, as well as additional supervisory and technical positions filled mostly by White men. There had clearly been major occupational shifts for women since the 1930s as well. Large numbers of African women had entered into full-time employment in the service sector and had become the majority of domestic servants; working White women had moved out of manufacturing jobs and taken up clerical and sales positions.

Despite these important changes, by the mid-1950s the racial and gender pattern of wage earning remained essentially intact. African men employed as laborers in secondary industry and commerce were earning about £13 a month – at most 20 percent of what skilled White men in the same sectors were earning. White women employed as shop assistants or clerks were earning from 50 to 65 percent of the earnings of their White male colleagues but about three times more than the male African laborers working in the same establishments. African women engaged as domestic servants in private homes received about £5 a month in cash wages, much less than half of what an African man who worked as a laborer received (Republic of South Africa, Bureau of Statistics, 1964, 1968a; South African Institute of Race Relations, 1957).

There was also substantial change in the pattern of African residence on the Rand. A series of government measures slowed the rate of African urbanization, and relentlessly sought to dismantle any area where Africans held freehold titles or lived as illegal squatters. After a prolonged and bitter struggle, most Africans in the Johannesburg area were forced to take up residence in Soweto, a conglomeration of government-owned and rigidly controlled locations some 13 kilometers to the southwest of the city center. A minority of Africans was able to avoid this fate by virtue of the fact that they lived in Alexandra, a township that the government was unable to eliminate, or that they were domestic servants residing on their employers' property. Although illegally, servants working in apartment buildings were sometimes able to have their families live with them in their crowded roof-top rooms – an arrangement which came to be known as "locations in the sky."

A series of studies of the urban African cost of living established that the gap between estimated household income and essential expenditure widened until the mid-1950s and probably began to narrow thereafter (Union of South Africa, 1944; Wix, 1951; Gibson, 1954; de Gruchy, 1960; Suttner, 1966). In the mid-1950s, the hypothetical minimum level of expenditure for an African family of five in Soweto was no less than £24 a month and the sustainable minimum level of expenditure was about £36 a month (Gibson, 1954: 33–35; South African Institute of Race Relations, 1957: 31). An average laborer's wage of £13 a month would cover just 54 percent of the hypothetical minimum, or 36 percent of the sustainable minimum. These proportions had deteriorated since the 1930s, as price rises for goods purchased by urban Africans outstripped wage increases.

In order to assess how this larger gap was bridged, it is necessary to consider the changes in the economics of two crucial sources of non-wage income – laundry work and beer brewing. As a consequence of the changing preferences of White households, and the added costs of transport from the more distant townships, the practice of taking in laundry started to decline after the Second World War, although it remained a valuable source of income for some women at least until the mid-1950s (Gibson, 1954).

In the 1940s, several factors began to undermine the practice of home brewing: changes in the labor force reduced the number of customers accessible to brewers in the townships; the opening of municipal beer halls created significant competition; advertising by commercial breweries made home-brewed beer less popular; harassment by the authorities intensified. During the 1950s, the resulting decline in home brewing did not abolish illegal liquor distribution as a source of non-wage income, but rather transformed it: township drinking establishments called *shebeens* thrived as distributors of commercially brewed liquor and beer (Rogerson and Hart, 1986). Proportionately far fewer township households were involved in the more commercially oriented *shebeen* trade than had been yard households in home brewing. As a consequence, beer consumption became an activity requiring expense for most African households. Although some new non-wage activities – such as home dressmaking and coffee-cart trading for women, and backyard manufacturing and operating pirate taxis for men – emerged during the postwar period (Beavon and Rogerson, 1986a), no single one could fully replace the cash income previously earned from brewing.

It thus remains to be explained how the huge gap between male wages and minimum levels of household expenditure was bridged during the 1950s. For many households the alternative to declining inputs of non-wage income was to send additional members out into the wage labor force. In the early 1950s, a survey of a Rand township determined that on average there were 1.3 wage earners per African family; 70 percent of the surveyed families had only one wage earner (Johannesburg, Non-European Affairs Department, 1951). A study in the early 1960s found an average of 1.6 wage earners per African household, with 54 percent of households containing two or more wage earners (Bureau of Market Research, 1963). It is evident that the average number of wage earners per household rose during the 1950s (Hlophe, 1977).

The additional wage earner in many households was a woman who, during earlier times, would have been engaged in brewing, laundry, or other market activities. The monthly wage of £13 from a male laborer and of £5 from a woman working in the service sector would together amount to £18, or about 75 percent of the hypothetical minimum level of household expenditure, or just 50 percent of the sustainable minimum. This clearly shows that an urban household consisting of a nuclear family, even with both parents working full-time, would be in dire circumstances. While some additional income-generating activities by adults or by children would have narrowed this gap somewhat, it seems likely that this household configuration did not provide a satisfactory urban existence.

The addition of another wage earner, particularly a man, would make for a far more viable household income. A working son and a father, for instance, would push the household's income from wages above the hypothetical minimum, leaving the wife to contribute further through either wage employment or a non-wage pursuit. This household configuration might reasonably be expected to cover 75 percent or more of the sustainable minimum level of expenditure. A daughter would earn lower wages, but would hold out the potential of bringing a cash *lobola* payment into the household, while a son might well have to save money in order to make this payment. For households without an older child in the labor force, an alternative would have been to incorporate an additional adult wage earner from outside the nuclear family.

Surveys on household composition during the postwar period indicate the frequent presence of a third adult member, household size approximating six rather than five persons (Bureau of Market Research, 1963). In some cases, this additional adult was a lodger paying a monthly rent; in others, a relative who was integrated into the household's income-pooling network. While it is difficult to estimate how much a third member would increase the minimum level of household expenditure, it is quite clear that the wage contribution of an additional man would far exceed the added cost associated with his consumption. An additional woman would have meant a smaller net cash contribution, but she would have lightened the housework and child care burden on a working wife.

The typical urban African household in the mid-1950s was more reliant on wage earnings than ever before. A decline in the capacity of a man's wage to cover essential expenditure resulted in intense pressure on households either to send an additional member into the wage labor force, or to incorporate an additional adult wage earner. A decline in brewing and laundry work meant that the proportion of cash needs met from market sources had probably decreased overall, though many households undoubtedly still earned significant income from market activities. Rogerson (1986) found, for instance, that coffee-cart trading in Johannesburg grew rapidly after the Second World War: there were at least a thousand carts operating in 1955. This activity now became increasingly dominated by women, which Rogerson attributes to the generally declining returns from coffee-cart trading and the improved employment opportunities for African men. Hawking of prepared foods, fruits and vegetables, and other household goods was an important source of income for many African households in the townships (Beavon and Rogerson, 1986b). Taking in lodgers was a more viable proposition than it had been in the inner city yards, and the opportunity of obtaining rental income had seemingly improved since the 1930s.

It is useful to think of two variants on an urban African household type for the mid-1950s. The first is a marginalized income-pooling unit made up of a nuclear family of five persons, but with a sixth person in residence who was a rent-paying lodger. This household could meet its cash needs by combining income from a man's wages (50 percent), a woman's wages (25 percent), rent from a lodger (15 percent), and other sources (10 percent). The second variant consisted of six persons in an income-pooling unit – an elementary family plus an additional man. This household could meet its greater cash needs from the combined income of two men's wages (75 percent), a woman's income from taking in laundry or other market sources (15 percent), and other sources (10 percent). The latter variant was much more likely to achieve an income that would have made possible a sustainable existence.

After the Second World War, virtually all urban White households received wages or salaries that situated them well above any existing measure of a minimum standard of living. On the average, White salary and wage earners had weekly incomes that exceeded the hypothetical minimum level of monthly expenditure for African households, while even comparatively low-paid White women workers received wages that would have more than covered the sustainable minimum level of expenditure for an African household. A budget survey of White families in 1955 indicated that the average family of a wage and salary earner in Johannesburg obtained 79 percent of its income from the "head of family's" wage (or salary), 10 percent from the "wife's" wage (or salary), and the remaining 11 percent from a mixture of other sources. In the last group, by far the most important source of income was "rent" on money (interest and dividends) and fixed property. These figures reflect overall averages, which hide the fact that in those households where women worked, they probably brought in 30 to 40 percent of total cash income. Even for the comparatively prosperous households of White workers, the male wage or salary was frequently supplemented by non-wage sources of cash income: in Johannesburg over one-third contained "working wives," and many relied on rent for part of their income.

In the early 1970s, a sharp increase in the price of gold and a resurgence of Black worker militancy created the conditions for an unprecedented rise in African wages: between 1971 and 1975 real wages grew an aggregate 44 percent, and nearly 12 percent in 1975 alone (Keenan, 1983). The gap between African and White wages, however, narrowed only slightly since Africans' wages had started at such a low level. By the mid-1970s on the Rand, the wages of African men working as laborers in secondary industry and commerce exceeded one-fifth of the earnings of skilled White workers for the first time. The earnings of African semiskilled workers were higher – amounting to perhaps one-third of the earnings of skilled Whites. The gender pattern of wage earnings proved to be more rigid. In many industries, the wages for African women were only half of those for African men, while in the services sector this fraction was even smaller (Bureau of Market Research, 1976; Republic of South Africa, Department of Statistics, 1977a, 1977b).

In response to the expansion of the Black consumer market in the 1960s, the University of South Africa's Bureau of Market Research (BMR) undertook a series of household surveys to assess changing patterns of Black income and expenditure.[4] The data pertaining to African household composition in Soweto (Johannesburg) are summarized in Table 17. In 1970 and 1975 household size was reported to be 5.1 persons, a figure which suggests that the average Sowetan household was smaller during the 1970s than it had been during either the early 1960s or the early to mid-1980s, when it was around 5.5 persons.[5] These data contradict the notion that average household size has been steadily declining.

Table 17 reveals also two striking trends in the composition of African households between 1962 and 1985: a sharp rise in the number of "female-headed" households, which grew as a proportion of all households from 14 to 29 percent; a major shift in average household membership as the proportion of "children over 18" increased from 11 to 25 percent, and as that of "other household members" increased from 6 to 20 percent. The first trend clearly shows that "female-headed" households became a major *urban* household type during the 1970s,[6] while the latter indicates a substantial growth in the proportion of African households containing adult members in addition to, or in lieu of, a conjugal couple. Increases in average household size, "female-headedness," and adult membership strongly indicate that the contemporary period has been marked by a sharp expansion of urban African household types other than that of the nuclear family. The growth in the number of "children over 18" probably reflects an increase in the number of multi-generational households, while that of "other household members" represents an increase in the number of extended households. A study of divorce and custody in Cape Town offers some insights into the latter development. Burman and Fuchs (1986) argue that a variety of pressures on Africans – such as extremely low wages for

Table 17. *African multiple member households in Johannesburg,*
1962–85

	1962	1970	1975	1980	1985
Average size	5.60	5.07	5.10	5.51	5.48
Proportion "female-headed"	14%	18%	25%	26%	29%
Average composition:					
Household heads[a]	18%	20%	20%	18%	18%
Wife	14%	15%	14%	12%	11%
Children under 7 years	23%	15%	11%	9%	6%
Children 7–18 years	29%	30%	30%	26%	19%
Children over 18 years	11%	9%	12%	19%	25%
Other household members[b]	6%	11%	13%	17%	20%
	100%	100%	100%	100%	100%
Average number of:					
Salary and wage earners	1.57	1.47	1.42	1.51	1.35
Other recipients of income[c]	0.15	0.23	0.21	0.32	0.58
Earners and other recipients	1.72	1.70	1.63	1.83	1.93
Dependency ratio[d]	3.26	2.98	3.13	3.01	2.84

Notes:

The data refer only to multiple member households. Households are defined as "one or more families or a group of two or more persons dependent on a common or pooled income, and usually living in the same house. ... Members of a household need not necessarily be related by blood or marriage."

[a] Defined as "the person recognised as the head by the others living in the household"; it is apparent that in practice this means a man in all cases where the household includes an adult male.

[b] Defined as relatives not the children of the "household head" and non-related household members. The Bureau does not specify the ages of "other members" and the discussion in this chapter assumes that they are predominately adults.

[c] Defined as "persons whose income derives only from sources other than salaries and wages."

[d] Calculated by dividing the average number of wage and salary earners and other recipients of income by average household size.

Source: Bureau of Market Research (1986).

women and rigid urban residency requirements – have resulted in abandonment, separation, or divorce among urban couples, with the consequence that children were often farmed out to rural relatives. They maintain that this has meant an increase in the number of urban households consisting solely of adults, as the former members of dissolved households either move in with siblings or relatives, or else establish householding arrangments with other unattached adults. They argue that the various arrangements which have emerged as a result of this process only superficially resemble past patterns of family extension.

In its 1975 report, the BMR calculated that the average household in Soweto had a monthly income of about R190. Wages accounted for 84 percent of total household income: "heads of households" contributed 58 percent, "wives" 13 percent, and "other" households members 13 percent. On average about 17 percent of household income was derived from non-wage sources, with rent from lodgers accounting for over half this amount (BMR, 1975). While these figures are undoubtedly quite poor indicators of the relative contributions of both household members and income sources, they do offer a basis for making some useful calculations of the adequacy of African wages.

For an average-size household in Soweto, a conservative estimate of the hypothetical minimum level of expenditure was R110, and of a sustainable minimum level is R165 per month.[7] Therefore, the average wage of R112 for a "household head" would barely cover the hypothetical, but would fall far short of the sustainable, minimum level of household expenditure. The BMR's estimate of R190 for average household income, however, would adequately cover the sustainable minimum level of expenditure for the average household, suggesting a major change occurring in the average level of urban African incomes since the mid-1950s. Yet, all descriptive accounts agree that by the 1970s tremendous differentiation had emerged among urban African households, and consequently the BMR's average figures do not adequately reflect the township reality of widespread deprivation and hardship. Only a small to medium-sized household with a steadily employed, semiskilled male worker would receive enough wage income from a single member to allow it to cover adequately the sustainable minimum level of expenditure. The household of an unskilled male worker would reach such a level only if it had additional members employed as wage earners, or else had access to significant sources of non-wage income. "Female-headed" households were in much worse shape. The BMR calculated that, for 1980, 57 percent of "female-headed" households lived below the sustainable minimum level of expenditure, while the comparable figure for "male-headed" households was 36 percent. Larger households also faced a much greater income shortfall than smaller ones (BMR, 1982). It is thus apparent that in the 1970s many urban African households were still living well below a sustainable minimum level of expenditure, and most of the remaining ones were in immediate peril of falling below this level.

The BMR surveys offer little insight into how households with wage incomes below the sustainable minimum managed to survive. Studies of urban poverty, "informal sector" activities, and women's work have begun to provide some clues, showing that many township households still have access to significant sources of subsistence and market income. A Health Department survey of one area of Soweto in the mid-1970s, for instance, found that nearly 40 percent of the residents maintained vegetable gardens (Shuenyane *et al.*, 1977: 496), while a report in the newspaper *New Nation* claimed that in Alexandra, a township only a fraction the size of Soweto, there were at least 1,000 "livestock farmers" providing themselves and, in some instances, other residents with milk and meat (June 25, 1987: 3).

Several studies have concluded that about one out of three township households participate in the "informal sector" on either a full-time or part-time basis (Matsetela *et al.*, 1980; Rogerson and Beavon, 1982; Pillay, 1984a). Popular activities include hawking, pirate taxi driving, operating *shebeens*, and "child minding." The latter activity has expanded rapidly in response to the growing demand for child care by African women working in wage employment. A study found that in Soweto there were at least 2,500, mostly older women, providing paid day care for about seven children (Cock *et al.*, 1986). The single most important source of market income for African households was derived from street trading. In every township, and in "White" business districts where it was allowed, hawkers sold items ranging from cooked food to knitted clothing, and from medicinal herbs to cassette tapes. The largest group of street traders was women engaged in the sale of food, and it was common to find "township aunties" selling fruits and vegetables at a low margin. Men typically hawked dry goods, and children or adolescent males were the main sellers of newspapers. While street traders were a heterogeneous group, Rogerson and Beavon (1982) found that about half of them earned amounts that would have to be combined with other sources of income in order to provide even a minimal household budget.

Other forms of household income included rents and transfer payments. Given the extreme shortage of housing in African residential areas, subletting part of a house, or yard space for building a shack, could provide significant income. The lack of a viable social welfare system for Africans meant that few households without a pensioned or disabled member received any transfer payments from the state. This point is dramatically illustrated by government figures for the early 1980s, which indicate that unemployed Blacks drew only 0.3 percent of their subsistence from state unemployment benefits (Meth and Piper, 1984). Unlike unemployed Whites, impoverished Blacks have been systematically excluded from state transfer payments and forced to appeal to kin, private charities, and/ or resort to begging.

In southern Africa, it should be noted that a narrow focus on household income obscures a crucial aspect of urban survival strategies: many township residents participate in inter-household networks of mutual assistance organized by the independent African churches, women's associations, and burial societies (Kramer, 1975; Matsetela *et al.*, 1980; Webster, 1984). A *stokvel*, for instance, is a group of women who have organized themselves into a rotating credit association, and which also has commonly served as a mechanism for facilitating the market activities of its members. One study claims that, during the 1970s, as many as two-thirds of the households in one area of Soweto participated in such associations (Matsetela *et al.*, 1980).

It is useful to contrast two configurations of urban African households during this period: the largely wage-dependent "male-headed" household, with the mixed-income "female-headed" household. The first type was probably reliant for 90 percent or more of its cash income on multiple wage earners. In small households consisting of a nuclear family, this would have been a husband and wife, or a father and older child. Such households would earn a sustainable level of income only if they were able to keep multiple earners in the labor force, or if the male earner was employed as a semiskilled laborer in a well-paying industry. In order for larger households to maintain this standard, it would have been essential for them to send additional members into the labor force. Unemployment and inflation each posed serious threats to the welfare of households of this type.

"Female-headed" households reliant on a mixture of different types of income were in an even more precarious position. Bush, Cliffe, and Jansen (1984) assert that the nucleus of these households was often two or three female relatives who were forced into income-pooling arrangements because of "proximity" rather than because of any customary rights or responsibilities. Such households would combine income from a variety of sources including wages, rent, pensions (from older or disabled members), market activities, and "exchanges of services." While such arrangements were so fluid that it is difficult to generalize about the proportions among the sources, it seems likely that many of these households would receive half or more of their cash income from non-wage sources.

Common to both of these household configurations was their reliance on massive work inputs by women. African women were not only trapped in the lowest-paying occupations, but they also bore full responsibility for housework and children. As one authority on domestic work in South Africa observed, "all recent research reports that men's involvement in domestic work is virtually non-existent among the African working class. The sexual division of labor within the home defines cooking, shopping, cleaning and child care very rigidly as 'women's work' " (Cock, 1987: 136).

With regard to the White population, government surveys indicate that their households were smaller in size than those of Africans, were composed predominantly of elementary families, and were frequent employers of African women as domestic servants (Republic of South Africa, Department of Statistics, 1977b, 1978). While these findings suggest a continuity in the structure of White households, other research challenges this conclusion. Based on a survey of mixed working-class and lower middle-class White households in Durban, Argyle (1977) cautions against an acritical acceptance of the "myth of the elementary family." He found that at least one-fifth of the households in his sample were either extended or multiple in structure (see also Simkins, 1986), and suggests that various factors – the effects of divorce, lower wages for White women than men, and lack of support facilities for the elderly – were encouraging the formation of multi-generational households among the White population.

Burman and Fuchs (1986) also maintained that the exceptionally high divorce rate among White South Africans – among the highest in the world – has caused the emergence of a new form of family extension, as people remarried and created households that were in some ways quite distinct from the conventional model of the nuclear family. In terms of income-pooling, when child support payments were made, they may have enmeshed some households into a system of transfers which could constitute a significant source of household income. While it is clear that extended and multi-generational households were much less common among Whites than among Africans, it seems plausible to argue that the proportion of White households that were complex in form has been increasing. Simkins suggests that the appropriate model for White households was "serial monogamy ... in strata (defined largely by race and class) where desertion is a common occurrence" (1986: 40). The implication is that during the contemporary period White households have been gravitating in terms of their composition toward the model of the African households, and not vice versa.

South Africa's economic prosperity of the mid-1970s faltered and then completely collapsed during the 1980s. The rate of growth in real wages for Africans at first slowed and subsequently reversed, while that of inflation and unemployment skyrocketed. Based on a recurring survey of a small sample of households, Keenan found that African unemployment in Soweto nearly doubled between 1981 and 1986, and that the proportion of households falling below a sustainable level of income had sharply risen. He maintains that African households' initial response to the deepening crisis was to reduce their "overall dependency ratio" either by "increasing the number of people in employment or by getting rid of 'unproductive' members of the household" (1986: 3). Many were able to pursue both strategies by sending additional, mostly female, members into the labor force and by dispatching children and old people to live with relatives in rural areas.[8] Other households were able to supplement their income by undertaking, or expanding participation in non-wage activities. In some areas of Soweto during the early 1980s, Keenan found that both the relative and absolute contribution of non-wage activities to household income had increased by around 50 percent (1986: 4), while the BMR data summarized in Table 17 indicate that the average number of household members earning non-wage income nearly tripled between 1975 and 1985. Over the same period, and despite an increase in average household size, the "dependency ratio" fell from 3.13 to 2.84 persons per income earner.

From around 1985, however, the rapidly deteriorating economic situation and escalating political conflict sharply intensified the pressures on urban households. Limits were reached as to the extent that households could reduce their size by shedding members, and/

or increase their wage income by sending additional persons into an already overcrowded labor market. Moreover, mounting unrest and repression began severely to hamper access by township residents to some sources of non-wage income. As Keenan observes:

With the closure and boycott of schools people have been unable to sell food and cold drinks to the children; many *shebeens* have been either destroyed, closed down or put out of business; consumer boycotts and transport difficulties have made it difficult for hawkers to get supplies; while the presence of troops and police in the streets have deterred many people from venturing into such activities. The net effect has been a very marked demise in the size of the informal sector in terms of both its absolute contribution to household economies and in terms of its proportion of total household income. (1986: 6)

The strains on the budgets of African households were further intensified by both a sharp rise in the rate of inflation and by the state's efforts to underwrite the cost of reforms by increasing rents, fees, and fares for township residents.

Underlying the political struggles that are rocking South Africa today is a profound crisis of reproduction: the incomes of African households have been undermined by stagnant real wages, escalating unemployment, new constraints on non-wage labor activities, and mounting pressures on household budgets. These conditions have fueled demands by workers and intensified opposition in the townships. The myriad struggles which have emerged over rents, services, education, relocation, and the policing of the townships must all be seen as part and parcel of the working-class challenge to capital and the state.

An historical examination of household changes over the last century shows that there has been no linear path of development culminating in a homogeneous mass of urban workers who are "fully dependent upon wages for subsistence." The vast majority of the Rand's labor force has belonged to households pooling incomes from a variety of activities, which we have categorized into the five major forms of wages, rents, market sales, transfer payments, and subsistence. Settlement in urban areas has certainly served to modify the character and combinations of non-wage activities, but has not led to the demise of any of these forms of income. On the Rand today, it is common to find Black households which derive substantial portions of their income from non-wage sources, as well as White households which are not completely reliant on wages.

It is also clear that households on the Rand have not become uniform in composition. Based on a review of the quantitative evidence available for urban households, Simkins has concluded that "Perhaps just over half of South African households are nuclear in structure; most of the rest are extended or multiple. If there is a trend towards the nuclear household, it is a very weak one" (1986: 41). Indeed, during the contemporary period such a trend appears to be non-existent. Among the African population one finds sharply increasing proportions of "female-headed" households and strong pressures toward multi-generational households, while among the White population soaring divorce rates, at the very least, force us to modify our conception of the nuclear family.

Once the imposition of a linear path of development for households is rejected, it becomes apparent that the labor force on the Rand has always been reproduced by a mixture of different household types. The formation of urban households by skilled White workers, for instance, went hand-in-hand with the transformation of rural African homesteads in Basutoland and elsewhere. As the labor force became increasingly urbanized, race played a prominent role in defining urban household types. But it is equally important to observe that at specific conjunctures both the White and African populations have included groups of households with quite different patterns of income pooling. Up to the 1930s, for example, the typical household of "poor Whites" was quite distinct from that of a skilled White worker; today, it is African households which are most differentiated in terms of income-pooling practices.

Moreover, each household type has developed according to its own individual pattern. That associated with skilled White workers, for example, established a stable pattern of income-pooling during the incorporation period. As the real value of wages rose between the mid-1890s and the First World War (an A-phase of the world-economy), the proportion of cash income derived from the wages earned by skilled workers rose to about 90 percent, with rent contributing the remaining 10 percent, proportions which subsequently stayed about constant. Also traceable to these years is the other important feature of this household type, its reliance on a paid servant to help with domestic work.

The typical "poor White" household, on the other hand, went through important changes in the interwar B-phase. Initially, it was based on the pooling of wages and non-wage forms of income, and had a standard of living approximately that of urban Blacks. Based on improved employment opportunities at first for White women, and subsequently for unskilled White men, it was rapidly transformed during the 1930s. By the end of the Second World War it had adopted income-pooling arrangements similar to those of the skilled White household type, and its standard of living improved. Three aspects of this transition are noteworthy: it occurred during a period of rapid local economic growth – a development that sharply distinguished the Rand from most of the rest of the world-economy at this time; it was facilitated by women's employment – a characteristic that differentiates this type from that of skilled Whites; it required extensive state intervention in the labor market on behalf of White workers. The last aspect has subsequently guaranteed the stability of this household type by keeping White unemployment levels at virtually zero.

By contrast, the African households that formed on the Rand during the interwar years followed a very different path of development. In the mid-1930s, the typical household of a steadily employed African man derived about half of its cash income from non-wage activities. This proportion fell sharply after the Second World War to an estimated 25 percent in the mid-1950s, and then to around 10 percent in the mid-1970s, a pattern indicating a rapid increase in the importance of wages during the postwar A-phase. Despite its apparent similarity with the White household type, in terms of the proportion of income derived from wages, many important differences remain: it exists at a much lower standard of living; it usually requires that multiple adult members be kept in the labor force; it is highly vulnerable to unemployment.

But there exists another important aspect of African households that not only further differentiates this group from White households but also challenges the view of a linear development in the importance of wages: the rapid growth in the number of "female-headed" households during the contemporary B-phase. Unlike households which include a steadily employed man, those which are "female-headed" were likely to obtain half of their income from non-wage sources, both in the 1930s and in the 1970s. The important difference was that, in the later period, their composition usually did not include an employed man. This development indicates that it is overly simplistic to argue – on the basis of the change in the household type of a steadily employed man – that all African households are consistently becoming more reliant on wages. In fact, it seems that non-wage sources of income constitute about half of the budget of what now appears to be the fastest-growing proportion of urban African households.

As this discussion of different household types and their divergent paths of development has shown, the growth in the importance of wages for the Rand's labor force has not followed a linear trajectory. Rather it has been cyclical in character, showing an overall increase during periods of economic expansion. This has occurred when established household types raised the proportion of their budgets derived from wage earnings: by higher real levels of pay (skilled White workers between the mid-1890s and the First World War), by benefiting from improved employment opportunities ("poor Whites" during the 1930s), or by sending additional wage earners into the labor force (African workers during the postwar years). These changes are related to – but not directly correlated with – the A-phases of the world-economy, since conditions on the Rand have always been mediated by a variety of locally influential factors. The countercyclical profits of gold production, for instance, established the economic conditions necessary for improvements in wage-earning opportunities for "poor Whites" during the 1930s.

It also appears that the relative importance of non-wage sources of income for the reproduction of the labor force has tended to increase during B-phases of the world-economy. The mechanism by which this development has unfolded on the Rand, however, is not simply a reversal of that which occurred during A-phases. In fact, while it does appear that established household types become more reliant on non-wage forms of income during periods of hardship, the increase has mainly been underwritten by the formation of new household types. Thus, during the interwar period the overall importance of non-wage incomes for the reproduction of the labor force increased as large numbers of African workers established urban households, while during the contemporary period it has again increased as "female-headed" Black households have become one of the major household types on the Rand.

NOTES

1 Available information has made it impossible to generalize about the household divisioning of labor between "madams" and domestic

servants, and how this may have changed over time. In his essay on domestic service during this period, van Onselen notes that the duties of "houseboys" tended "to vary according to the class of the employer, the size and age of the family, the number of staff kept and the individual experience and attributes of the servant himself. In most homes, however, the 'houseboys' were responsible for making fires, cleaning stoves, sweeping, washing dishes, preparing morning and afternoon tea, keeping the yard clean, and doing such routine garden work as weeding and watering" (1982b: 30). It is clear that the "madam" in the household of a skilled worker did a variety of significant and necessary household tasks, which included cooking, shopping, supervision, and possibly some aspects of cleaning and laundry. The lack of labor time studies for the Rand has made it impossible to estimate meaningfully the divisioning of labor between servants and employers for this or subsequent periods. However, this should not be allowed to obscure the fact that the household divisioning of labor for the majority of working-class White women in South Africa varied significantly from core areas, where women of a comparable class level were unlikely to have had a domestic servant under their command. It also should be noted that White children in South Africa probably did less household chores than their counterparts elsewhere because of the widespread presence of domestic servants.

2 For estimates of the relative adequacy of the male wage during this period see the Johannesburg Joint Council of Europeans and Natives (1928); the Native Economic Commission (Union of South Africa, 1932b: testimony of Major H. S. Cooke, Director of Native Labor); Hellmann (1948); the report of the Unofficial Commission (Appointed by the South African Temperance Alliance and the South African Institute of Race Relations) on the "illicit liquor problem" (1935: testimony of two African residents of the Klipspruit Location); the Industrial Legislation Commission (Union of South Africa, 1935: testimony of J. D. Rheinallt Jones, Advisor, South African Institute of Race Relations); Janisch (1941); and the report of the Bus Commission (Union of South Africa, 1944).

3 Based on the pioneering work of Edward Batson during the early 1940s, the hypothetical minimum level of expenditure has become widely known as the "Poverty Datum Line" (or PDL), and the 50 percent higher figure as the "Effective Minimum Level." Batson maintained that the former reflected the "barest minimum upon which health can theoretically be achieved," while the latter represents the minimal amount that a household would have actually to spend in order to sustain itself over an extended period of time (cited in Union of South Africa, 1944: 12–13).

4 It should be noted that the BMR data are plagued by many shortcomings

in the manner in which they have been collected and reported. Among other problems, they rely on a procedure which surely underestimates the contribution of non-wage sources of income, and they are reported as average figures that undoubtedly conflate significant differences among quite distinct household types. Nevertheless, they remain useful since they have been collected in a uniform fashion over a period of years. In contrast, the government census data have been compiled in a form that provides virtually no useful information about African households.

5 These figures undoubtedly underestimate actual household size, though it should be noted that unlike many other calculations they are not based simply on residence under a common roof (see the BMR definition of households in Table 17). Other recent research gives substantially higher figures – Keenan and Sarakinsky (1987), for instance, maintain that actual household size in Soweto is 7–8 persons, while Pillay maintains that most township households "accommodate an extra 2 persons per dwelling that are not family (i.e., lodgers or tenants)" (1984b: 5).

6 Unlike in rural areas, the growth of the urban "female-headed" household cannot be explained as a direct effect of the migrant labor system. Van der Vliet (1984) maintains that "staying single" has been adopted as a survival strategy by urban women, who found that men were frequently poor net contributors to household budgets.

7 The BMR (1976) calculated that a "minimum living level" for an average-sized African household in Soweto was R100 a month, while a "supplemented living level" was R133 a month. Other evidence, however, suggests that these figures are too low. The Institute of Planning Research at the University of Port Elizabeth established a "household subsistence level" for Africans in Johannesburg at R120 per month, while the Johannesburg Chamber of Commerce estimated that a "minimum living level" for an African family of five in Soweto was R109 per month (South African Institute of Race Relations, 1976). I have thus taken a figure of R110 per month as roughly corresponding to the hypothetical, and R165 (a figure 50 percent higher) as the sustainable minimum levels of expenditure. Even these figures, however, are extremely conservative and do not represent what the trade unions with the broadest-based Black support would consider a "living wage"; on this point see Jack (1987).

8 This formulation at first appears to be inconsistent with the BMR's data showing increases in average household size during this period. Part of the explanation may be that a decrease in the "dependency ratio" can be achieved either by sending away "unproductive" members, or by enlarging the number of "productive" members. A viable option for some "female-headed" households may be to increase the number of

persons living together, thereby simultaneously cutting the "dependency ratio" and enlarging the households. The increase in the proportion of "other members" may also represent the bringing in of new members in order to decrease the "dependency ratio."

CHAPTER 2

Lesotho: the creation of the households

William G. Martin

Southern Africa's great cities are colonial creations, born of the overseas expansion of the European world-economy. As such they drew upon local and global resources, of which none was more important than continuing inflows of labor to provide the sinews of mineral and then industrial production. The process of labor force formation was considerably complicated by the circulating character of the African migrant flow. Dictated at first by the structure of mining production and African communities, and later by the imposition of state control, many Black households have sustained substantive ties to their rural area of origin. The households of urban Black workers for much of the past century were households split over geographic space. Even within a continent marked by labor migration, these movements have been so large and enduring that southern Africa has long been called "Africa of the labor reserves."

These urban–rural movements have been central to production and of great concern to state authorities. Numerous studies by state commissions, by private enterprises involved in hiring migrant workers, and by academic researchers have described the contours of migration for almost as long as it has taken place. We know, for example, much about the direction and volume of total migrant flows, especially to the gold mines of South Africa. Great attention has also been paid to the private and public institutions that have controlled migration. Yet when one turns to the rural areas, the literature is curiously underdeveloped.

In large part this reflects several decades of concern with the political structuring of the flows, and the exact manner by which they have sustained the system of "cheap labor." From this perspective the story of rural areas has been one of unremitting decline. The implementation of apartheid in the post-1945 era is explained by the drive to replace, via political and institutional mechanisms, the previous "precapitalist" agricultural subsidy to wages that allowed capital "to pay the worker *below* the cost of his reproduction" (Wolpe, 1972: 434). Yet, capital has always and everywhere paid less than the cost of reproducing the labor force. What actually needs explanation is how changing social structures have sustained over time urban labor forces through shifting balances of waged and non-waged incomes. This entails a study of rural–urban networks. Recent local histories, born of the last ten years' upsurge of social and oral history, have begun to fill this gap (Beinart and Bundy, 1987; Beinart *et al.*, 1986; Bozzoli, 1983). Nevertheless, the drive to recover rural history has yet to generate a consistent, long-term assessment of urban–rural household formation. Indeed the success-ful thrust to break through a simplistic depiction of rural decline, to recapture rural history in its own right, would appear to be having the effect of undermining, or at least forestalling, the search for any consistent historical patterns of rural labor reproduction in relation to urban developments.

Conceived as a supplementary study to that of households in Johannesburg, we are confronted with an historical and methodo-logical dilemma. On the one hand, there is no single rural area that can depict, in even ideal-typical fashion, the relationship between rural areas and Johannesburg over time. As production processes on the Rand have changed from mining to industry and services, so too have rural areas become increasingly differentiated between sites of commercializing settler and peasant farming and simple rural labor reserves. One result has been consistent transformations in the gender and income structure of urban–rural households, as well as in the stability of their composition. On the other hand, the lack of time series data on the rural origins and ties of Johannesburg's population makes it difficult to shift focus among rural areas as Johannesburg's rural links have changed over time – even if we were to be satisfied with abandoning the study of household formation in a single site over time.

We have thus settled on a less than comprehensive solution, but one we hope is fruitful nevertheless. We have chosen to examine one particular rural area, Lesotho.[1] The Basuto have had a long and sustained relationship with labor force formation in South Africa, and the area has been as extensively studied as any rural part of southern Africa. It nevertheless remains the case that data on household size and income-pooling, for example, are absent for most of the last century. Although this is undoubtedly the case for most peripheral areas of the world, it seems particularly evident for areas like Lesotho that were incorporated into the world-economy only during the late nineteenth and early twentieth century. A prior set of processes, however, requires initial investigation: the uneven process of the creation of household structures out of the web of a precapitalist mode of production, as the Basuto first came into contact with the capitalist expansion from the coast of southern Africa. As we shall see, the pattern of Basuto household activities, gender and age stratification, and income-pooling practices is inextricably bound up with the determinants of the dissolution of precapitalist ways of life and rule.

The essential starting point for any analysis of household formation in rural southern Africa is an appreciation of the precapitalist organization of production and labor activities. While this may be briefly characterized as a lineage mode of production, it would be specious to assert that in these social formations household structures existed, since both the control over productive resources (land, cattle, etc.) and labor (particularly women's labor) rested on social and political networks far larger than "households." Chiefs, for example, not only allocated land and lent out vast cattle herds, but called forth labor tribute to work their own lands, and garnered the benefits of hunting, war, and trade. Male elders retained control over the resources necessary to marry. Thus while homesteads, i.e., large residential units with multiple conjugal groups, remained a principal locus for crop production, the essential determinants of access to the means of production and reproduction were determined beyond the homestead's boundaries. As Kimble notes for this period:

Although the homestead formed an important centre of productive activity in the Sotho social formation, the social organisation of production was dependent on the existence of chieftainship which was maintained through the surplus labour of the direct producers . . . These links were still decisive in determining the patterns of production. (1982: 129)

Two successive waves of prosperity and expansion in surrounding settler colonies began the process of incorporating Lesotho into the world-economy: first, the growth of pastoral and particularly wool production between 1850 and 1870; and secondly, the discovery and rapid exploitation of the Kimberley diamond fields between 1870 and 1882. For the Basuto, contact with expanding colonial markets first took the form of migration to farms in the Cape Colony, which was followed by expanded waves of migration to the new Kimberley diamond fields in the 1860s. After Basuto lands were incorporated into the Cape Colony, this process was furthered by the imposition of the 10s. tax in 1869. By 1875, 15,000 men were getting passes to work outside of the territory out of an estimated population of 127,325. Ten years later this number was reported to have doubled (Ashton, 1967: 162). At this latter time, the interval of absence from the territory was no longer, however, a full year, but well below six months.

Wages from migration were new, and of considerable importance in Basutoland. Yet it would be specious to assert that cash incomes were always pooled within household structures. The existing evidence suggests strongly that early migration, especially to the Kimberley fields, was directed by chiefs, and served largely, if not wholly, their interests. Many chiefs sent out migrants in search of guns and ammunition, which they subsequently distributed. Chiefs often imposed taxes as well on their young subjects engaged in wage labor. The same could be said for the growing export trade in cereals, which offered an alternative source of money incomes in the last half of the nineteenth century, and for a while displaced labor migration as the principal source. Close both to Kimberley and to the Rand, the Basuto rapidly responded to the growth of markets for grains. In 1873, 100,000 bags of grain and 2,000 bags of wool were exported, while imports of a wide variety of goods reached approximately £150,000 (Murray, 1981: 11). Clearly chiefs' production units, still able to call upon tributary male labor, were best placed to take advantage of such new opportunities. At the same time, it is clear that the penetration of new goods and wants was widely diffused, as is evident, for example, by the expansion in the number of both traders' stations and plows (circa 2,749 in 1875). As the *Grahamstown Journal* optimistically put it at the end of the 1870s:

Inhabited by an industrious race, and constantly stimulated by the demands of a growing civilization which are daily becoming more diversified, Basutoland is in the process of rapidly transforming its pastures into arable lands and its production is such that it is not unlikely that it may one day become one of the main sources from which the [Cape] Colony will derive its supply of cereals. (Cited in Germond, 1967: 325)

In terms of well-being, this period stands out as one of the best in the last 125 years, with high levels of crop and pastoral production for self-use and market sale supplemented by migrant labor incomes.

Thus, by 1885, the impact of labor migration and cash-crop production was significant. But, as was the case in many other parts of the world, the initial effect of the world-economy was to enhance the precapitalist stratification rather than to dissolve the historic patterns of the organization of social life.

Early participation in labor and commodity markets by the Basuto was based upon favorable land/labor ratios in Basutoland, labor shortages in expanding colonial markets, and the distance of interior markets from the coast. All these factors were swept away with the permanent establishment of vibrant mining centers in the interior. In the course of this transition, the precapitalist system of production and reproduction was increasingly rendered inoperative. This latter process, and the fitful emergence of households sending migrants to the Rand, is the essential story of the period from 1865 to the eve of the First World War.

By the time of the establishment of the mining industry in the Rand in the 1880s, the struggles of the Basuto to defend their lands had come to an end. Wars with Afrikaner settlers in the 1850s and 1860s had led to the loss of much fertile land. It was only by accepting British protection that the Basuto were able to retain the central parts of their kingdom. The creation of the Protectorate of Basutoland in 1869, often heralded as the successful defense of the Sotho kingdom, marked rather the integration of Sotho political authority within the rules of the interstate system. While Protectorate status precluded White-owned farms from being established, it changed the social role of the chiefs. In precolonial days, chiefs relied upon tribute and returns from hunting, war, trade, and their regulation of productive resources. As Basutoland was surrounded and penetrated by colonial forces, the position of the chiefs became dependent upon controlling access to the fruits of colonial political and economic networks, while their reciprocal obligations to their communities – hitherto the guarantors of their positions – concomitantly lapsed. It is hard to overestimate the importance of this transformation, despite the fact that the chiefs continued to utilize the ideological symbols of the precapitalist epoch. Insofar as chiefs were successful in becoming mediators for the British colonial state, the formal shell of precapitalist authority remained. Yet this hardly marked the preservation of precapitalist modes of political rule and social organization.

Parallel disintegrative processes were similarly induced from below as the commoner's relationships with colonial markets were radically altered. Whereas both labor and grain exchanges in the middle of the nineteenth century first appeared as trade in preciosities, this gave way to exchanges based on world market values. This change in the density, penetration, and value basis of commodity markets had a dramatic effect on the ability of the Basuto to garner the cash incomes that were increasingly necessary to fulfill tax and consumption needs. Indeed, it is quite clear that a great change in the fortunes of the Basuto occurred after 1880. If expanding crop production in the 1860s and 1870s led visitors to argue that the "Basuto are rapidly enriching themselves," ten to fifteen years later warnings of disaster were in the air. A missionary note of 1888 captures the processes at work quite well:

Basutoland has become impoverished. First the [Gun War of 1881] against the [Cape] Colony was detrimental to her prosperity; next followed three years of drought. This year the lands have yielded a plentiful crop, but the opulence of old has not returned. The diamond fields, the Free State, and the Colony which formerly provided an outlet for Basutoland are henceforth closed to her. The railway line from the Cape to Kimberley is throwing foreign wheat on the market at a low price, and the products of Basutoland which would have to be brought at great cost in ox-wagon, cannot compete. To these causes ... it is necessary to indicate another. Contact with the Whites during the war has created new needs among the natives. (Cited in Germond, 1967: 462, 470)

Like Afrikaner farmers in the interior, the Basuto found that full integration of the interior into the world-economy removed cost disparities between frontier and world market production values. Further evidence of this trend is indicated in the changes in local labor markets. The early years both of diamond and particularly of gold mining were marked by relatively high wages for unskilled African workers, reflecting in part the existence of African alternatives: both subsistence and cash-crop production. The closure of both the expansion of land and the commodity market for grain, at a time when the need for cash incomes had increased, made the melding of income from labor migration with production on the land all the more important. Yet at the same time mining capital on the Rand effectively reduced wages through the collective dictation of wage rates and the creation of monopsonistic recruiting organizations. By the First World War, mining magnates were committed to reducing their Black wage bill (Richardson and van Helten, 1982).

Among those seeking wage labor on the Rand, the Basuto figured prominently. Distant areas like Basutoland were especially important suppliers of labor as little labor could be coerced from the areas surrounding the mines, since these latter areas were controlled by Afrikaner settler farmers who used their own state-machinery to prevent the recruitment of Black labor. The 1896 census revealed that Black workers in Johannesburg were drawn overwhelmingly from beyond the borders of the Transvaal (at that time an independent Afrikaner republic). Of the total population of 102,078 persons, Blacks represented just about half. Of this latter figure, only 754 persons fell into the "Transvaal and undefined" African category (Johannesburg, Sanitary Department, 1896: Part 1, Return II). Basutos were reported to represent 8.154 persons or 16 percent of the total Black population. The 1904 census reported that 21 percent of the Rand's Black population was of Basuto origin (29,711 persons). The overwhelming proportion of Basuto were engaged in "industrial" (includes mining) pursuits (15,678 males), while domestic service contributed the next largest category by far (4,881 males and 2,235 females) (Transvaal Colony, 1906: Tables XXV, XLIX, LIII).

This increasing importance of labor migration was apparent in Basutoland itself. By 1911, 22 percent of the total male population, and 3 percent of the female population, was recorded as absent at the time of the census (Murray, 1981: 4). Total migration figures would be considerably higher given that many circulating migrants would have been home at the time of the census. Yet, at least in the early years of the century, migrants maintained their ability to demand relatively high wage rates, and to migrate at their convenience. Migrants avoided the gold mines for very clear reasons: among all the avenues of labor open to them, the mines offered the lowest incomes, and required at least a six months' contract. As multiple evidence before the Transvaal Labour Commission of 1903 indicated, Basuto refused low wages and long contracts in favor of shorter trips at higher wages (Sloley, 1904: 2–7, 147–52).

Clearly a transition from discretionary participation in frontier markets to a continuous engagement in labor and commodity exchanges had become widespread. This led to a dependence on resources from a combination of sources: migrant wage labor, subsistence production, and the sale of surplus agricultural products, that is, to the emergence of income-pooling practices typical of household structures in the capitalist world-economy. We have already noted that the position of the chiefs during this period became increasingly dependent upon the economic and political networks of the world-economy. For commoners the changes were no less dramatic, although they led not to greater rewards but to deepening poverty. A key factor was the decline in per capita availability of fertile lowland acreage. This led to smaller holdings, although it is impossible to gauge the extent to which greater inequality in landholdings emerged. Yet even under the implausible assumption that stable or increasing agricultural exports were equally distributed, by all accounts the pace of depenence upon cash incomes far outpaced incoming receipts from the sale of cereals and pastoral products. Accounts of increasing agricultural production thus need to be set against increasing need for cash incomes. When the Resident Commissioner of Basutoland of the time, H. C. Sloley, was asked if the Basuto were getting more wealthy and independent through their agricultural production, he replied:

No, I should say that is not the case. They have got very wealthy of late years; they have markets for their produce and such things, but until late years they did not. But at the same time their wants have increased proportionately, and I have no doubt that they have not only a great deal more money than they used to get, but they have a great more to do with it. (Sloley, 1904: 207)

Under these conditions the emergence of young male migrant labor as an essential generator of resources for the broader community – as opposed to chiefly and elder control over land, cattle, and women – posed a considerable threat to the maintenance of practices that bound multiple conjugal units into homestead settlements, and commoner homestead settlements to chiefs. The earliest indicator of such changes occurred at the extensive network of mission stations in Basutoland, where missionaries encouraged their converts to abandon practices of labor tribute, cattle loans, and brideprice – all the essential mechanisms that bound individuals' productive activities into a broader network of precapitalist control and redistribution. It was thus on the mission stations that the new units of production and reproduction, which we call households, were first evident.

By the First World War, such pressures for closer control of resources affected a much broader proportion of the population. Whereas previously elders controlled young males through their domination of access to cattle and bridewealth, migration now increasingly placed resources directly in the hands of younger men. Throughout the opening decades of the twentieth century, a continual battle was fought by chiefs and elders to control the labor of young men, a fight that even divided the chiefs from the colonial state over the issue of whether to tax homesteads or individuals (the latter implying all young men). To tax unmarried men was a contradictory process from the standpoint of the chiefs. On the one hand, it could well lead to further migration of the young, and thereby increase further their social independence. On the other hand, the increasing dependence of chiefs upon tax incomes made such a prospect appealing. As one statement of 1916 noted:

Most of the boys of 18, 19, and so on look after their fathers' stock at the mountains. There are some boys of these ages who run away to the mines. I would say let these boys be made to pay and not those who look after the cattle of their fathers ... If our boys are compelled to pay then they will leave our cattle at the mountains and go to Johannesburg. (Cited in Kimble, 1985: 54)

Such statements most often applied to wealthier homesteads who had considerable local resources, and whose access to cash incomes was particularly dependent upon agricultural surpluses and/or the sale of mohair and wool, which had emerged as a key export commodity. For those allied to the missions and for the increasing number of persons affected by overcrowding on the land, even the promise of cattle through service to elders disappeared. And, as consumption goods and even inputs to agriculture became linked to wage earnings, men continued to migrate after marriage. As Resident Commissioner Sloley noted as early as 1904, "I do not quite agree with the theory that the Basuto goes out to get a wife and buys a few cattle. He is continually earning money and spending it" (cited in Kimble, 1985: 210). Under these conditions it was impossible to retain even the semblance of precapitalist links. The result was that the precapitalist homestead increasingly gave way to the household participating in the capitalist world-economy, which managed its own production and consumption needs.

This change has been widely observed throughout southern Africa. It is important to note, however, that we are not asserting the demise of extended families and the rise of nuclear families. The size of households alone has very little to do with the substantive processes at work. As we have indicated, what was important here is the emergence of bounded units of production and consumption that regulated relations to labor and commodity markets. As long as precapitalist relationships retained their force, participation in both labor and commodity markets could be subject to precapitalist political control and, possibly, resistance in defense of precapitalist life. The emergence of household structures was thus part and parcel of the transformation of precapitalist form of rule.

Throughout the 1920s, the general tendencies of increasing land pressure, the deepening commodification of life, and the insertion of the chiefs into the colonial system of rule continued unabated. Together these factors inexorably pressed toward higher levels of dependence upon cash incomes, which for many households came increasingly from migrant labor. Accounts of the period suggest that households were in fact splitting into two forms, with one smaller, wealthier (often chiefly) group, reliant upon income from agricultural and pastoral production, and another more impoverished segment, increasingly reliant upon wage income in order to meet needs that could only be fulfilled through the market. The interwar period clearly marked the end of any expectation that the vast majority of the Basuto could ever gain sufficient cash income from rural productive activities. One immediate cause was the continual pressure on land, a factor enhanced by the increasing lack of rural employment opportunities in South Africa. By the 1930s, it was evident that many households had insufficient access to land in Basutoland itself. By this time, available land was almost completely under cultivation in both lowland and highland areas, eliminating lowland grazing areas (Ashton, 1967: 136ff). This process was accompanied by an increasing number of chiefs in the countryside, as the sons of chiefs continued to be "placed," as well as by an increasing power of the headmen in the allocation of land. Whereas in previous periods land surpluses allowed homestead heads to allocate land to members of their settlement group, by the 1930s "owing to the general shortage of land, few family holdings [were] left and practically all the land, especially the little remaining virgin land, [came] under the headman's control" (Ashton, 1967: 145). Larger numbers of marginal producers appeared, with newly formed households often waiting years before being allocated lands.

For households now dependent upon labor migration not only at the beginning but throughout their life cycle, agricultural practices were severely undermined by the absence of male labor. As noted above, the Basuto in the late nineteenth century quickly adopted plows and increased productivity in the process. Labor migration within smaller household units removed such sources of labor. In the 1930s,

The full human team consists of a small boy as leader, a youth as driver and an experienced man as ploughman. Owing to the dearth of males, due to labour migration, the most varied combinations may be found. Sometimes there is no leader, at other times boys of twelve or thirteen may have to take the plough and girls and women often have to inspanned as drivers or ploughmen. The effect of this absence of men is serious ... (Ashton, 1967: 124)

More and more households were also forced to merge their meager resources with those better off: contributing labor if plows were absent, or sharecropping in return for labor assistance. While this type of arrangement fell within precolonial arrangements of reciprocity, by the 1930s these practices could more accurately be described as the selling of labor power and the renting of land. All this occurred within the context of traditional terminology, which served to mask growing class stratification.

Continual adherence to the regulation that every married man had rights to land allocation served to check the expansion of the stratification through the creation of a large body of permanently landless. Still more important, however, for the income patterns and composition of the households was the worldwide agricultural crisis of the mid-1930s. Prices for primary products – both cereals and wool, the essential products of the Basuto – began to fall after very high peaks in the early 1920s. With the crash of 1929, prices plummeted. Given the tendencies outlined above, this put ever greater pressure on rural cultivators throughout southern Africa. Those who depended upon agricultural production for income found their incomes slashed. Grain exports steadily declined. By the end of the First World War exports equaled imports. After the crash, grain imports accelerated (Murray, 1981: 18), these years being further marked by devastating droughts that killed a high percentage of livestock. The result was a greater push toward wage employment in South Africa, where industrial growth was accelerating after 1924, and the mineral sector was booming after the revaluation of gold in 1933.

Households which pooled income from marginal agricultural production and migrant labor thus became increasingly common in the years after the great crash. At the same time, a new significant feature emerged: the permanent outmigration of entire households and their reformation as urban households in South African cities. While single males had in previous decades remained in the urban areas of South Africa, the crushing conditions of rural life in the 1930s accelerated this tendency considerably. In the 1946 census, an actual drop in the population of Basutoland was recorded for the first time. As Great Britain's *Annual Report on Basutoland* noted at the time:

It is generally agreed that this fall is not due to faulty enumeration, but to certain economic factors such as land scarcity, soil poverty and a succession of bad harvests which has inevitably resulted in a larger exodus to the industrial centres of the Union [of South Africa], where many have probably become permanently resident . . . The three districts most affected . . . besides being the biggest sources of labour for the mines, are also from an agricultural point of view the most poverty-stricken . . . (Great Britain, Colonial Office, 1947: 17)

Most commentators have attributed migrant flows simply to an increasing dependency on the mines. However, the Basuto, drawn by the industrial boom under way in South Africa, and ever aware of wage differentials, appeared to have been attracted rather to the higher-paying opportunities in industry whenever such were available. Whereas in the 1910s and 1920s the mining companies achieved their desired goal of recruiting larger numbers of Basuto on increasingly long contracts (extending from six to nine months), in 1948 employment had fallen to 35,136 males from 47,470 in 1936, because of the diversion of labor to new South African industries such as steel (Great Britain, Colonial Office, 1947: 17).

In succeeding decades, migration to South Africa continued to rise. Absentees as a percentage of population went from 15.8 percent in 1936 to 19.5 percent in 1956, with women migrants almost doubling in number over these two decades, to a figure of 41,992 out of an absent population of 154,782 in 1956 (Murray, 1981: 4). The dispersion of the Basuto migrant laborers across sectors within South Africa is also suggested by the returns on the destination of migrants issued passes: through the early 1950s, up to half were employed outside the mining sector where wages were by now far above those in the mines (Great Britain, Colonial Office, 1952: 15).

The absence of men throughout the year became the accepted norm in every village. Activities formerly dependent upon resident males, or at least upon a male complement during crucial periods of the agricultural cycle, were most profoundly affected. Whereas previous divisions of labor by sex had allocated the care of cattle and plowing to men, women were now increasingly engaged in these activities. The loss of male labor time undercut both the capital and labor resources for plowing. By the mid-1950s, roughly one-half of Basuto households thus lacked the necessary oxen to form a plowing team. As a result, plowing became an item either paid out of migrants' cash remittances or exchanged for rights to fields or by crop-shares. Under these conditions, a small group of resident males, with greater control and access to both agricultural and pastoral lands, appeared to be emerging as capitalist farmers. This was particularly true in areas where significant incomes were derived from wool and mohair sales; here 45 percent of families had few or no small stock (Sheddick, 1954: 84, 99–102, 189). While chiefs were especially effective in controlling access to the remaining grazing areas in mountainous areas, a small group of wealthier commoners appeared to be emerging as well.

An immediate effect of these changes was the continuing transformation of class relations as these increasingly pivoted on relations to South African capital and not to local controllers of the means of production which were generating ever smaller returns. Indeed this could be seen in the increasing inability of chiefs and headmen to control resident populations. Both tribute labor and court fines payable to chiefs were abolished while remaining chiefly privileges were restricted to an appointed few. The proliferation of minor chiefs and the onerous burdens they placed on commoners were thus finally contained.

For the vast majority of commoner households now engaged in migrant labor, these new divisions of labor and income sources became entrenched. With agricultural production rarely meeting fully even foodstuff needs, the labor of women and children became increasingly important in rural areas. Migrant remittances served to underwrite both continued agricultural production and consumption needs. Household budgets, which were first collected in the 1950s and 1960s, indicate this quite well. The most optimistic assessor of rural production, Vernon Sheddick, shows that even under the assumption of good crops, returns from agricultural production for landholders could barely meet restricted subsistence needs in the late 1940s (1954: 97). Sandra Wallman's profiles of thirty households in 1961–63 show that, while grain sales often contributed significantly to income in the period after harvest, over the calendar year income from migrant wages was far more important (1969: 73–75). And it was equally clear that all thirty households frequently fell below the official poverty line.

It took a particular set of conditions to ensure the viability of these emergent migrant labor households. On the one hand, continued productivity of land was required to maintain rural income sources; on the other hand, continued access to South Africa's labor market was necessary to ensure cash incomes. Around the mid-1950s, radical changes occurred which undercut both these features. First, there was a dramatic shift in wage-earning opportunities within South Africa attendant upon the extension of apartheid. Beginning in the 1950s and accelerating in the 1960s, the South African state restricted foreign labor flows by gender and location. This had been a state objective for a long time. What was new was the ability to enforce these regulations through an expanded bureaucracy of influx control and border posts. The effect of these restrictions was to limit migration to single males, and to direct these males to the mining sector. This reversed the permanent outflow of previous decades, which had served to relieve land pressures within Lesotho itself, and had generated the formation of Sotho households in urban South Africa. It also narrowed wage employment to the lowest-paying sector within South Africa, thereby restricting income-earning possibilities for Basuto migrants.

By the mid-1970s, the dependence of the Basuto on migration was striking. Within Lesotho itself the opportunities for wage labor were exceedingly small. In the mid-1970s, total employment in Lesotho totaled 22,000, with 7,000 in the public sector and 15,000 in the private sector, out of an active labor force of approximately 460,000 persons (Ström, 1978: 23). Such figures pale in relation to a migration flow of approximately 200,000 persons in 1975 (van der Wiel, 1977: 22) and migrants' earnings far exceeding Lesotho's Gross Domestic Product. No country in Africa by this time had a higher involvement in, and dependency upon, labor migration.

The destination of the vast majority of Basuto migrants was the gold mining sector, which had been isolated over the course of the 1960s and 1970s as a low-wage sector set apart from the urban-industrial labor market. Of the 81 percent of migrants engaged in the mines, approximately 30 percent were in the Rand areas. The predominance of mining as a sector of employment confirms the overwhelmingly male character of the migrant flow by the mid-1970s. Surveys of migration rates for male age groups illustrate the importance of migration. Migration rates reached a high point in the 25–29 years age cohort, showed a slight decline in the 30–34 age group, and dropped sharply after age 39. More than three-quarters of the males between 20 and 29 years of age were working in South Africa (van der Wiel, 1977: 32). As these figures suggest, there was in the mid-1970s no significant body of adult males permanently resident over their lifetime in Lesotho itself.

If male migration to mining centers formed the central linkage between South Africa and Lesotho, it remains to be determined how incomes from migration were shared as part of household consumption funds. Unfortunately the overall volume of miners' remittances to their households in Lesotho is difficult to ascertain. Even though restricted to tightly policed compounds, miners had many ways to spend their income. Remittances moreover flowed through many avenues: via recruiting agencies' facilities, through the post office, through friends returning home, and carried home by the miner himself. One survey in the mid-1970s reported that migrants spent 41 percent of their salary on themselves, 31 percent on other household members, 19 percent on communal household items (livestock, furniture, etc.), and 9 percent distributed to other households (especially here payments of "bohali" or "brideprice" to the wife's parents) (van der Wiel, 1977: 82). The small amount that actually was spent on persons outside the migrant's household indicates the tight circle that encapsulated transfers.

If migrant labor constituted the primary economic activity of adult males, agricultural production remained the primary activity of those women, children, and male elders left in the Lesotho countryside. Income or resources derived in this latter respect from both crop production and livestock raising. Distribution of land was far more equitable in Lesotho than in most surrounding territories. Not only were there no settler farmers, but the historical system of land tenure granted, in principle, usufructuary rights in some arable land to every married male taxpayer. Even where this practice continued, it clearly excluded many women and the unmarried, with the result that the landless households increased in the post-1945 period (from reported census figures of 7 percent in 1950, to 9 percent in 1960, to 13 percent in 1970). At the same time, landholdings became smaller, although it remained the case that the size of holdings corresponded to size of households (Murray, 1981: 89–90). Livestock were much more inequitably distributed, with an estimated 50 percent of households in the mid-1970s holding no stock at all. Here too evidence suggests, nonetheless, a correlation between household size and size of livestock holding. Yet successful crop production and livestock raising clearly did not offer alternative avenues for income from migration, as they might have done in earlier periods, even for those whose crop yields significantly worsened in the 1960s and 1970s. Rather, all evidence suggests that migrant incomes were essential to the provision of key agricultural inputs (tools, seeds, hiring of plows, etc.) as well as for the purchase of livestock.

The necessity of combining income from migrant wage labor and income-generating activities in Lesotho itself were reflected in household size and income distributions. Field studies suggest that household patterns in the mid-1970s exhibited two modes in the frequency of household size at two and six persons per household. A large part of the explanation for these modes lies in the life cycle of household formation and dissolution. Small households were predominantly composed of newly formed households or widows; in addition one must note households in which the husband/father had defaulted. Larger households, often composed of three generations, signified not the "traditional extended family," but households in the middle of their life cycle with resident parents, young children, and often women from broken conjugal unions.

Moving beyond household size, it is evident that income-pooling and stratification patterns divided along a fault line between households which had a male member in wage employment and those who did not. This factor, far more than any other such as access to land, determined total household income levels. Data from a mid-1970s survey indicated this quite clearly (see Table 18). Only for the two lowest income strata did agriculture contribute a considerable proportion of total household income. The majority of households in the low-income group consisted of widows living with young

Table 18. *Household size and sources of income*

	Annual income in rands			
	0–199	200–599	600–999	1,000 plus
Household characteristics				
Percentage of households	27	20	27	26
Average income	66	408	859	1,739
Average size	3.1	4.9	5.1	7.7
Sources of income in percentage				
Crops	39	16	3	4
Livestock	30	21	6	12
Off-farm	23	10	9	13
Migrant	8	53	81	71

Source: Adapted from van der Wiel (1977: 84, 88).

children. The two middle groups comprised mainly nuclear families with an absent male migrant, while the highest income stratum was composed of larger households often with more than one wage earner. If we relate household incomes to absolute poverty levels, it becomes apparent that approximately three-quarters of rural households were below even the inadequate official poverty datum line (van der Wiel, 1977: 89–90; cf., however, Murray, 1981). Even for those with access to all of a miner's wage, poverty could not be avoided: the starting wage paid by the mines in the mid-1970s was only 70 percent of the income required to satisfy an average household's basic needs.

The narrowing of employment opportunities during the 1960s and 1970s to low-wage male mining labor suggests that gender relationships must have undergone significant changes. In "traditional" custom, women were marginal members of Basuto society. They are subordinate in status both as daughters to one family and daughters-in-law to another family (Murray, 1981: ch. 7; Gordon, 1981: 113–30). By the mid-1970s, especially with the decline both in female migration and in the viability of incomes from crop production, women were especially dependent upon male migrant remittances. What this obscures are processes that cannot be hidden under "traditional/tribal" norms, and that pinpoint women as crucial regulators of household reproduction and thus, indicate the indirect contribution the women of Lesotho made to the South

African labor force. While males are, for example, often recorded as household heads, "in practice nearly 70 percent of rural households are effectively managed by women" (Murray, 1981: 155). Caught between their status position and dependence upon male wages – or even worse the lack of a male household member in paid employment – women were filled with uncertainty regarding their day-to-day survival. A considerable degree of conflict in the countryside revolved around the failure of men to support their families. Contributions from agricultural production managed by women offered only small returns for the considerable labor expended. And women were particularly at risk given the lack of a steady stream of remittances even when husbands were employed. Informal sector activities abounded and appeared to be particularly important to small, "female-headed" households. These activities included beer brewing and selling, petty trading, drug trading ("dagga," or marijuana, smoking being a longstanding custom), seasonal labor on wealthier farmers' land, and "concubinage." While essential to the survival of small households, they hardly provided a substitution for wage incomes, and those dependent upon them found themselves in the poorest situation of all rural households.

Over the course of the last century, many rural areas of southern Africa have at one time or another supplied labor to South Africa's mines and industries. Yet the rural social structures that have emerged have not unilaterally duplicated the path of those in Lesotho. In some areas, agricultural production for self-consumption and market sale has been sustained, even as migrant labor became entrenched; in others, alternative wage employment has emerged. Two critical factors underlay such differences. First, the character of rural resources and class formation has varied to a wide degree. For the Basuto, as we have seen, local class and cultural factors have often determined the possibilities of obtaining incomes from wage employment and agricultural production and their combination into household consumption funds. Secondly, and more relevant for us here, was the deepening relationship with South African labor force formation. As the latter altered over time, household structures and income-pooling took on divergent trajectories. In the nineteenth century, there opened up the possibility of production for the market and historically high wages; in the interwar period, wage employment created migrant-subsistence patterns and drew Basuto from their land to form urban households; in the postwar period, low-wage migrant incomes became entrenched as the center of household budgets. These transformations, and the different household structures and income-pooling practices that concomitantly dominated during each period, moved hand-in-hand with the industrialization of South Africa.

South Africa's movement into the semiperiphery in the late interwar period initiated a growing divergence in employment and income opportunities between South Africa and neighboring territories, and between different sectors within South Africa (Martin, 1990). Yet labor flows were far more difficult to control than commodity flows. Basuto grain could be excluded from the South African market, but the continued migrant inflow to South Africa's urban areas allowed Basuto (like South African Blacks) to move into higher-paying positions. As accumulation in southern Africa increasingly pivoted around South Africa in the postwar period, however, far more specific channeling of labor was established.

When South Africa plunged into a depression in the 1980s, and internal unemployment and resistance escalated, it no longer remained clear how long the postwar pattern would hold. After the mid-1970s, South African mines, benefiting from the rise in the gold price and fearing the potential effects of independence in Angola, Mozambique, and Zimbabwe, successively reduced recruiting of foreign miners. By comparison to other supplying areas, Lesotho has suffered the least, although how the higher wages for fewer migrants will remold household structures in Lesotho remains to be fully explored. Yet, without a resolution of the unemployment and political crisis in South Africa, the prospects for continuing wage contributions to Sotho households remain most uncertain in the short to medium run. After a century of close entrapment within South African developments, the Basuto face the loss of their previously easy access to the South African wage labor market.

NOTE

1 Lesotho is the name of the country since independence in 1966. It was called Basutoland when it was a British Protectorate. Basuto is the name of the people collectively. Each person is a Mosotho. The language is Sesotho. Basuto and Sotho are the adjectival forms.

V

Conclusion

Core-periphery and household structures

Immanuel Wallerstein and Joan Smith

We laid out in the introductory chapter how (and why) we reconceptualized the household as an income-pooling unit, with boundaries subject to continuing change. We suggested that households were socially constituted entities subject to pressures deriving from the cyclical rhythms of the world market and from the state-machineries. We argued that ethnicity was a principal modality of socializing household members into particular economic roles, and that these very norms of socialization kept changing under the influence of the multiple pressures generated by the ongoing operation of the world-system. Once formulated, this reconceptualization served as the premise of our collective research.

We proceeded to try to observe how households were constructed and reconstructed in eight "regions" of three parts of the world over a period of a century or so. This empirical work has been presented in Parts II, III, and IV. As the reader will readily observe, we discovered a complex picture, but one which our concepts rendered clearer, or at least so we believe. However, there are no simple conclusions that we can draw from what inevitably was (and was always conceived to be) an exploratory study. We wanted to see if our concepts were usable, and whether they revealed patterns that were prima facie plausible. Obviously, we were plagued by the problem of inadequate and incomparable data. New concepts seldom find already existing data that closely fit their needs of empirical measurement. We did not find ideal data in this case either. We discuss this problem in the Postscript.

The question, of course, is what have we learned from this exploratory effort. How can we now make explicit some tentative hypotheses that could be the subject of systematic further research? We started out with the strong suspicion that there was something wrong with the way the historical social sciences had traditionally conceptualized wage labor. At one point we thought this suspicion could be summarized in the phrase, "wages are not enough." Now, it seems to us, we should make a stronger assertion: In a capitalist system, wages can never be the sole or even principal mode of payment of the vast majority of the world workforce. Wages must always be combined with other forms of income. These other forms of income are never negligible. The rare exception might be a household composed of a married couple without children, both of whom are highly paid professional employees of large institutions – say, two yuppies in mid-Manhattan in the 1980s. These are not worker households.

The fact, however, that wages are always combined with other forms of income does not at all mean that they are always combined in the same ways. In fact, it seems clear that the combinations are different in patterned ways, and that these patterns are correlated substantially with the two characteristics of the world-economy we built into our research design: core/periphery, and A/B (or expansion/stagnation) phases.

To see this clearly, we must go back to the starting point. A basic belief of social science as it has been written now for 150 years or so is that once upon a time people produced by themselves in order to reproduce themselves. This is generally called living on subsistence. The usual model proffered is that, over historical time, and particularly (some would say only) in historical capitalism, this pattern of production/reproduction shifted in the direction of one in which most workers produced within enterprises controlled or owned by others and received money wages for the time thus spent. Having obtained the money in this fashion, the workers then purchased commodities in the market in order to reproduce themselves. We, along with many others, have been quite critical of this formulation of historical transformation. We do not think this is a good summary of modern history. Nevertheless, at this point, we wish to stress that, of course, this statement is not totally false. There is a small kernel of truth in it. This kernel however is so incomplete as to be misleading, and has in fact misled very many.

Still, this kernel of truth is well illustrated in the material covered in the Lesotho case study. It is indeed the case that, as late as the late nineteenth century, there were some parts of the world in which something near a "subsistence economy" continued to exist. What is important to underline is that, in such areas, it was also the case that what we today call a household – a relatively small, circumscribed unit largely responsible for gathering in sufficient income for reproduction – probably did *not* exist. That is to say, in such areas the unit guaranteeing reproduction tended to be much larger, what is sometimes called a "community" (Wallerstein, 1984). When such an area is incorporated into the world-system (Hopkins *et al.*, 1987), one of the many consequences is the disappearance, or at least the reduction in the economic role, of such communities and the creation of household structures such as we have been describing in this work. This process was harder to observe in any of the other material we collected, since in these other areas such a process when it occurred did so by and large earlier than the point in time for which we collected the material. What we are calling "households" were already in existence by the period for which we collected the data.

One of the basic processes of the historical trajectory of the capitalist world-economy has been the deepening of the distinction between, and the polarization of, core and periphery. Core and periphery are not discrete entities. They are a relational antinomy. Core-like and peripheral processes are opposite sides of a single coin. Peripherality exists only in relation to, and by contrast with, coreness. They are thus concepts grounded in space, but it is a complex space. There are multiple layers of coreness and peripherality (Wallerstein, 1978, 1987). Thus, we may use North–South as a metaphor for core-periphery. But we can of course also find core-periphery relations within a single country, with internal spatial implications, as within South Africa, or even within the United States.

The most interesting outcome of our research is the evidence that there seems to be a type of household structure that binds people to core-like activities and therefore to areas primarily engaged in such activities and another household structure that seems to bind people to peripheral activities and therefore to areas primarily engaged in peripheral activities. (It follows that semiperipheral states should probably show a fairly even mixture of the two household types.) This typological polarity shows up first of all in the *kinds* of non-wage activities that are closely integrated with wage work in such households. If this has not been obvious heretofore, it is because households do not start out historically in such a polarized way, but develop historically over time in that direction. Only analyses over long periods of time bring the patterns to the surface. One may refer to this whole process as housewifization, as Werlhof does (1984), provided that we remember that the "housewife" phenomenon is not totally gender-based (as Werlhof herself notes), but also provided that we remember that there are two distinct models, not merely one model, of housewifization.

In the areas that are being peripheralized, we find on the surface what many have hitherto described as an incomplete proletarianization. Wage income exists, but it is clearly insufficient to cover the living costs of a household. The wages are both too low and in most cases too sporadic. Therefore it seems the household is still partially self-subsistent, in the traditional sense of providing food, shelter, and clothing for themselves by means of non-market operations. In these cases, it seems there is an inverse relationship between wages and subsistence. Whenever wages decline for whatever reason (say unemployment), the household resorts to increased subsistence activity.

No doubt, there is some such pattern. But this is indeed a declining pattern over time. The question is with what it is being replaced. It is not being replaced with truly wage-centered households. Rather a different pattern has been emerging over time which is perhaps the very mark of peripheralization.

The pattern is not the combination of wages and subsistence, but the combination of wages and petty market operations. We call it petty market operations and not petty commodity production, because commodity production is only one kind of remunerative market activity. The retail sale of factory-produced matches (one at a time) by a 10-year-old boy in a Third World urban center is also remunerative market activity. The sale of living quarters space and services to a "boarder" is also a remunerative market operation. Illegal transactions of multiple varieties are also market operations.

The point of all these activities is that they earn cash, however little, and the peripheral household structure is in desperate need of cash, even very small amounts. It is in desperate need of cash precisely because the process of peripheralization is undermining, reducing, sometimes even destroying totally the possibility of obtaining resources out of traditional subsistence activities. A very clear example of this process is described in the chapter on rural Mexico where the land redistribution led rural residents to become market-oriented peasants who, however, because of the size of the plots, had to obtain wage work as well. Thus we see that not only are wages not enough, but most often market-oriented operations are also "not enough." The widespread combination of wages and market operations as the effective base of lifetime household income is indeed the signal mark of peripheralization.

It is in this fashion that we may interpret or reinterpret the enormous recent literature on "marginalization" and the "informal sector." Much of this literature emphasizes the "newness" of this phenomenon. Insofar as the process of peripheralization is a continuing trend in a polarizing capitalist world-economy, we are seeing more and more households of this archetypal peripheral variety, and seeing the pattern more and more clearly (Castells and Portes, 1989). But of course the basic phenomenon is not really new; it is more that it has been newly described.

The Black women who have engaged in beer brewing in the Rand in order to pool this market income with the inadequate wages of the male members of their household did not begin to do this only in the last fifteen to twenty years. To be sure, always and everywhere in peripheralized areas, some households are more "marginalized" than others, if by that we mean the proportion of lifetime wage income is even lower for some (most) than for a minority who are better connected with wage employment possibilities. But it is clear that even the latter (the better-connected households) engage in the combination of wage and market activities, as we can see for example even for the households of skilled laborers in Mexico City in the post-1945 period.

The contrast with the core pattern is clear. But even here, we can discern it only if we see it as a trend over time. If we look at Polish workers in Detroit or the rural Pennsylvanian shoe workers in Binghamton at the turn of the twentieth century, they seem to be following the same trajectory of peripheralization: going through a transition from a wages plus subsistence combination (of inverted proportions) to a wages plus market operations combination. Indeed, this is what marks them out as "working class" in the 1890–1914 US (or even the 1890–1945 US) as opposed to being "middle class."

The "middle class" has had a different household pattern. In the period following the Second World War, it is clear from our Detroit, Binghamton, and New York data that the working class (or at least part of the working class) moved to adopt a pattern similar to that the middle class already had. This was of course true of only part of the working class. This was not true of say the ghetto populations in Detroit or New York.

But what patterns are they we are describing as the core working-class household patterns? They are no more wage-exclusive income patterns than is the peripheral pattern. Here too wages are a crucial element but (except for a very tiny minority) can never be adequate. We are all familiar with the realities. The wages for contemporary workers in industrialized countries tend to be above minimal level, sometimes very much above this minimum. Nonetheless, they are so "insufficient" (in terms of income expectancies) that more and more women (erstwhile mere "housewives") have entered the labor market to secure a "second" wage income for the household. Sometimes this is part-time work (but part-time is an expression often used for up to 30 hours a week); sometimes it is full-time. Sometimes it is home work (a revived form of the putting-out system), but this home work turns out in effect to be disguised wage employment (and of course low-wage remuneration).

Now we discover however that not only is one wage not enough, but that two wages are also not enough, even if one of them (at least) is above the minimum level. These combined wages must still be supplemented if the household is to "survive," as it socially defines survival. Where is this supplementary income found? It is not by and large found in market operations.

At this point, as our US data make clear (and the pattern seems to be the same in western Europe), there are two different principal sources of supplementing the inadequate wage income. There is the pattern of the "poor," and there is the pattern of those above poverty level. The pattern of the "poor" is well known. The "poor" supplement inadequate wage income with inadequate government transfer payments ("welfare" of all varieties), to make up an inadequate overall package. Welfare is politically unpopular and the government programs are constantly under political attack. But what is the alternative to welfare? The only real alternative is the "peripheral" household pattern which is a wages plus market operations combination. Insofar as the state and large corporations wish to eliminate or reduce the petty market operations for a variety of reasons (ranging from the elimination of competition to police control to the aesthetics of urban life), welfare is essential. Insofar as there is a reduction in welfare, there must necessarily be a resurgence in petty market operations (including of course those that are formally illegal; street drug operations are one well-known example).

Whichever the solution, the poor remain poor, that is, with insufficient access to the large range of consumer durables that define acceptable living standards in the core zones of the world-economy. Subsistence (in the traditional sense) has ceased, however, to be an alternative for them. If the wages are cut back, and/or the welfare is cut back, few "return to the farm," for such "farms" no longer exist by and large. Instead, the "poor" who suddenly become poorer scrounge in the ghettos and barrios to find whatever petty market outlets they can in order literally to survive. In New York in the depression of the 1930s, Blacks still turned to market operations to supplement wage income – a peripheral pattern. Poor Whites were already utilizing transfer payments. By the 1970s downturn, both Blacks and Whites were utilizing transfer payments.

The second pattern, for those above the poverty level, is strikingly different, and approaches the middle-class pattern. The two-income household (of skilled workers, and therefore a fortiori of professionals) finds their cash income insufficient. But they have a solution available. It is paradoxically subsistence income. It is however a fundamentally different kind of subsistence income from that which centered in the primary production (of food and textiles) that we have long associated with the term. Such traditional subsistence activities have gone out, even in the updated form of garden plots and sewing dresses, which were widespread in the nineteenth century and even early twentieth century. Binghamton households were finding such activities uneconomical already in the 1930s.

The new subsistence has been termed "self-provisioning" (Pahl, 1984; Smith, 1987). Self-provisioning works in the following manner. The double-wage household, whose wages are above poverty level, use a part of their cash wages to purchase "means of production" – both basic tools, and maintenance supplies – with which to create additional resources into which they must necessarily pour their labor in order to have a consumable product.

The washing machine requires an initial investment. It does enable the household to wash clothes often and efficiently, but it requires that someone spends time at it. To be sure, one may argue that such labor is not physically onerous, but it remains time-consuming nonetheless. One could multiply the examples: the whole range of do-it-yourself activities; the pervasive wild-game hunting which assumes that the household has a freezer; the home accounting that presumes the household has a personal computer; chauffeuring children, which presumes the ownership of a car (if not of two).

Furthermore, it is not as though the households had any viable alternative. Not only can they not afford normally to purchase these services that they perform for themselves, but the services are increasingly not even available on the market, or at least not available at prices that are reasonably priced (as opposed to services available for the wealthy few at very high cost). For example, inexpensive furniture is increasingly only available in an assemble-it-yourself form. Many foods are now readily available only in a half-finished form which requires further household work and machinery.

Thus, the core household type that is emerging does not take the form of the classical image of the "proletarian" household, one that draws all its income from wages and does not own the "means of production." Quite the contrary. The core household type of the majority who are above the poverty level but beneath the level of high wealth is a household that combines wage income, property that takes the form of means of production (not for the market but for the household), plus self-provisioning labor.

In this picture how do the A/B phases of economic expansion and contraction affect the picture? The primary effect on the world labor force is a worldwide reduction in wage employment opportunities (although for a minority of zones and sectors the situation may remain stable or even improve). Wage income seldom disappears but it is a smaller percentage of total household income. Total income normally drops. Households compensate in whatever ways they can: petty market operations, transfer payments, increased self-provisioning (though the material base for this depreciates in a long contraction). People cope as best they can, and most often not too well. The attention of everyone including that of social scientists is suddenly drawn to the non-wage components of total household income. The polarization of household incomes and therefore of household patterns is accentuated. The "poor" in the core may be politically (and temporarily) forced back into "peripheral" household patterns. But the next A-phase seems to restore the distinction.

Nineteenth-century thought bequeathed to us a basic model of household structures: from subsistence to wage income. It is true in the sense that primary subsistence production has been disappearing, and virtually all households are today wage income recipients. Capitalism does indeed involve the "commodification of everything," and the cash nexus is its defining ideal. But it is not at all true that cash can only be obtained through wages. Petty market operations and rent on the one hand and transfer payments on the other hand provide cash, and that large percentage of the world's population who live poorly cannot survive without such other forms of cash income to supplement wages. Nor is there any likelihood that this need will diminish as we project ahead. The peripheral household pattern seems to be in the process of becoming ever more encrusted for the large majority of world labor.

There remains the better-off minority of world labor, those whose combined household wage incomes are above the "poverty level." These are the beneficiaries of so-called Fordism. The Fordist compromise (let us not forget the origin of the term) requires there be a large stratum of better-off workers who can purchase the so-called mass consumption items whose sale forms a key element of contemporary global profit. But the Fordist compromise contains a catch. The mass consumption items are *grosso modo* sold incomplete. They require self-provisioning labor. They require, that is, the consumer to add him or herself to the productive worker as a source of surplus-value to the economic enterprise that produces the item. Thus the productive workers (male and female) contribute surplus-value twice, once as wage worker and once as self-provisioning consumer. The better-off working-class households may be better off in terms of the range of items they consume. They are not better off in the amount of labor time invested in producing their income. They do not have really more leisure time. Rather, their leisure time is in large part self-provisioning labor.

The truly wage-centered household is the household of a very small minority indeed. If this minority grows larger worldwide (in the order of going from say 1 percent to 5 percent), what we will be witnessing is the process of bourgeoisification and not the process of proletarianization. The ultimate paradox is that it is the well-to-do professional or executive who is most often the true full-time wage worker; the proletarian is condemned to remain a partial wage worker. Thus do we live out the social polarization predicted by nineteenth-century social science in ways quite different from the patterns they thought would express this polarization.

A postscript on method

Joan Smith, with Jamie Sudler

In the studies reported here we have attempted quite broadly to measure the relative value to the household of the income accessible to it but derived from sources other than wages per se. The very nature of our study presented us with one of our fundamental problems. The usual precision associated with measuring the value of economic activities was altogether lacking.

There were the usual twin problems associated with large-scale historical studies of any kind: lack of data on many topics, and the incommensurability of the kinds of data that exist. But there was a more fundamental issue at stake, namely, how the range of analysis of economic activities may be extended beyond the set of assumptions that flow from and define the formal market. This issue goes to the heart of the intellectual and political debate that surrounds non-wage labor and its role in the capitalist world-economy.

The widely shared insight that non-waged work activities are as important to the world-economy as formally organized labor belies a striking inability or reluctance actually to measure that labor in such a way that comparisons may be made across place and time. The joke about the college professor marrying his housekeeper and thereby reducing the gross national product is no longer very funny. However, the absence of measurements of non-waged work is not simply the result of bureaucratic decisions but is entwined in the political definition of labor activities of every form. Quantification is always about control, and different forms of labor control always and everywhere are about political possibilities and necessities. Thus, the very effort to create an exact yardstick for non-waged labor in some very fundamental ways does violence to the character of that labor and its role in the world-economy.

In any case, in order to develop our argument we had to put some kind of value on the relative degree to which households depend upon non-waged labor to sustain themselves. In developing some rough and ready measurements of the value of non-waged labor (which we describe below) we were conscious that ours was hardly a novel attempt. However, after reviewing the debates concerning the proper measurement techniques we came to two related conclusions: First, there exists no standard accepted method for imputing value to non-waged labor activities. Secondly, whatever the methods employed, they are the product of a wide variety of assumptions concerning the nature of economic activities – the way economic value is created, appropriated, and assigned. We are not immune to such assumptions and have attempted to be clear about them. We have, however, constructed our accounts not so much upon the precision of our measurements but on the plausibility of our arguments.

Our argument is not new. Over the course of the past two decades many theorists, especially those concerned with so-called development processes and feminists concerned with the real economic contributions and condition of women, have pointed to the central role of non-waged labor in the dynamics of the household and the world-economy (Deere, 1979). What we have attempted here is to demonstrate two points. First, there is a pattern, worldwide in scope, in the degree to which non-waged labor activities supplement earnings from wages. Secondly, these non-waged labor forms are the product of constraints specific to the capitalist world-economy. We demonstrate that these informally organized relations are not some survival from a precapitalist past nor are they just a method of subordinating women, although there is hardly any question that they have this effect. Non-waged labor is, in terms of the modern world-system, no less "capitalist" than the labor in the most advanced robotized plant (Smith, 1984a). In what follows, we describe briefly the issue of measurement of non-waged labor and how this issue is addressed from a number of perspectives. Before turning to the details, a brief overview would be helpful.

Numerous scholars have insisted that non-waged labor, as carried out under the aegis of the household unrelated to a formal labor market, falls outside any contemporary notion of value per se. The value of this labor is said to be quite literally incalculable. A second group insists on the notion that non-waged activities of any kind can be calibrated on exactly the same sort of scale as waged work – whether that scale be one of "preferences" or of time spent in the activity. A third insists on the unitary character of all labor that can be expressed in monetary terms. From this point of view, informal labor is simply disguised waged work. Finally, a fourth group of theorists remain agnostic about the "essential" character of non-waged labor and instead impute to it values based either on the assumed value of labor inputs or on the market value of the product of that labor, while cautioning that these are inexact measures developed for heuristic purposes only. In the regional studies reported in this volume we have taken the fourth stance, a position that is consonant with the kinds of data that were available to us in the different sites covered by our research.

We begin our review of these methodologies, perhaps paradoxically, by noting that a very consequential debate has revolved around the notion that household-based labor, labor that takes place apparently outside of the formal economy and apparently independent of the constraints of the formally organized labor market, is quite literally invaluable (Sahlins, 1974; Meillassoux, 1981; Chayanov, 1966). The labor performed in this non-economic setting cannot be measured against any other activity. There is no substitute for it. Rather than being based on narrow self-interest, intra-household transactions and the labor that is at the root of these transactions are relations of altruism and thus are not interchangeable with other forms of impersonal economic activities. There is a set of processes in the sphere of the private household that are absolutely specific to the household and responsive almost exclusively to those household relations.

It is here that the idea of a separate sphere denotes labor forms that are entirely different than those that are "statistically visible, taxable and accountable" (Redclift, 1985: 94). In this separate sphere, whether it be the household economy proper or subsistence production of "commodities," consumption and individual livelihoods are shaped "through personal bonds, existing in dualistic opposition to the 'public' world of production and accumulation" (Redclift, 1985: 95).

Of the many theorists who subscribe to the notion of a separate sphere, an important subgroup argues that this private domain of production is nonetheless fundamental to the broader economic system. Nevertheless, they argue that, because this non-waged labor, whether it be purely for household consumption or in order to produce "things and services" that will be purchased in the informal market economy, is not subject to the logic of capital, it is incommensurate with market values and for that reason cannot be properly speaking measured at all (Bernstein as cited in Redclift, 1985: 95; Whitehead, 1981: 110).

Interestingly, this idea of a separate domain wherein value, as formally defined, plays no part in the household economy was at the heart of early twentieth-century budget studies in both the US and Great Britain (May, 1984; Barrett and McIntosh, 1980).

The very earliest US budget studies recognized the value of non-waged labor to the household. Most of these studies were anecdotal as opposed to what subsequent reformers defined as "scientific." In the later studies, calculations of the household's income fund were based entirely on the income of the male "head of household." There was a reason. The social reformers who compiled the later budget studies had a political agenda and saw the world through their own moral imperatives. Politically, the studies had to be taken seriously by those in power – they had to be "scientific." Morally, they were shaped by an understanding of proper family organization – real work was to be reserved for adult males. Since both housework and informal market activities were "incalculable" and since they were carried on by women and children, these forms of informal labor activities soon disappeared from calculations of households' income (May, 1984: 63ff).

The most extensive debate concerning the value of informally organized labor revolved around the character of domestic activities (Seccombe, 1974). In insisting that women's domestic work was unique, these feminist scholars were conceding the argument that non-waged labor is incommensurable with values generated in the formally organized economy. Non-waged domestic labor, it was argued, has a privatized character which formed the material basis for the autonomy of women's oppression in the home outside of the controlling domain of the formal economy; hence, the notion of a capitalist patriarchy (Hartmann, 1981).

Because domestic labor was not subject to the discipline of the competitive market, the amount of labor time expended could vary wildly between producers (Himmelweit and Mohun, 1977). In this version of the debate concerning the valorization of non-waged labor activities, the very idea of socially necessary labor time as both a method of labor control and the only possible basis of quantification was entirely absent.

Ironically, it was the neoclassical economists who insisted on the comparability of all forms of labor activities, not because non-wage labor is part of the public domain of production but because, from the point of view of their theory, even wage labor activities are part of the private world of tastes and preferences. Just like individuals, households act rationally. They optimize their quality of life by a rational distribution of their resources, given opportunity costs and productivities. In the neoclassical version, households are not different from factories. They combine capital goods, raw materials, and labor to produce useful commodities. The kind of labor chosen is a function of market conditions (Stigler and Becker, 1977; Becker, 1965).

There are many problems with this model, not the least of which is the assumption concerning a joint household utility function (Folbre, 1986). For our purposes, however, we are interested in a slightly different though related issue. How can the value of opportunity costs and productivities be arrived at independently of the socially ascribed roles that flow directly from patterns in formally organized labor activities? In short, there is a circularity here that confounds the issues. Because some "types" of workers can command so little in the formally organized labor market, their greater time spent in non-waged labor is appropriate, i.e., more valuable than the wage labor forgone. But since these "types" of workers spend so much time outside the formally organized labor market, their wages are lower, making non-wage labor more valuable. Not only do we have a chicken-and-egg problem here, in the pursuit of the kind of exact quantifications necessary for the empirical work of neoclassical economics, but we also have the final bow to intrinsic differences between different "types" of workers (Becker, 1981: 21). Other neoclassical economists sensitive to the implicit circularity of the argument, and the gendered biases invoked, have tried to correct the neoclassical model by adding fresh variables: psychic rewards; orientation of wives; perceived importance of the tasks are included as exogenous variables in comparing the value of waged labor to that of non-waged work (Berk, 1985: 34ff).

The neoclassical economists (and the sociologists influenced by neoclassical models of behavior) address a very specific question. Their issue is not the contribution of non-waged labor activities to the formally organized economy, either directly as part of worldwide commodity chains or indirectly as a supplement to the wage, but how household members appropriate their labor between different tasks that are themselves given in the very nature of things. Since in their model there is little difference *theoretically* between life-and-death decisions and deciding to go to a movie, the final outcome of the process of household decisions establishes the value of non-waged labor. Whatever is chosen is by definition more valuable to the household than that which was forgone.

In contrast to household-based research, a whole range of studies focuses on the total value to the national economy of the so-called informal sector. Characteristic of these studies is the assumption that the distinguishing feature of this informal labor is that it is not included in official statistics because it falls outside (or evades) obligatory reporting procedures. For purposes of measurement, its dollar value is no different than its counterpart in the formally organized economy.

The Internal Revenue Service in the United States, for example, with its all too obvious interest in income from all sources, uses a sampling technique to estimate the size of the so-called "shadow economy" through indirect measures of reporting compliance (Internal Revenue Service, 1977). Similarly, other studies employ sampling techniques to estimate how much households spend on commodities and services available through the informal sector, and from those expenditure accounts generate estimates of the size of the informal economy (Smith, 1985). The velocity of checks and currency relative to the gross national product and changes in currency levels relative to demand deposits are other indices employed in measuring the "shadow" economy (Tanzi, 1986).

These studies take as their starting point the presumed fundamental unity of economic activities. The major difference they see between labor in formal sectors and informally organized labor is that the latter somehow slipped out of the clutches of state officials. In these accounts, the informal character of the work is nothing more than a thin disguise for wage labor. And of course the more difficult question of "house work" is, from this point of view, dismissed altogether as non-economic in character. Thus, the issue of measurement is simply a question of proper enforcement and accounting by the state. A mechanic in his own garage, a neighbor providing babysitting services, or a purveyor of goods in a garage sale are, in terms of the value of their labor, comparable to their colleagues whose work is organized by the formally reported wage mechanisms recorded by the state's agencies.

It is precisely this unity that has been dismissed by other theorists who argue, as we do, that the economy of the field, bazaar, household, and backyard has indeed undergone a transformation in all regions of the modern world-economy, but the consequence of that transformation process has not resulted in a singular labor form hiding behind a variety of disguises. It has produced a multiplicity of labor forms all of which yield value, changes in which have enormous implications for alterations in the formally organized wage labor force.

Having said that though, the problem still remains: how best to calibrate those values in order to create an historically coherent account of the processes we believe are integral to this world-economy. To this end, we have opted for an eclectic approach precisely because of these measurement problems. Data were incomparable across different regions and time periods. Sometimes we knew the value of "similar" forms of labor and sometimes we did not. And of course we were all too conscious of the problems inherent in ascribing to very different labor *relations* notions of comparability that arise from the ostensible similarity in the product of that labor. Sometimes we knew the value of the commodities for which the informal labor processes we studied were a substitute and sometimes we did not. Sometimes we were able to calculate the exact cash value of non-waged labor and sometimes this sort of calculation was altogether impossible. So we employed a variety of techniques in an attempt to generate an account that did not, on one hand, sacrifice historical or regional scope for precision of measurement nor, on the other hand, abandon quantification altogether in order to make a theoretical point. In short, we did the best we could within the parameters of our research question and our understanding of the character of informally organized labor within the capitalist world-economy.

Our definition of the value contributed to the household income fund through labor that was not organized via the formal mechanisms of the market was based on its proportional contribution to the total household pool of resources. In turn, we employed one of two devices to measure the value of this non-waged labor depending upon the available data: the market value of the goods and services it produced or the market value of the labor itself. We define the household as the set of relations between adults and children that imposed an obligation to share resources that were generated through any number of kinds of labor relations. In that sense, household relationships overlapped with and, in some important way, defined other productive relationships. What we did not assert, however, was there existed a parity among household members in the division of labor that generated these resources nor in their final distribution.

There is little question that ideas about equity between household members are historically specific and of recent origins, in most cases more a pious hope than an established fact (Tilly and Scott, 1978). Furthermore, the gender division of labor within and outside of these household relations obviously has an impact on changes in both the total amount of resources available to the household and how these resources are distributed. Though we have not turned our attention to gender-specific forms of exploitation established by virtue of these household relations, we have illustrated that what has passed for "women's work" rooted in the natural order of things is nothing of the sort. Instead we proceeded by defining the so-called domestic economy as a subset of non-waged labor in general. We have argued elsewhere that non-waged work is certainly not "of-a-piece" but in fact constitutes a wide variety of labor relations with very different determinations (Smith, 1987). But for our purposes the congruence between different forms of informal labor relations was at the center of our analysis.

Along with other writers, we have insisted on the radical distinction between households and genealogical relations (Harris, 1981). If they do overlap in practice, it is more the result of social policy than of some naturally occurring coincidence. As has been noted elsewhere there is, in our view, a very good reason to identify biological "relationships" with those that are political in origin (Wallerstein, 1988).

We have proceeded with our research in the various sites by assuming that the resources available through household relations were hardly fixed but were themselves subject to changes in the world-economy. It was the character of these changes that drew our attention to the effect on non-waged labor of long waves of expansion followed by periods of economic contraction. Yet there is a contradiction. If there is a marked and increasing instability in the degree to which members of a wage labor force can count on subsidies to their wages, at the same time such subsidies continue to be a crucial feature of the accumulation process as it extends and deepens throughout the world. In short, we began our research noting that the very processes that required the continued sharing of resources generated outside of the wage relationship proper were the same processes that threatened these non-waged relations. The upshot was the reconstitution at the level of the state, the modern household posing as something preordained by nature itself (Donzelot, 1979). However the household was constituted and however recruitment took place, to be a member of a household, for our purposes, meant legitimate access to the pie even if the portion alloted was a paltry one.

It is precisely the permeability of the household, the absence of a wall separating it from a putative "wider" economy, that has led us to treat the product of domestic labor as commensurate with the product of all other social relations of production. In other words, domestic labor, as well as other forms of non-waged labor, are linked in our model to commodity chains which are themselves created and recreated by processes of the world-economy.

We have used the notions of sharing and pooling not to mark out a privileged terrain of equitable relations influenced by moral elements nor the presence of a beneficent head of household in charge of allocation (Harris, 1981: 143ff), but simply to indicate that for the purposes of our research we took as given the degree to which workers could assume relative access to the resources generated outside of the wage relationship proper. Both our analytical interests and the limitations of our data prevented us from considering the norms and relationships that governed the actual distribution of resources among household members, and how that distribution affects the division of labor within the household or in the broader economy (Pahl, 1988). By definition, we argued that *some* sharing took place among household members, but we were not at all governed by the notion that this sharing was based on principles of altruism or equity. Thus, while we note their importance, the specific character of relations between household members did not play a substantial role in our research. This was not our research question.

Obviously, we faced all sorts of technical measurement difficulties, most of which stem from either a circularity in comparable measurements or in measurements that by their very nature did not easily yield comparable data across time and region. The measurement techniques we finally adopted and their related problems are discussed at length in Goldschmidt-Clermont (1987) with specific reference to domestic labor. We list them here briefly, as we extended them to cover all forms of labor organized outside of the formal economy.

1. Estimates of value of non-waged labor based on the volume of inputs:

The starting point of this technique is to evaluate non-waged labor on the basis of the volume of labor inputs in terms of either the number of workers or the number of hours of the household's time spent in informal labor activities. While this method generated information on the degree to which non-waged labor absorbs the household's time and thus was a good measure at any single point in time and in any single region of proportional contributions to the household's income fund, it has a serious problem from the point of view of our research interests. As a comparative measure across time and region, it was insensitive to differences in the productivities of informally organized labor. The same amount of labor time could yield considerably more or considerably less value to the overall pool of resources at a different time and place. While this method for evaluating the strategies employed by individual households in allocating their time has considerable merit, for our purposes it proved least useful.

2. Estimates based on the value of inputs:

In this method the value to the household consumption fund is calculated in terms of the monetary value of the labor time expended as measured by the imputed value of that labor on the formal market. In some of the regions studied, we used the wages of what a paid worker would receive for the "same" work contributed by the unpaid household member. In others, we used as a benchmark the wages forgone as a result of engaging in the informal labor activities. There were problems with both these techniques. Though allowing comparative analysis they rested, as we noted above, on imputed market prices which were themselves sensitive to the degree to which the labor in question was or was not commodified.

Secondly, as Goldschmidt-Clermont (1987) points out, it is not altogether clear which categories of wages should be used in order to make the proper imputation – wages for substitute workers, wages paid to workers doing similar activities in the formal market, or forgone wages of household members. When we did employ this method, as in the case of our Binghamton site study, we chose for purposes of imputation the wages that would have had to be paid for substitute household workers.

3. Estimates based on the value of goods produced in non-wage-based production:

This is the evaluation technique we primarily used to measure the monetary value of informal labor activities. If the final product of these informal activities was actually purchased, we imputed to the household consumption fund estimates of the price of the goods less the value of the goods and materials that went into their production. Laundry, tacos, a room and bed, homemade beer, all had real "market" prices, and it was this price whenever possible that we used as the basis for our judgment concerning the income to the household. It should be noted that most of the goods produced and sold via this informal labor are the surplus of goods and services produced for "own-use" consumption; thus the actual prices of capital inputs is, relatively speaking, quite low. The economies of scale inherent in this kind of production are exactly what is disrupted over the long haul and which eventually renders these forms of petty-market production uneconomical. It is exactly this dynamic that is not captured in the neoclassical argument about tastes and preferences.

On the other hand, if the labor in question produced a good or service that was exclusively for domestic consumption, the value imputed to that labor whenever possible was calculated at what would have been the price of the goods or service had it been purchased on the formal market – keeping in mind, of course, the relationship between market prices and the availability of substitutes.

Finally, let us say a word about the proportion of the total pool of resources contributed by wages generated in the formal wage labor force. First, it should be noted that we quickly dismissed the idea that the "norm" was a single wage contributed by a head of household. The only thing remarkable about the existence of a family wage system is the extent to which it is honored in the breach rather than in practice. Only one site that we considered had a set of households that were organized overwhelmingly on the basis of the wages of a male head of household. This was among skilled White workers on the Rand in the early part of the century. And of course, as is all too well known, it required a draconian system of labor control over African workers in order to create the circumstances that would allow such a family wage system to exist.

In most households and in all sites, a number of household members found places in the wage labor force, if not permanently, then at least sporadically. And of course no household, outside those of White workers on the Rand, lacked members engaged in all sorts of domestic labor. Where available, as in the case of New York, Binghamton, and Detroit, we used household budget studies to establish broad estimates for total wage income. When we did not have such budget studies, we turned to wage studies of specific classes of workers and extrapolated from these estimates of total household waged income, given what we knew about the patterns of wage labor force participation among various family members and what we knew about family composition among groups of workers.

Let us conclude this review of the methods associated with calibrating the value of non-waged labor with this observation: The degree to which the actual nature, extent, and limitations of non-waged labor presents methodological difficulties is no measure of their centrality in the world-economy. Quite the contrary! By shrouding such activities behind a veil, their important contribution has been secured, while at the same time minimizing the kind of political struggles that would ensue if the real nature of non-waged work were culturally admitted. It is for this reason we believed that, rather than letting these methodological difficulties call a halt to our investigations, they should be a spur to research for anyone who is concerned with the historical character of the capitalist world-economy.

References

Acevedo, Marta (1982). *El 10 de mayo*. México: Cultura/Secretaría de Educación Pública.

Aglietta, Michel (1979). *A Theory of Capitalist Regulation*. London: New Left Books.

Aiken, Alexander (1907). *The Cost of Living in Johannesburg*. London: Spottiswoode.

Alonso, Jorge (1984). "Mujer y trabajo en México," in Asa Cristina Laurell *et al.*, *El obrero mexicano*, II: *Condiciones de trabajo*. México: Siglo XXI.

Andrews, Benjamin (1935). *Economics of the Household*. New York: Macmillan.

Argyle, John (1977). "The Myth of the Elementary Family: A Comparative Account of Variations in Family Household Structure amongst a Group of South African Whites," *African Studies*, 36, 2, 105–18.

Arizpe, Lourdes (1973). *Parentesco y economía en una sociedad nahua: Nican Pehua Zacatipán*. México: Secretaría de Educación Pública, Instituto Nacional Indigenista.

　(1980). *La migración por relevos y la reproducción social del campesinado*. México: Centro de Estudios Sociológicos, Colegio de México.

　(1984). "Agrarian Change and the Dynamics of Women's Rural Out-Migration in Latin America," in UNESCO, *Women on the Move: Contemporary Changes in Family and Society*. Paris: UNESCO.

Arrom, Silvia (1985). *The Women of Mexico City, 1790–1857*. Stanford, CA: Stanford University Press.

Ashton, Hugh (1967). *The Basuto*. London: Oxford University Press.

Babson, Steve (1984). *Working Detroit: The Making of a Union Town*. New York: Adama Books.

Bach, Frederico (1935). "Un estudio del costo de la vida," *El Trimestre Económico*, 2, 5, 12–49.

Baerga, María del Carmen (1984). "Wages, Consumption, and Survival: Working-Class Households in Puerto Rico in the 1930s," in J. Smith, I. Wallerstein, and H. D. Evers, eds., *Households and the World-Economy*. Beverly Hills, CA: Sage.

Banco de México (1966). *Encuesta sobre ingresos y gastos familiares en México, 1963.* México: Banco de México.

Bancroft, Hubert (1893). *Resources and Development of Mexico.* San Francisco: Bancroft.

Bandelier, Adolph (1884). *Report of an Archaeological Tour in Mexico in 1881.* Papers of the Archaeological Institute of America, Vol. II. Boston: Cupples, Upham; reprinted New York: AMS Press, 1976.

Barba de Piña Chan, Beatríz (1960). "Bosquejo socio-económico de un grupo de familias de la ciudad de México," *Anales del Instituto Nacional de Antropología e Historia,* 11, 87–154.

Barrett, M. and Maureen McIntosh (1980). "The 'Family-Wage': Some Problems for Socialists and Feminists," *Capital and Class,* No. 11, 51–72.

Bartra, Roger (1974). *Estructura agraria y clases sociales en México.* México: UNAM, Instituto de Investigaciones Sociales & Ediciones Era.

Bayor, Ronald (1978). *Neighbors in Conflict: The Irish, Germans, Jews, and Italians of New York City, 1929–1941.* Baltimore, MD: Johns Hopkins University Press.

Bazant, Jan (1973). "Peones, arrendatarios y aparceros en México, 1851–1853," *Historia Mexicana,* 23, 90, 330–57.

Beals, Ralph (1970). *Cherán: A Sierra Tarascan Village.* Westport, CT: Greenwood Press.

Beavon, K. S. O. and C. M. Rogerson (1986a). "The Changing Role of Women in the Urban Informal Sector of Johannesburg," in David Drakakis-Smith, ed., *Urbanisation in the Developing World.* London: Croom Helm.

  (1986b). "Temporary Trading for Temporary People: The Making of Hawking in Soweto." Paper presented to the I.G.U. Working Group on Third World Urbanization, Madrid, August 27–30. Johannesburg: Department of Geography and Environmental Studies, University of Witwatersrand.

Becker, Gary (1965). "A Theory of Allocation of Time," *Economic Journal,* 75, September, 493–517.

  (1981). *A Treatise on the Family.* Cambridge, MA: Harvard University Press.

Beinart, William and Colin Bundy (1987). *Hidden Struggles in Rural South Africa.* Johannesburg: Ravan.

Beinart, William, Peter Delius, and Stanley Trapido (1986). *Putting a Plough to the Ground.* Berkeley: University of California Press.

Belshaw, Michael (1967). *A Village Economy: Land and People of Huecorio.* New York: Columbia University Press.

Berk, Richard and Sara Fenstermaker Berk (1979). *Labor and Leisure at Home.* Beverly Hills, CA: Sage.

Berk, Sara Fenstermaker (1985). *The Gender Factory: The Apportionment of Work in American Families.* New York: Plenum Press.

Bernstein, Harvey (1979). "African Peasantries: A Theoretical Framework," *Journal of Peasant Studies*, 6, 4, 421–43.

Bigelow, Howard F. (1953). *Family Finance*. Philadelphia, PA: Lippincott.

Boris, Eileen and Bardaglio, Peter (1987). "Gender, Race, and Class: The Impact of the State on the Family and the Economy, 1790–1945," in N. Gerstel and H. E. Gross, eds., *Families and Work*. Philadelphia, PA: Temple University Press.

Bortz, Jeffrey (1987). *Industrial Wages in Mexico City, 1939–1975*. Unpubl. Ph.D dissertation, University of California, Los Angeles. Washington: Library of Congress, Cataloging-in-Publication Data.

Boserup, Ester (1970). *Woman's Role in Economic Development*. London: Allen & Unwin.

Bozzoli, Belinda, ed. (1983). *Town and Countryside in the Transvaal*. Johannesburg: Ravan.

Brink, Elsabe (1986). "The Garment Workers and Poverty on the Witwatersrand, 1920–1945." Seminar paper, African Studies Institute, University of Witwatersrand.

Broome County Oral History Project (BCOHP) (n.d.). Oral History Interviews: Transcripts of interviews conducted for the Broome County Oral History Project. Broome County Historical Society, Binghamton, New York.

Bundy, Colin (1979). *The Rise and Fall of the South African Peasantry*. London: Heinemann.

Bureau of Market Research (BMR), University of South Africa (UNISA) (1963). *Income and Expenditure Patterns of Urban Bantu Households: South-Western Townships, Johannesburg*, by F. E. Radel, C. de Koning, and G. R. Feldmann-Laschin, Research Report No. 6. Pretoria: BMR, UNISA.

(1975). *The Minimum and Supplemented Living Levels of Non-Whites Residing in the Main and Other Selected Urban Areas of the Republic of South Africa, August 1975*, by M. Loubser, Research Report No. 47. Pretoria: BMR, UNISA.

(1976). *Income and Expenditure Patterns of Urban Black Households in Johannesburg*, by J. H. Martins, Research Report No. 50.3. Pretoria: BMR, UNISA.

(1982). *Income and Expenditure Patterns of Urban Black Multiple Households in Johannesburg, 1980*, by P. A. Nel, Research Report No. 94.7. Pretoria: BMR, UNISA.

(1986). *Income and Expenditure Patterns of Urban Black Multiple Households in Johannesburg, 1985*, by J. H. Martins, Research Report No. 130.9. Pretoria: BMR, UNISA.

Burman, Sandra and Rebecca Fuchs (1986). "When Families Split: Custody and Divorce in South Africa," in Sandra Burman and Pamela Reynolds, eds., *Growing Up in a Divided Society: The Contexts of Childhood in South Africa*. Johannesburg: Ravan.

Bush, Ray, Lionel Cliffe, and Valery Jansen (1984). "The Crisis in the Reproduction of the Cheap Labour Economics of Southern Africa." Paper presented to the 1984 Review of African Political Economy Conference, September 29–30, University of Keele.

Bustamante, Benigno (1861). "Memoria geográfica y estadística de Guanajuato," *Boletín de la Sociedad Mexicana de Geografría y Estadística*, primera época, 1, 54–95.

Busto, Emiliano (1880). *Estadística de la República Mexicana*, 3 vols. México: Ignacio Cumplido.

Cabrera, Luis (1975). "Discurso sobre el problema agrario," in M. Contreras and J. Tamayo, *México en el siglo XX, 1900–1913: Textos y documentos*, 1. México: Centro de Estudios Latinoamericanos.

Cardoso, Ciro (1983). *México en el siglo XIX (1821–1910): Historia económica y de la estructura social*. México: Ediciones Nueva Imagen.

Carnegie Commission (1932). *The Poor White Problem in South Africa*, 1: *Rural Impoverishment and Rural Exodus*, by J. F. W. Grosskopf. Stellenbosch: Pro Ecclesia.

Castells, Manuel and Alejandro Portes (1989). "World Underneath: The Origins, Dynamics, and Effects of the Informal Economy," in A. Portes, M. Castells, and L. A. Benton, eds., *The Informal Economy*. Baltimore, MD: Johns Hopkins University Press.

Centro de Estudios Históricos del Movimiento Obrero Mexicano (CEHSMO) (1975). *La mujer y el movimiento obrero mexicano en el siglo XIX: Antología de la prensa obrera*. México: CEHSMO.

Centro de Investigaciones Agrarias (CDIA) (1973). "Tenencia de la tierra, población y empleo," in Leopoldo Solis, *La economía mexicana*, II: *Política y desarrollo*. México: FCE.

Chapin, Robert Coit (1909). *The Standard of Living Among Workingmen's Families in New York City*. New York: Charities Publication Committee, Russell Sage.

Chayanov, A. V. (1966). *The Theory of Peasant Economy*. Homewood, IL: R. D. Irwin.

City of Detroit, Planning Department (1983). *A Profile of Detroit: 1980*.

Claghorn, Kate Holladay (1901). "The Foreign Immigrant in New York City," in U.S. Industrial Commission, *Reports*, IX. Washington, DC: Government Printing Office.

Clapp & Mayne, Inc. (1980). *Ingresos y gastos de las familias, Puerto Rico 1977*, 2 vols. San Juan: Negociado de Estadísticas del Trabajo.

Clark, Sue Ainslie and Wyatt, Edith (1911). *Making Both Ends Meet: The Income and Outlays of New York Working Girls*. New York: Macmillan.

Coatsworth, John (1984). *El impacto económico de los ferrocarriles en el Porfiriato*. México: Ediciones Era.

Cock, Jacklyn (1987). "Trapped Workers: Constraints and Contradictions

Experienced by Black Women in Contemporary South Africa," *Women's Studies International Forum*, 10, 2, 133–40.

Cock, Jacklyn, Erica Emdon, and Barbara Klugman (1986). "The Care of the Apartheid Child: An Urban African Study," in Sandra Burman and Pamela Reynold, eds., *Growing Up in a Divided Society: The Contexts of Childhood in South Africa*. Johannesburg: Ravan.

Cockcroft, James (1983). *Mexico: Class Formation, Capital Accumulation, and the State*. New York: Monthly Review Press.

Cohen, Miriam (1977). "Italian-American Women in New York City, 1900–1950: Work and School," in M. Cantor and B. Laurie, eds., *Class, Sex, and the Woman Worker*. Westport, CT: Greenwood Press.

(1982). "Changing Educational Strategies among Immigrant Generations: New York Italians in Comparative Perspective," *Journal of Social History*, No. 15, March, 443–66.

Coleman, Cindy, Karl Debus, Fred Freundlich, Amy Halpern, Lynn Marshal, Doug Meurs, Arn Pearson, Sharon Porter, Kate Welch, Randy Wilson, and Thomas Wong (1984). "Binghamton: Case Studies in Urban and Economic Development." Report prepared by the Workshop in Local Economic Analysis, Department of City and Regional Planning Community Design Assistance Program, Cornell University.

College Settlements Association (CSA) (1894). *Fifth Annual Report*.

Committee on Human Resources (1959). *Unemployment, Family Income and Level of Living in Puerto Rico*. San Juan: Estado Libre Asociado.

(The) Conference Board (1975). "The New York Market 1972/1973." New York: The Board, Conference Report No. 649.

Conk, Margo Anderson (1978). *The United States Census and Labor Force Change: A History of Occupation Statistics, 1870–1940*. Ann Arbor, MI: UMI Research Press.

Cook, Sherburne and Woodrow Borah (1971). *Essays in Population History*, 1: *Mexico and the Caribbean*. Berkeley, CA: University of California Press.

Cowan, Ruth (1983). *More Work for Mother*. New York: Basic Books.

Cross, Harry (1978). "Living Standards in Rural Nineteenth Century Mexico: Zacatecas, 1820–1880," *Journal of Latin American Studies*, 10, 1, May, 1–19.

Daines, Marvel (1940). *Be It Ever So Tumbled: The Story of a Suburban Slum*. Detroit.

Daniel, Annie (1905). "The Wreck of the Home: How Wearing Apparel is Fashioned in the Tenements," *Charities*, 14, 1, April 1, 624–29.

de Barbieri, Teresita (1984). *Mujeres y vida cotidiana*. México: Secretaría de Educación Pública.

Deere, Carmen D. (1979). "Rural Women's Subsistence Production in the Capitalist Periphery," in R. Cohen, P. C. W. Gutkind, and P. Brazier, eds., *Peasants and Proletarians: The Struggles of Third World Workers*. New York: Monthly Review Press.

de Gortari, Hira (1982). "Los años difíciles: una economía urbana: el caso de la ciudad de México (1890–1910)," *Iztapalapa*, 3, 6, 101–14.

de Gruchy, Joy (1960). *The Cost of Living for Urban Africans*. Johannesburg: South African Institute of Race Relations.

de Jesus Toro, Rafael (1982). *Historia económica de Puerto Rico*. Cincinnati, OH: South Western Publishing.

de Kieweit, C. W. (1957). *A History of South Africa: Social and Economic*. London: Oxford University Press (first published in 1941).

Detroit Area Study (1956). *A Social Profile of Detroit, 1955*. Ann Arbor: University of Michigan.

Detroit United Community Services (1921). *Minimum Budget for Wage Earner's Family*. United Community Services Collection (Box 5, Folder 36), Reuther Library, Wayne State University.

Dietz, James L. (1986). *Economic History of Puerto Rico*. Princeton, NJ: Princeton University Press.

Diffie, Bailey W. and Justine W. Diffie (1931). *Porto Rico: A Broken Pledge*. New York: Vanguard Press.

Dinerman, Ina (1978). "Patterns of Adaptation among Households of US-Bound Migrants from Michoacán, México," *International Migration Review*, 12, 4, 485–501.

Dirección General de Estadística, México (1941). *Anuario estadístico de los Estados Unidos Mexicanos, 1939*. México.

(1943). *Anuario estadístico de los Estados Unidos Mexicanos, 1941*. México.

Donzelot, Jacques (1979). *The Policing of Families*. New York: Pantheon.

Dubofsky, Melvyn (1975). *Industrialization and the American Worker, 1865–1920*. Arlington Heights, IL: AHM Publishing.

Eaton, Isabel (1895). "Receipts and Expenditures of Certain Wage-Earners in the Garment Trades," *Quarterly Publications of the American Statistical Association*, June, 4–38.

Eckstein, Susan (1977). *The Poverty of Revolution: The State and the Urban Poor in Mexico*. Princeton, NJ: Princeton University Press.

Eisenstein, Zillah R. (1979). *Capitalist Patriarchy and the Case of Socialist Feminism*. New York: Monthly Review Press.

Everett, Mike (1980). "La evolución de la estructura salarial mexicana, 1939–1963," *Revista Mexicana de Sociología*, 41, 4, 93–103.

Ezekiel, Raphael (1984). *Voices From the Corner: Poverty and Racism in the Inner City*. Philadelphia, PA: Temple University Press.

Feige, Edgar L. (1986). "A Reexamination of the Underground Economy in the U.S.," *International Monetary Fund Staff Papers*, 33, 4, 768–81.

Fernández y Fernández, Ramón (1946). *Los salarios agrícolas en 1944*. México: Secretaría de Agricultura y Fomento.

Fine, Sidney (1975). *Frank Murphy: The Detroit Years*. Ann Arbor: University of Michigan Press.

Folbre, Nancy (1986). "Cleaning House: New Perspectives on Households and Economic Development," *Journal of Development Economics*, 22, 1, 5–40.

Freund, Bill (1989). "The Social Character of Secondary Industry on the Witwatersrand, 1915–45," in Alan Mabin, ed., *Organisation and Economic Change*, Southern African Studies, Johannesburg: Ravan.

García, Brígida, Humberto Muñoz, and Orlandina de Oliveira (1982). *Hogares y trabajadores en la Ciudad de México*. México: El Colegio de México.

——— (1984). "La familia obrera y la reproducción de la fuerza de trabajo en la ciudad de México," in P. González, S. León, and I. Marván, eds., *El obrero mexicano*, 1: *Demografía y condiciones de vida*. México: Siglo XXI.

Gauger, William and Kathleen Walker (1981). *The Dollar Value of Housework*. New York State Department of Agriculture, Bureau of Home Economics.

Gay, Judith S. (1980). "Basuto Women Migrants: A Case Study," *Bulletin, Institute of Development Studies*, 11, 4, 19–28.

Gereffi, Gary and Peter Evans (1981). "Transnational Corporations, Dependent Development, and State Policy in the Semiperiphery," *Latin American Research Review*, 16, 3, 31–64.

Germond, Robert C., assembler and trans. (1967). *Chronicles of Basutoland*. Lesotho: Morija Sesuto Book Depot.

Gibson, Olive (1954). *The Cost of Living for Africans: The Results of an Enquiry into the Cost of Living for Africans in the Locations and African Townships in Johannesburg and Alexandra*. Johannesburg: South African Institute of Race Relations.

Glazer, Sidney (1965). *Detroit: A Study in Urban Development*. New York: Bookman Associates.

Golding, Philip R. (1976). "The Conditions of Employment for White Workers in Urban Industry, 1880–1948, with Particular Reference to the Changing Influence of the Gold Mining Industry." Unpubl. M.A. thesis, University of Witwatersrand.

Goldschmidt-Clermont, Luisella (1987). *Economic Evaluations of Unpaid Household Work*. Geneva: International Labour Office.

González, Luis (1979). *Pueblo en vilo: microhistoria de San José de Gracia*. México: El Colegio de México.

González Montes, Soledad (1986). "Trabajo femenino y avance del capitalismo en México rural a fines del Porfiriato: El distrito de Tenango, 1900–1910." Paper presented at the VII Reunión de Historiadores Mexicanos y Norteamericanos, Ciudad de Oaxaca.

González Navarro, Moisés (1957). *Historia moderna de México*, IV: *El porfiriato: La vida social*. México: Editorial Hermes.

——— (1974). *Población y sociedad en México: 1900–1970*, 2 vols. México: Universidad Nacional Autónoma de México, Facultad de Ciencias Políticas y Sociales.

González y González, Luis, Emma Cosio Villegas, and Guadalupe Monroy (1956). *Historia moderna de México*, III: *La república restaurada: La vida social*. México: Editorial Hermes.

Goode, William J. (1963). *World Revolution and Family Politics*. New York: Free Press.

Gordon, Elizabeth (1981). "Easing the Plight of Migrant Workers' Families in Lesotho," in W. R. Bohning, ed., *Black Migration to South Africa*. Geneva: International Labour Office.

Graebner, William (1986). "Coming of Age in Buffalo: The Ideology of Maturity in Postwar America," *Radical History Review*, No. 34, 53–74.

Great Britain, Colonial Office (1947). *Annual Report for Basutoland for the Year 1946*. London: HMSO.

——— (1952). *Annual Report, Basutoland*. London: HMSO.

Gregory, Peter (1986). *The Myth of Market Failure: Employment and the Labor Market in Mexico*. Baltimore, MD: Johns Hopkins University Press.

Guerrero, Julio (1901). *La génesis del crimen en México*. México: Lib. Bouret.

Gutman, Herbert G. (1976). *The Black Family in Slavery and Freedom, 1750–1925*. New York: Pantheon.

Hacker, Andrew, ed., (1983). *U.S.: A Statistical Portrait of the American People*. New York: Viking Press.

Hammack, David (1982). *Power and Society: Greater New York at the Turn of the Century*. New York: Russell Sage Foundation.

Hanson, Alice and Manuel A. Pérez (1947). "Incomes and Expenditures of Wage Earners in Puerto Rico," *Puerto Rico Department of Labor*, Bulletin No. 1, May 1.

Hanson, Earl Parker (1955). *Transformation: The Story of Modern Puerto Rico*. New York: Simon & Schuster.

Harris, Olivia (1981). "Households as Natural Units," in Kate Young, Carol Wolkowitz, and Roslyn McCullagh, eds., *Of Marriage and the Market: Women's Subordination Internationally and Its Lessons*. London: Routledge & Kegan Paul.

Hartmann, Heidi (1981). "The Family as the Locus of Gender, Class and Political Struggle: The Example of Housework," *Signs*, 6, 3, 366–94.

Haynes, George E. (1969). *Negro Newcomers in Detroit*. New York: Arno Press.

Hellmann, Ellen (1948). *Rooiyard: A Sociological Survey of an Urban Native Slum Yard*. Cape Town: Oxford University Press.

Henry Street Settlement Studies, No. 9 (Henry St. 9). "Soup Kitchens." Helen Hall Settlement Papers Collection, Manuscripts, Columbia University Library, New York.

Hernández, Enrique and Jorge Córdoba (1982). *La distribución del ingreso en México*. México: Centro de Investigación para la Integración Social.

Hernández, Luisa (1983). "Auge y decadencia de la industria de la aguja en Puerto Rico: 1914–1940." Unpubl. Ph.D. dissertation, UNAM, Mexico.

Herrero, José Antonio (1974). *La mitología del azúcar*. Rio Piedras: CEREP.

Herrmann, Gretchen M. and Stephen M. Soiffer (1984). "For Fun and Profit: An Analysis of the American Garage Sale," *Urban Life*, 12, 4, 397–421.

Herzfeld, Elsa (1905). *Family Monographs*. New York: James Kempster.

Hewitt de Alcántara, Cynthia (1977). *Ensayo sobre la satisfacción de necesidades básicas del pueblo méxicano entre 1940–1970*. México: Centro de Estudios Sociológicos.

Hill, Joseph A. (1929). *Women in Gainful Occupations, 1870–1920*. Census Monograph, IX. Washington, DC: Government Printing Office.

Himmelweit, Susan and Simon Mohun (1977). "Domestic Labour and Capital," *Cambridge Journal of Economics*, 1, 1, March, 15–31.

Hindson, Doug C. (1987). *Pass Controls and the Urban Proletariat in South Africa*. Johannesburg: Ravan.

History Task Force (1979). *Labor Migration under Capitalism: The Puerto Rican Experience*. New York: Monthly Review Press.

Hlophe, Stephen (1977). "The Crisis of Urban Living under Apartheid Conditions: A Socio-Economic Analysis of Soweto," *Journal of Southern African Affairs*, 2, 3, 343–54.

Hopkins, Terence K. *et al.* (1987). "Incorporation into the World-Economy: How the World-System Expands," *Review*, 10, 5/6 (Supplement), Summer/Fall.

Howe, Irving (1976). *World of Our Fathers*. New York: Harcourt, Brace, Jovanovich.

Hughes, James and George Sternlieb (1978). *Jobs and People: New York City 1985*. New Brunswick, NJ: The Center for Urban Policy Research and Citizen's Housing and Planning Council of New York.

Ibarra Olivares, Felipe (1946). "El trabajo y el salario de la mujer," *Trabajo y Previsión Social*, 28, 99, 19–47.

Inglis, William (1935). *George F. Johnson and His Industrial Democracy*. Endicott, NY: Endicott-Johnson.

Internal Revenue Service (1977). *Estimates of Income Unreported on Individual Income Tax Returns*. Washington, DC: Government Printing Office.

Iturriaga, José (1951). *La estructura social y cultural de México*. México: Fondo de Cultura Económica.

Jack, Abner (1987). "Towards a 'Living Wage': Workers Demands over Sixty Years," *South African Labour Bulletin*, 12, 3, 77–94.

Janisch, Miriam (1941). *A Survey of African Income and Expenditure in 987 Families in Johannesburg*. Johannesburg: Radford Aldington.

Johannesburg Joint Council of Europeans and Natives (1928). *The Native in Industry*. Johannesburg: Hortors.

Johannesburg, Non-European Affairs Department (1951). *Report on a Sample Survey of the Native Population Residing in the Western Areas of Johannesburg*. Johannesburg: Non-European Affairs Department.

Johannesburg, Sanitary Department (1896). *Census, 15th July, 1896: Report of the Director of the Census*. Johannesburg: Standard and Diggers' News.

Jones, Jacqueline (1985). *Labor of Love, Labor of Sorrow: Black Women, Work and the Family from Slavery to the Present.* New York: Basic Books.

Juárez, Antonio (1984). "La clase obrera y sus condiciones de vida en México," in Pablo González, Samuel León, and Ignacio Marván, eds., *El obrero mexicano, 1: Demografía y condiciones de vida.* México: Siglo XXI.

Katz, Friedrich (1974). "Labor Conditions on Haciendas in Porfirian Mexico: Some Trends and Tendencies," *Hispanic American Historical Review*, 54, 1, 1–47.

Keenan, Jeremy (1983). "Trickle Up: African Income and Unemployment," in South African Research Service, ed., *South African Review*, 1: *Same Foundations, New Facades?* Johannesburg: Ravan.

(1986). "A Socio-Economic Profile of Soweto Households during the 'Reform' Era, 1978–1986." Mimeo., University of Witwatersrand.

Keenan, Jeremy and Michael Sarakinsky (1987). "Black Poverty in South Africa," *South African Labour Bulletin*, 12, 4, 108–18.

Keller, Suzane (1968). *The American Lower Class Family.* State of New York, Division for Youth, Albany.

Kessler-Harris, Alice (1968). "The Lower-Class as a Factor in Reform: New York, the Jews, and the 1890s." Unpubl. Ph.D dissertation, Rutgers University.

(1982). *Out to Work: A History of Wage-Earning Women in the United States.* New York: Oxford University Press.

Kessner, Thomas and Betty Boyd Caroli (1978). "New Immigrant Women at Work: Italians and Jews in New York City, 1880–1905," *Journal of Ethnic Studies*, 5, 4, Winter, 19–31.

Kimble, Judy (1982). "Labour Migration in Basutoland, c. 1870–1885," in Shula Marks and Richard Rathbone, eds., *Industrialisation and Social Change in South Africa.* London: Longman.

(1985). "Clinging to the Chiefs," in Henry Bernstein and Bonnie K. Campbell, eds., *Contradictions of Accumulation in Africa.* Beverly Hills, CA: Sage.

Kiser, Clyde Vernon (1969). *Sea Island to City: A Study of St. Helena Islanders in Harlem and other Urban Centers.* New York: Atheneum (first published in 1932).

Knapp, Eunice (1951). "Family Budget of City Worker, October 1950," *Monthly Labor Review*, 72, 2, February, 152–55.

Koch, Eddie (1983). " 'Without Visible Means of Subsistence': Slumyard Culture in Johannesburg, 1918–1940," in Belinda Bozzoli, ed., *Town and Countryside in the Transvaal: Capitalist Penetration and Popular Response.* Johannesburg: Ravan.

Korrol, Virginia E. Sanchez (1983). *From Colonia to Community.* Westport, CT: Greenwood Press.

Kramer, Julian (1975). *Self Help in Soweto: Mutual Aid Societies in a South*

African City. Bergen, Norway: Department of Social Anthropology, University of Bergen.

Kreps, Juanita Morris (1979). *Economic Study of Puerto Rico*, 2 vols. Washington, DC: US Department of Commerce.

Kyrk, Hazel (1953). *Economic Problems of the Family*. New York: Harper.

Lamale, Helen H. and Margaret S. Stoz (1960). "The Interim City Worker's Family Budget," *Monthly Labor Review*, 83, 8, August, 785–808.

Lara y Pardo, Luis (1908). *La prostitución en México*. Paris and México: Lib. Bouret.

León, Nicolás (1943). "El matrimonio entre los tarascos pre-colombianos y sus actuales usos," originally published in 1889, reprinted in *Aspectos del pensamiento michoacano*. Gobierno de Michoacán.

Lewis, Jon (1984). *Industrialisation and Trade Union Organisation in South Africa, 1924–55: The Rise and Fall of the South African Trades and Labour Council*. Cambridge: Cambridge University Press.

Lewis, Oscar (1959). *Five Families: Mexican Case Studies in the Culture of Poverty*. New York: Basic Books.

  (1963). *Life in a Mexican Village: Tepoztlán Restudied*. Urbana: University of Illinois Press.

Lomnitz, Larissa (1975). *Cómo sobreviven los marginados*. México: Siglo XXI.

Lopez, Adalberto (1974). "The Puerto Rican Diaspora," in A. Lopez and J. Petras, eds., *Puerto Rico and Puerto Ricans*. Cambridge, MA: Schenkman.

López Cámara, Francisco (1984). *La estructura económica y social de México en la época de la Reforma*. México: Siglo XXI.

McCraw, Louise (1977). "Family Budget Costs Continued to Climb in 1976," *Monthly Labor Review*, 100, 7, 35–39.

McGuire, Ross and Nancy Grey Osterud (1980). *Working Lives: Broome County, New York, 1800–1930*. Binghamton, NY: Roberson Center for the Arts and Sciences.

Maldonado Lee, Gabriel (1977). *La mujer asalariada en el sector agrícola*. México: CENIET.

Mandle, Jay (1978). *The Roots of Black Poverty*. Durham, NC: Duke University Press.

Manning, Caroline (1934). "The Employment of Women in Puerto Rico," *U.S. Department of Labor, Bulletin of the Women's Bureau*, No. 18.

Martin, William G. (1990). "Region Formation under Crisis Conditions: South versus Southern Africa in the Interwar Period," *Journal of Southern African Studies*, 16, 1, March, 112–38.

Martin, William G. and Mark Beittel (1987). "The Hidden Abode of Reproduction: Conceptualizing Households in Southern Africa," *Development and Change*, 28, 2, 215–34.

Matsetela, T., M. Matshoba, D. Webster, P. Wilkinson, J. Yawitch, and

H. Zarenda (1980). "Unemployment and 'Informal' Income-Earning Activity in Soweto." Seminar paper, African Studies Institute, University of Witwatersrand.

May, Martha Elizabeth (1984). "Home Life: Progressive Social Reformers Prescriptions for Social Stability, 1890–1920." Unpubl. Ph.D dissertation, State University of New York at Binghamton, Department of History.

Mayor's Unemployment Committee (1932). *The Effect upon Detroit of the Three Years of the Depression*. Detroit.

Meillassoux, Claude (1981). *Maidens, Meal and Money*. Cambridge: Cambridge University Press.

Mejía Fernández, Miguel (1979). *Política agraria en México en el siglo XIX*. México: Siglo XXI.

Mendieta y Nuñez, Lucio (1938). *La economía del indio*. México.

Menegus Bornemann, Margarita (1980). "Ocoyoacac – una comunidad agraria en el siglo XIX," *Historia Mexicana*, 30, 1, 33–78.

Meth, Charles and Solveig Piper (1984). "Social Security in Historical Perspective," Carnegie Conference Paper, No. 250. Cape Town: Second Carnegie Inquiry into Poverty and Development in Southern Africa.

Michigan Bureau of Labor and Industrial Statistics (1892). *Ninth Annual Report*. Lansing.

(1896). *Thirteenth Annual Report*. Lansing.

Mintz, Sidney (1974). *Worker in the Cane: A Puerto Rican Life History*. New York: Norton.

Molina Enríquez, Andrés (1909). *Los grandes problemas nacionales*. México: A. Carranza.

Morales Otero, Pablo and Manuel A. Pérez (1937). "Health and Socio-Economic Conditions on a Sugar Cane Plantation," *The Puerto Rican Journal of Public Health and Tropical Medicine*, 12, 4, June, 4–81.

(1941). "Second Survey of the Lafayette Area," *The Puerto Rican Journal of Public Health and Tropical Medicine*, 15, 4, June, 548–615.

Morales Otero, Pablo, Manuel A. Pérez, *et al.* (1939). *Estudios sanitarios y económico-sociales de Puerto Rico*, Part II. San Juan: Health Division, Puerto Rico Reconstruction Administration and School of Tropical Medicine.

More, Louise Bolard (1907). *Wage-Earner's Budgets: A Study of Standards of Living in New York City*. New York: Henry Holt; reprinted Arno Press, 1971.

Morgan, Winona (1939). *The Family Meets the Depression*. Minneapolis: University of Minnesota Press.

Morley, Morris (1974). "Dependence and Development in Puerto Rico," in A. López and J. Petras, eds., *Puerto Rico and Puerto Ricans: Studies in History and Society*. Cambridge, MA: Schenkman.

Motts, Irene (1973). *La vida en la Ciudad de México en las primeras décadas del siglo XX.* México: Editorial Porrúa.

Muñoz, Humberto, Orlandina de Oliveira, and Claudio Stern (1982). *Mexico City, Industrialization, Migration and the Labour Force.* Paris: UNESCO.

Murphy, Arthur and Henry Selby (1981). "A Comparison of Household Income and Budgetary Patterns in Four Mexican Cities," *Urban Anthropology*, 10, 3, 247–67.

Murray, Colin (1981). *Families Divided: The Impact of Migrant Labour in Lesotho.* Cambridge: Cambridge University Press.

Napolska, Sister Mary Remigia (1946). *The Polish Immigrant in Detroit to 1914.* Chicago: Polish Roman Catholic Union of America.

National Industrial Conference Board (NICB) (1921). *Family Budgets of American Wage Earners: A Critical Analysis*, Research Report No. 41. New York: The Century Co.

(1926). *The Cost of Living in New York City, 1926.* New York: NICB.

Nearing, Scott (1914). *Financing the Wage-Earner's Family: A Survey of the Facts Bearing on Income and Expenditures in the Families of American Wage-Earners.* New York: B. W. Huebsch.

New York City (NYC, RM) (1935). *Report of Mayor LaGuardia's Committee on Unemployment Relief.* New York City.

New York City, Community Service Society (NYC, CSS) (1977). "Applying for Public Assistance in New York City: A Study of Families at an Income Maintenance Center."

New York City, Council on Economic Education (NYC, CEE) (1973). "Challenges of the Changing Economy of New York City, 1973," *Proceedings of the Sixth Annual Institute of the New York City Council of Economic Education, April 11.*

New York City, Tenement House Department (NYC, THD) (1902–03). *First Report*, 1.

New York State Commission of Youth and Delinquency (NYSCYD) (1956). *Final Report.* Albany: State of New York Division for Youth.

New York State Department of Labor (NYSDL).

(1967a). *Structure of Earnings and Hours in New York State Industries*, IV: *Women Workers.* Albany: New York State Department of Labor, Division of Research and Statistics.

(1967b). *Employment Statistics*, III. Albany: New York State Department of Labor, Division of Research and Statistics.

(1971). *Employment Statistics*, IV. Albany: New York State Department of Labor, Division of Research and Statistics.

(1973a). *Earnings and Hours. Wage Bulletins.* Albany: New York State Department of Labor, Division of Research and Statistics.

(1973b). *Labor Research Report No. 17. Minimum Wage Certificates for Under-*

18 Workers. Albany: New York State Department of Labor, Division of Research and Statistics.

(1977). *Earnings and Hours in New York State Industry*. Albany: New York State Department of Labor.

Nutini, Hugo, Pedro Carrasco, and James Taggart (1976). *Essays on Mexican Kinship*. Pittsburgh, PA: University of Pittsburgh Press.

Nutini, Hugo A. and Barry Isaac (1974). *Los pueblos de habla náhuatl de la región de Tlaxcala y Pueblo*. México: Secretaría de Educación Pública, Instituto Nacional Indigenista.

Nutini, Hugo A. and Timothy D. Murphy (1970). "Labor Migration and Family Structure in the Tlaxcala–Puebla Area," in W. Goldschmidt and H. Hoijer, eds., *Social Anthropology of Latin America: Essays in Honor of Ralph Beals*. Los Angeles: University of California, Latin American Center.

Oestreicher, Richard Jule (1979). "Solidarity and Fragmentation: Working People and Class Consciousness in Detroit, 1877–1895." Unpubl. Ph.D dissertation, University of Michigan.

Ogburn, W. F. and M. F. Nimkoff (1955). *Technology and the Changing Family*. Boston: Houghton Mifflin.

Oppenheimer, V. (1982). *Work and the Family: A Study in Social Demography*. New York: Academic Press.

Orton, Lawrence D. (1981). *Polish Detroit and the Kolasinski Affair*. Detroit: Wayne State University Press.

Ovington, Mary (1911). *Half a Man: The Status of the Negro in New York*. New York: Longmans, Green.

Padilla, Enrique (1968). "La historia de México y los ciclos económicos," *El Trimestre Económico*, 25, 140, 707–30.

Padrón de la Ciudad de México (1882). Collected by the Municipalidad de la Ciudad de México in 1882; currently bound in numbered vols. 3423–30. Archivio de la Ciudad de México, Mexico City.

Pahl, J. (1988). "Earning, Sharing, Spending: Married Couples and Their Money," in Gillian Parker and Robert Walker, eds., *Money Matters*. London: Sage.

Pahl, R. E. (1984). *Divisions of Labour*. Oxford: Basil Blackwell.

Pani, Alberto (1917). *Hygiene in Mexico*. New York: Putnam.

Pantojas, Emilio (1985). "Desarrollismo y lucha de clases: Los límites del proyecto populista en Puerto Rico durante la decada del 1940," *Revista de Ciencias Sociales*, 24, 3 & 4, 353–90.

Paré, Luisa (1977). *El proletariado agrícola en México: Campesinos sin tierra o proletarios agrícolas*. México: Siglo XXI.

Parsons, Talcott (1955). *Family Socialization and Interaction Processes*. Glencoe, IL: Free Press.

Pérez, Erick (1984). "La condición obrera en Puerto Rico: 1898–1920," *Plural*, 3, 1 & 2, 157–70.

Pérez, Manuel A. (1939). *Estudio preliminar de las condiciones de vida en los arrabales de San Juan*. San Juan: Puerto Rico Reconstruction Administration.

(1942). "Living Conditions among Small Farmers in Puerto Rico," *Research Bulletin in Agriculture and Livestock*. San Juan: Department of Agriculture and Commerce of Puerto Rico.

Perloff, Harvey (1950). *Puerto Rico's Economic Future*. Chicago: University of Chicago Press.

Phillips, Ray E. (1938). *The Bantu in the City: A Study of Cultural Adjustment on the Witwatersrand*. Cape Province: Lovedale.

Picó, Fernando (1986a). "Cafetal Adentro: Una historia de los trabajadores agrícolas en el Puerto Rico del siglo XIX," *Revista El Sol*, 3, 1, 4–36.

(1986b). Las trabajadoras del tabaco en Utuado, Puerto Rico según el censo de 1910," *Homines*, 9, 1 and 2, 269–82.

Picó, Isabel (1980). "Apuntes preliminares para el estudio de la mujer puertorriqueña y su participación en las luchas sociales de principios de siglo," in E. Acosta Belén, ed., *La mujer en la sociedad puertorriqueña*. Río Piedras: Ediciones Huracán.

Pillay, P. N. (1984a). "Alexandra: An Analysis of Socio-Economic Conditions in an Urban Ghetto," Carnegie Conference Paper No. 19. Cape Town: Second Carnegie Inquiry into Poverty and Development in Southern Africa.

(1984b). "Poverty in the Pretoria-Witwatersrand-Vereeniging Area: A Survey of Research," Carnegie Conference Paper No. 18. Cape Town: Second Carnegie Inquiry into Poverty and Development in Southern Africa.

Piven, Frances Fox and Richard Cloward (1971). *Regulating the Poor*. New York: Vintage Press.

(1982). *The New Class War*. New York: Pantheon.

Platt, Robert (1942). *Latin America: Countrysides and Regions*. New York: McGraw-Hill.

Pleck, Elizabeth (1979). "A Mother's Wages: Income Earning among Married Italian and Black Women, 1896–1911," in N. Cott and E. Pleck, eds., *A Heritage of Her Own*. New York: Simon & Schuster.

Pollak, Hansi P. (1931). "An Analysis of the Contribution to Family Support of Women Industrial Workers on the Witwatersrand," *South African Journal of Science*, 28, 572–82.

(1933). "Women Workers in Witwatersrand Industries," *South African Journal of Economics*, 1, 1, 58–68.

Poniatowska, Elena (1982). *El último guajolote*. México: Cultura/Secretaría de Educación Pública.

Pope, Jesse E. (1905). *The Clothing Industry in New York*. Social Science Series, No. 1. Columbia: University of Missouri Press.

Portes, Alejandro and Saskia Sassen-Koob (1987). "Making It Underground: Comparative Material on the Informal Sector in Western Market Economies," *American Journal of Sociology*, 93, 1, July, 30–61.

Powell, T. (1974). *El liberalismo y el campesinado en el centro de México (1850–1870)*. México: Secretaría de Educatión Pública (SEP Setentas).

Puerto Rico, Departamento de Instrucción Pública (1934). *Rural Life in Puerto Rico*. San Juan: Department of Education.

Puerto Rico, Departmento del Trabajo (1914). *Informe sobre las condiciones de vivenda de los trabajadores de Puerto Rico*. San Juan: Bureau of Supplies, Printing, and Transportation.

   (1959). *Ingreso y gastos de las familias en Puerto Rico en el año 1953*. San Juan: Negociado de Estadísticas del Trabajo, División de Estudios Económicos.

   (1960). *Ingreso y gastos de las familias, 1953*. San Juan: Negociado de Estadísticas del Trabajo, División de Estudios Económicos.

Puerto Rico, Oficina del Gobernador (1974). *Planificación social y grupos no participantes*. San Juan: Oficina del Gobernador.

Puerto Rico Reconstruction Administration (PRRA) (1938). *Censo de Puerto Rico: 1935*. Washington, DC: Government Printing Office.

Quintero, A. G. (1978). *Conflictos de clase y política en Puerto Rico*. Río Piedras: Ediciones Huracán.

   (1982). "El crecimiento de la lucha económica y el surgimiento del Partido Socialista: 1910–1924," in G. García and A. G. Quintero, eds., *Desafío y solidaridad: Breve historia del movimiento obrero puertorriqueño*. Río Piedras: Ediciones Huracán.

Ramos Arizpe, Guillermo and Salvador Rueda Smithers (1984). *Jiquilpan, 1895–1920: Una visión subalterna del pasado a través de la historia oral*. Jiquilpan, Michoacán: Centro de Estudios de la Revolución Mexicana "Lázaro Cárdenas."

Redclift, Nanneke (1985). "The Contested Domain: Gender, Accumulation and the Labour Process," in Nanneke Redclift and Enzo Mingione, eds., *Beyond Employment: Household, Gender, and Subsistence*. New York: Basil Blackwell.

Redclift, Nanneke and Enzo Mingione, eds. (1985). *Beyond Employment: Household, Gender, and Subsistence*. New York: Basil Blackwell.

Redfield, Robert (1949). *Tepoztlán: A Mexican Village*. Chicago: University of Chicago Press.

Republic of South Africa, Bureau of Statistics (1964). *Statistical Year Book, 1964*. Pretoria: Government Printer.

   (1968a). *Statistics of Houses and Domestic Servants, 1938–1965: Nine Principal Urban Areas in South Africa*, Report 11-03-01. Pretoria: Government Printer.

   (1968b). *Population Census, 6th September, 1960*, Vol. VII, Nos. 1 and 2. Pretoria: Government Printer.

Republic of South Africa, Central Statistical Services (1985). *Population Census, 1980*, Reports 2-80-04, 05. Pretoria: Government Printer.

Republic of South Africa, Department of Statistics (1977a). *Labour Statistics: Wage Rates, Earnings and Average Hours Worked in the Printing and*

Newspaper Industry, Engineering Industry, Building Industry, and Commerce, September 1975, Report 01-20-04. Pretoria: Government Printer.

(1977b). *Statistics of Houses and Domestic Servants, October 1975, and of Flats, May 1975: Eleven Principal Urban Areas in South Africa*, Report 11-03-11. Pretoria: Government Printer.

(1978). *Survey of Household Expenditure, 1975*, Reports 11-06-05, 06. Pretoria: Government Printer.

Reynolds, Clarke (1970). *The Mexican Economy*. New Haven, CT: Yale University Press.

Richardson, Peter and Jean Jacques van Helten (1982). "Labour in the South African Gold Mining Industry, 1886–1914," in Shula Marks and Richard Rathbone, eds., *Industrialisation and Social Change in South Africa*. London: Longman.

Rischin, Moses (1962). *The Promised City*. Cambridge, MA: Harvard University Press.

Rivera Quintero, Marcia (1979). "The Development of Capitalism in Puerto Rico and the Incoporation of Women into the Labor Force," in E. Acosta Belén, ed., *The Puerto Rican Woman*. New York: Praeger.

(1980). "Incorporación de las mujeres al mercado de trabajo en el desarrollo del capitalismo," in E. Acosta Belén, ed., *La mujer en la sociedad puertorriqueña*. Río Piedras: Ediciones Huracán.

(1986). "Puerto Rico, 1986: An Overview." Dossier prepared for the meeting of the *Council on Women and the Church*, Presbyterian Church, at the Mayagüez Hilton, Mayagüez, Puerto Rico, February 27.

Robinson, John (1977). *How Americans Use Time*. New York: Praeger.

Rodríguez, Clara (1979). "Economic Factors Affecting Puerto Ricans in New York," in *Labor Migration under Capitalism*, History Task Force, Centro de Estudios Puertorriqueños. New York: Monthly Review Press.

Rodríguez, Jaime (1983). *Down From Colonialism: Mexico's Nineteenth Century Crisis*. Los Angeles: Chicano Studies Research Center, University of California.

Rogerson, C. M. (1986). "Feeding the Common People of Johannesburg, 1930–1962," *Journal of Historical Geography*, 12, 1, 56–73.

Rogerson, C. M. and K. S. O. Beavon (1982). "Getting by in the 'Informal Sector' of Soweto," *Tijdschrift voor Economische en Sociale Geografie*, 72, 4, 250–65.

Rogerson, C. M. and D. M. Hart (1986). "The Survival of the 'Informal Sector': The Shebeens of Black Johannesburg," *GeoJournal*, 12, 2, 153–66.

Romero, Matías (1898). *Mexico and the United States*, 1. New York: Putnam.

(1975). "El pensamiento porfirista sobre las relaciones entre obreros y patronos," in M. Contreras and J. Tamayo, *México en el siglo XX, 1900–1913: Textos y documents*, 1. Mexico: Centro de Estudios Latinoamericanos.

Roniger, George (1974). "Metro New York, and Economic Perspective." New York: First City National Bank.

Rosenwaike, Ira (1972). *Population History of New York City.* Syracuse, NY: Syracuse University Press.

Rosenzweig, Fernando, ed. (n.d.). *Estadísticas económicas del Porfiriato*, II. *Fuerza de trabajo y actividad económica por sectores.* México: El Colegio de México.

Rostow, W. W. (1979). *The World Economy: History and Prospect.* Austin: University of Texas Press.

Ruiz, Elizabeth (1971). "Spring 1970 Cost Estimates for Urban Family Budgets," *Monthly Labor Review*, 94, 1, January, 59–61.

Ruiz Harvell, Rafael (1978). "Aspectos laborales de la mujer en México, 1900–1970," *Revista Mexicana de Trabajo*, 1, 3, 77–108.

Sahlins, Marshall (1974). *Stone Age Economics.* Chicago: Aldine.

Sartorius, Carlos (1870). "Memoria sobre el estado de la agricultura en el partido de Huatusco," *Boletín de la Sociedad Mexicana de Geografía y Estadística*, Segunda época, 2, 141–97.

Sassen-Koob, Saskia (1983). "Labor Migration and the New Industrial Division of Labor," in J. Nash and M. P. Fernandez-Kelly, eds., *Women, Men, and the International Division of Labor.* Albany, NY: SUNY Press.

(1985). "Capital Mobility and Labor Migration," in S. Sanderson, ed., *The Americas in the International Division of Labor.* New York: Holmes & Meier.

Schejtman, Alejandro (CEPAL) (1982). *Economía campesina y agricultura empresarial: tipología de productores del agro mexicano.* México: Siglo XXI.

Sears, Robert, Eleanor Maccoby, and Harry Levin (1957). *Patterns of Child Rearing.* Evanston, IL: Row, Peterson.

Seccombe, Wally (1974). "The Housewife and Her Labour under Capitalism," *New Left Review*, No. 83, 3–24.

Secretaría de Agricultura y Fomento, México (1934). *El salario mínimo en el sector agrícola.* México.

Secretaría de Hacienda, México (1911). *Memoria de Hacienda y Crédito Público, 1909–1910.* México: Oficina Impresora de Estampillas.

Secretaría de Programación y Presupuesto, México (1981). *Encuesta nacional de ingresos y gastos de los hogares, 1977.* México: SPP.

Severinghaus, C. W. and C. P. Brown (1982). *History of the White-Tailed Deer in New York, Addendum.* New York State Department of Environmental Conservation.

Sheddick, Vernon (1954). *Land Tenure in Basutoland.* London: HMSO.

Shuenyane, E., S. Mashigo, C. Eyberg, B. D. Richardson, N. Buchanan, J. Pettifor, L. MacDougal, and J. D. L. Hansen (1977). "A Socio-Economic, Health and Cultural Survey in Soweto," *South African Medical Journal*, 51, April 9, 495–500.

Shulman, Harry Manuel (1938). *Slums of New York.* New York: Albert & Charles Boni.

Shumann, C. G. W. (1938). *Structural Changes and Business Cycles in South Africa, 1806–1936*. London: P. S. King.

Sierra Padilla, Elena (1962). "Algunos de los problemas más frecuentes de la obrera mexicana, visto a través del trabajo social." Thesis, Universidad Nacional Autónoma de México.

Silvestrini, Blanca (1979). *Los trabajadores puertorriqueños y el Partido Socialista: 1932–40*. Río Piedras: Editorial Universitaria.

Simkhovitch, Mary Kingsbury (1938). *Neighborhood: My Story of Greenwich House*. New York: Norton.

Simkins, Charles (1986). "Household Composition and Structure in South Africa," in Sandra Burman and Pamela Reynolds, eds., *Growing Up in a Divided Society: The Contexts of Childhood in South Africa*. Johannesburg: Ravan.

Sloley, Resident Commissioner H. C. (1904, Cd. 1897). *Reports of the Transvaal Labour Commission. Minutes of Proceedings and Evidence*. London: HMSO.

Smith, James D. (1985). "Market Motives in the Informal Economy," in W. Gaerter and A. Wenig, eds., *The Economics of the Shadow Economy*. New York: Springer Verlag.

Smith, Joan (1984a). "Nonwage Labor and Subsistence," in Joan Smith, Immanuel Wallerstein, and Hans-Dieter Evers, eds., *Households and the World-Economy*. Beverly Hills, CA: Sage.

(1984b). "The Paradox of Women's Employment: The Importance of Being Marginal," *Signs*, 10, 2, Winter, 291–310.

(1987). "Transforming Households: Working-Class Women and Economic Crisis," *Social Problems*, 24, 5, December, 416–36.

Smith, Joan, Immanuel Wallerstein, and Hans-Dieter Evers, eds. (1984). *Households and the World-Economy*. Beverly Hills, CA: Sage.

South African Institute of Race Relations (1957). "African Poverty," mimeo., RR 67/57. Johannesburg: South African Institute of Race Relations.

(1976). *A Survey of Race Relations, 1975*, compiled by Muriel Horrell and Tony Hodgson. Johannesburg: South African Institute of Race Relations.

Stack, Carol (1970). *All Our Kin: Strategies for Survival in a Black Community*. New York: Harper & Row.

Stahl, C. W. (1981). "Migrant Labour Supplies, Past and Present and Future, with Special Reference to the Gold Mining Industry," in W. R. Bohning, ed., *Black Migration to South Africa*. Geneva: International Labour Office.

Starr, Frederick (1900). *Notes upon the Ethnography of Southern Mexico*. Reprinted from Volume VIII, Proceedings of Davenport Academy of Natural Sciences, Davenport, Iowa. Putnam Memorial Publication Fund.

Stecker, Margaret Loomis (1971). *Inter-city Differences in Costs of Living in*

March, 1935 – 39 Cities. New York: DaCapo Press. Reprint of 1937 publication.

Steward, Julian (1956). *The People of Puerto Rico.* Urbana: University of Illinois Press.

Stigler, George J. and Gary S. Becker (1977). "De gustibus non est disputandum," *American Economic Review,* 67, 2, 76–90.

Stiglitz, Joseph E. (1973). "Approaches to the Economics of Discrimination," *American Economic Review, Papers and Proceedings of the 85th Annual Meeting,* 63, 2, May, 287–95.

Ström, G. W. (1978). *Underdevelopment and Dependence in Lesotho, the Enclave of South Africa.* Uppsala: Scandinavian Institute of African Studies.

Suttner, Sheila (1966). *Cost of Living in Soweto, 1966.* Johannesburg: South African Institute of Race Relations.

Taggart, James (1975). *Estructura de los grupos domésticos de una comunidad nahuatl de Puebla.* México: Secretaría de Educación Pública, Instituto Nacional Indigenista.

Tanzi, Vito (1986). "Underground Economy and Tax Evasion in the U.S.: Estimates and Implications," in Vito Tanzi, ed., *The Underground Economy in the U.S. and Abroad.* Lexington, MA: Lexington Books.

Thompson, Lanny (1989). "Households and the Reproduction of Labor in Mexico, 1876–1970," Unpubl. Ph.D dissertation, State University of New York at Binghamton. Ann Arbor: University Microfilms International.

Tilly, Louise and Joan Scott (1978). *Women, Work and Family.* New York: Holt, Rinehart & Winston.

Transvaal Chamber of Mines (1914). *Twenty-Fourth Annual Report for the Year 1913.* Johannesburg: Argus.

(1937). *Forty-Seventh Annual Report, 1936.* Johannesburg: Hortors.

Transvaal Colony (1903). *Report of the Transvaal Labour Commission.* Johannesburg: Argus.

(1906). *Results of a Census of the Transvaal Colony and Swaziland.* London: Waterlow.

(1908). *Report of the Transvaal Indigency Commission, 1906–08,* TG 13-1908. Pretoria: Government Printer.

Union of South Africa (1913). *Report of the Small Holdings Commission (Transvaal),* UG 51-1913. Cape Town: Cape Times, Government Printer.

(1914). *Report of the Economics Commission,* UG 12-1914. Pretoria: Government Printer.

(1926). *Report of the Economic and Wage Commission,* UG 14-1926. Cape Town: Cape Times.

(1932a). *Report of the Cost of Living Commission,* UG 36-1932. Pretoria: Government Printer.

(1932b). *Report of the Native Economic Commission,* UG 22-1932. Pretoria: Government Printer.

(1935). *Report of Industrial Legislation Committee*, UG 37-1935. Pretoria: Government Printer.

(1944). *Report of the Commission Appointed to Inquire into the Operation of Bus Services for Non-Europeans on the Witwatersrand and in the District of Pretoria and Vereeniging, 1944*, UG 31-1944. Pretoria: Government Printer.

(1946). *Census of Europeans, 6th May, 1941: Report on the Wages of Domestic Servants*, UG 46-1946. Pretoria: Government Printer.

Union of South Africa, Board of Trade and Industries (1945). *Investigation into Manufacturing Industries in the Union of South Africa*, BTI Report 282. Cape Town: Cape Times.

Union of South Africa, Bureau of Census and Statistics (1957). *Survey of Family Expenditure – November, 1955*, Report No. 3. Pretoria: Government Printer.

Union of South Africa, Census Office (1912). *Census of the Union of South Africa, 7th May, 1911*, UG 31-1912. Pretoria: Government Printer.

Union of South Africa, Department of Native Affairs (1942). *Report of the Inter-Departmental Committee on the Social, Health and Economic Conditions of Urban Natives*. Pretoria: Government Printer.

Union of South Africa, Office of Census and Statistics (1921). *Third Census of the Union of the Population of the Union of South Africa, Enumerated 3rd May, 1921, Report with Summaries and Analysis of the Detailed Tables*, UG 37-1924. Pretoria: Government Printer.

(1937). *Report on the Inquiry into the Expenditure of European Families in Certain Urban Areas, 1936*, UG 21-1937. Pretoria: Government Printer.

(1938a). *Census of Industrial Establishments, 1935–36*, UG 24-1938. Pretoria: Government Printer.

(1938b). *Sixth Census of the Union of South Africa, Enumerated 5th May, 1936*, I: *Population*, UG 21-1938. Pretoria: Government Printer.

(1942). *Sixth Census of the Union of South Africa, Enumerated 5th May, 1936*, VII: *Occupations and Industries*, UG 11-1942. Pretoria: Government Printer.

United States Bureau of the Census (USBC) (1890a). *Census of Population*. Washington, DC: Government Printing Office.

(1890b). *Population*, I. Washington, DC: Government Printing Office, 1895.

(1890c). *Compendium*, III, *Population*. Washington, DC: Government Printing Office, 1897.

(1890d). *Manufacturing Industries*. Washington, DC: Government Printing Office.

(1910a). *Abstract, with Supplement for New York*. Washington, DC: Government Printing Office, 1913.

(1910b). *Census of Manufacturing*. Washington, DC: Government Printing Office.

(1910c). *Census of Population*. Washington, DC: Government Printing Office.

(1910d). *States*, iii; *Occupations*, iv. *Population*. Washington, DC: Government Printing Office, 1914.

(1910e). *United States Census of Puerto Rico*. Washington, DC: Government Printing Office.

(1920a). *Occupations*, iv. *Population*. Washington, DC: Government Printing Office.

(1920b). *United States Census of Puerto Rico*. Washington, DC: Government Printing Office.

(1930a). *Fifteenth Census of the United States: Population*. Washington, DC: Government Printing Office.

(1930b). *Occupations*, iv; *Families*, vi. *Population*. Washington, DC: Government Printing Office.

(1930c). *United States Census of Puerto Rico*. Washington, DC: Government Printing Office.

(1940a). *Manufactures 1939*, i, State series, New York. Washington, DC: Government Printing Office, 1942.

(1940b). *Population*. Washington, DC: Government Printing Office.

(1940c). *Sixteenth Census of the United States: Population*. Washington, DC: Government Printing Office.

(1940d). *United States Census of Puerto Rico*. Washington, DC: Government Printing Office.

(1940e). *Sixteenth Census of the United States: Housing*, ii. *General Characteristics*, Part iv, New York. Washington, DC: Government Printing Office, 1943.

(1950a). *Census of Manufacturing*. Washington, DC: Government Printing Office.

(1950b). *Characteristics of the Population*, New York, ii, 32. Washington, DC: Government Printing Office.

(1950c). *Seventeenth Decennial Census of the United States: Census of the Population*. Washington, DC: Government Printing Office.

(1950d). *United States Census of Puerto Rico*. Washington, DC: Government Printing Office.

(1958). *Manufactures*, iii. Washington, DC: Government Printing Office, 1961.

(1959). *Census of Manufacturing*. Washington, DC: Government Printing Office.

(1960a). *Census of Population*, i: *Characteristics of the Population*. Washington, DC: Government Printing Office.

(1960b). *United States Census of Puerto Rico*. Washington, DC: Government Printing Office.

(1970a). *Census of Manufacturing*. Washington, DC: Government Printing Office.

(1970b). *Characteristics of the Population*, New York, i, 34, 1. Washington, DC: Government Printing Office, 1973.

(1970c). *United States Census of Puerto Rico*. Washington, DC: Government Printing Office.

(1977). *Manufactures*, III, 2. Washington, DC: Government Printing Office.

(1980a). *Census of Population*, I: *Characteristics of the Population*. Washington, DC: Government Printing Office.

(1980b). *United States Census of Puerto Rico*. Washington, DC: Government Printing Office.

United States Bureau of Foreign Commerce (1882). "Living in the City of Mexico," *United States Consular Reports*, No. 20, 223–31.

(1885). *U.S. Consular Reports: Labor in America, Asia, Africa, Australasia, and Polynesia*. Washington, DC.

(1886). "Mexico: The State of Agricultural Labor," *United State Consular Reports*, No. 67, 525–69.

United States Bureau of Labor Statistics (USBLS) (1935–36). *Family Income and Expenditures in New York City 1935–1936*, No. 643, 2 vols. Washington, DC: Government Printing Office, 1939, 1941.

(1950). *Study of Consumer Expenditures, Incomes, and Savings*, 2 vols. University of Pennsylvania, 1956.

United States Department of Labor (1901). *Labor Conditions in Puerto Rico*, by Azel Ames, Washington, DC: Government Printing Office.

(1940). "Report on Puerto Rico: The Needlework Industry," mimeo., Washington, DC.

United States Immigration Commission (USIC) (1911). *Immigrants in Cities*. Reports of the Immigration Commission 26, 61st Cong., 2nd sess., S. Doc. 338. Washington, DC: Government Printing Office.

United States War Department (1900). *Informe sobre el Censo de Puerto Rico: 1899*. Washington, DC: Government Printing Office.

Unofficial Commission (Appointed by the South African Temperance Alliance and the South African Institute of Race Relations) (1935). *The Illicit Liquor Problem on the Witwatersrand*. Johannesburg: South African Temperance Alliance and the South African Institute of Race Relations.

Vallens, Vivian (1978). *Working Women in Mexico during the Porfiriato, 1880–1910*. San Francisco: R & E Research Associates.

van der Horst, Sheila (1971). *Native Labour in South Africa*. London: Frank Cass (first published 1942).

van der Vliet, Virginia (1984). "Staying Single: A Strategy against Poverty," Carnegie Conference Paper No. 116. Cape Town: Second Carnegie Inquiry into Poverty and Development in South Africa.

van der Wiel, A. C. A. (1977). *Migratory Wage Labour*. Mazenod, Lesotho: Mazenod Book Centre.

Vanek, Joan (1973). *Keeping Busy: Time Spent in Housework, United States 1920–1970*. Ann Arbor: University Microfilms International.

van Onselen, Charles (1982a). *Studies in the Social and Economic History of the Witwatersrand, 1886–1914*, I: *New Babylon*. London: Longman.

(1982b). *Studies in the Social and Economic History of the Witwatersrand, 1886–1914*, II: *New Nineveh*. London: Longman.

Vázquez Calzada, José (1978). *La población de Puerto Rico y su trayectoria histórica*. San Juan: Escuela de Salud Pública.

(1979). "Demographic Aspects of Migration," in *Labor Migration under Capitalism: The Puerto Rican Experience*, History Task Force, Centro de Estudios Puertorriqueños. New York: Monthly Review Press.

Vietorisz, Thomas and Bennett Harrison (1970). *The Economic Development of Harlem*. New York: Praeger.

Waite, Warren (1928). *Economics of Consumption*. New York: McGraw-Hill.

Wallace, Phyllis Ann (1974). *Pathways to Work: Unemployment among Black Teenage Families*. Lexington, MA: Lexington Books.

Wallerstein, Immanuel (1978). "World-Systems Analysis: Theoretical and Interpretative Issues," in B. H. Kaplan, ed., *Social Change in the Capitalist World-Economy*. Beverly Hills, CA: Sage.

(1984). "Household Structures and Labor-Force Formation in the Capitalist World-Economy," in J. Smith, I. Wallerstein, and H.-D. Evers, eds., *Households and the World-Economy*. Beverly Hills, CA: Sage.

(1987). "Periphery," in J. Eatwell *et al.*, eds., *The New Palgrave: A Dictionary of Economics*. London: Macmillan, vol. III.

(1988). "The Ideological Tensions of Capitalism: Universalism versus Racism and Sexism," in Joan Smith, Jane Collins, Terence K. Hopkins, and Akbar Muhammad, eds., *Racism, Sexism and the World-System*. New York: Greenwood Press.

Wallerstein, Immanuel, William G. Martin, and Torry Dickinson (1982). "Household Structures and Production Processes: Preliminary Theses and Findings," *Review*, 5, 3, Winter, 437–58.

Wallman, Sandra (1969). *Take Out Hunger*. New York: Humanities Press.

Wandersee, Winifred (1983). "The Economics of Middle-Income Family Life: Working Women During the Great Depression," in L. Scharf and J. Jensen, eds., *Decades of Discontent*. Westport, CT: Greenwood Press.

Warman, Arturo (1976). *Y venimos a contradecir: Los campesinos de Morelos y el estado nacional*. México: Centro de Investigaciones Superiores del INAH.

Webster, David (1984). "The Reproduction of Labour Power and the Struggle for Survival in Soweto," Carnegie Conference Paper No. 20. Cape Town: Second Carnegie Inquiry into Poverty and Development in Southern Africa.

Wells, Henry (1969). *The Modernization of Puerto Rico: A Political Study of Changing Values and Institutions*. Cambridge, MA: Harvard University Press.

Werlhof, Claudia v. (1984). "The Proletarian is Dead; Long Live the Housewife?" in J. Smith, I. Wallerstein, and H.-D. Evers, eds., *Households and the World-Economy*. Beverly Hills, CA: Sage.

Whetten, Nathan (1948). *Rural Mexico*. Chicago: University of Chicago Press.

Whitehead, Ann (1981). "I'm hungry, Mum: The Politics of Domestic Budgeting," in Kate Young, Carol Wolkowitz, and Roslyn McCullagh, eds., *Of Marriage and the Market: Women's Subordination Internationally and Its Lessons*. London: Routledge & Kegan Paul.

Widick, B. J. (1972). *Detroit: City of Race and Class Violence*. Chicago: Quadrangle Books.

Wilkie, James (1970). *The Mexican Revolution: Federal Expenditure and Social Change Since 1910*. Berkeley: University of California Press.

(1974). *Statistics and National Policy*. Los Angeles: University of California, Latin American Center.

Wilkie, James and Paul Wilkins (1981). "Quantifying the Class Structure of Mexico, 1895–1970," in J. Wilkie and S. Haber, eds., *Statistical Abstract of Latin America*. Los Angeles: University of California, Latin American Center.

Williams, Faith (1956). "Standards and Levels of Living of City-Worker Families," *Monthly Labor Review*, 79, 9, September, 1015–23.

Winckler, Judith (1985). *Child Care Data for Broome County*, Broome County Child Development Council, Binghamton.

Wix, Ethel (1951). *The Cost of Living: An Enquiry into the Essential Requirements for African Families Living in Johannesburg, Pretoria and Reef Towns, August–December, 1950*. Johannesburg: South African Institute of Race Relations.

Wolf, Eleanor Paperno and Charles N. Lebeaux (1969). *Change and Renewal in an Urban Community: Five Case Studies of Detroit*. New York: Praeger.

Wolpe, Harold (1972). "Capitalism and Cheap Labour-Power in South Africa: From Segregation to Apartheid," *Economy and Society*, 1, 4, 425–56.

Womack, John (1970). *Zapata and the Mexican Revolution*. New York: Vintage Books.

(1978). "The Mexican Economy During the Revolution," *Marxist Perspectives*, 1, 4, 80–123.

Wrobel, Paul (1979). *Our Way: Family, Parish, and Neighborhood in a Polish-American Community*. Notre Dame, IN: University of Notre Dame Press.

Zeluck, Stephen (1952). "The Effect of the Federal Minimum Wage Legislation upon the Puerto Rican Needlework Industry," Unpubl. Ph.D dissertation, University of Chicago.

Zuid-Afrikaansche Republiek (1897). *Report of the State Mining Engineer*.

Pretoria: Gedrukt ter Staatsdrukkerij der Zuid-Afrikaansche Republiek.

Zunz, Olivier (1982). *The Changing Face of Inequality: Urbanization, Industrial Development Immigrants in Detroit, 1880–1920*. Chicago: University of Chicago Press.

Index

301

Studies in Modern Capitalism